More Reviews

"Heartfelt greetings to the readers o[illegible] Russia to Australia'. The tragic r[illegible] overtook Imperial Russia in the 20th Century deprived Russia of millions of its countrymen. A large number, found themselves in the Far East and eventually many of them established a second homeland on the continent of Australia. Their faith, fortune, suffering and struggle for a worthwhile life should not be forgotten. Vassilieff's book presents an important contribution in preserving the historical legacy of the Russian Diaspora."

— Maria Romanova, HIH The Grand Duchess of Russia, Head of the Russian Imperial House

"A captivating read, personifying a series of significant – historical broad ranging events – as lived through by the author and his family, spanning the 20th Century of Russia, China and Australia. A heritage left for the future generations in its intimate account of what it's like to lose part of one's family and homeland and finally reach Australian shores to ultimately call it home."

— Vladimir Kouzmin, Editor *Unification*
(Russian Weekly National Newspaper)

This was truly an Odyssey lived through by many but told by very few, which makes the book not only interesting but also valuable as a documentary.

— Dr Paul A Urtiew,
ORUR Snr Scm (Chief Sct ret'd), San Francisco

ODYSSEYA

AN EPIC JOURNEY FROM RUSSIA TO AUSTRALIA

A. Vassilieff

Alexander Vassilieff

To 13/4/10

Bob & Denise

ABOUT THE AUTHOR

Alexander Vassilieff is a descendent of the colonists who are personified in his first epic novel – a biography of his family. Alex was born in Shanghai, China. At the age of three, he was taken to Harbin and at nine, in 1951, to Sydney, Australia. After an active career as a Professional Engineer and service to community life, he retired and lives with his wife Alexandra. They have two children and four grandchildren.

Printed and bound in Australia by Griffin Press

First published in Australia 2008
This edition published 2008

Cover design, typesetting: Chameleon Print Design

Vassilieff, Alexander
Odysseya
EAN13: 978-0-646-48901-8
pp486

This book is dedicated to **Klava** – my Mother – who gave so much and received so little.

O God thy sea is so great
And my boat so small

Breton's Fisherman's Prayer

My family's journey

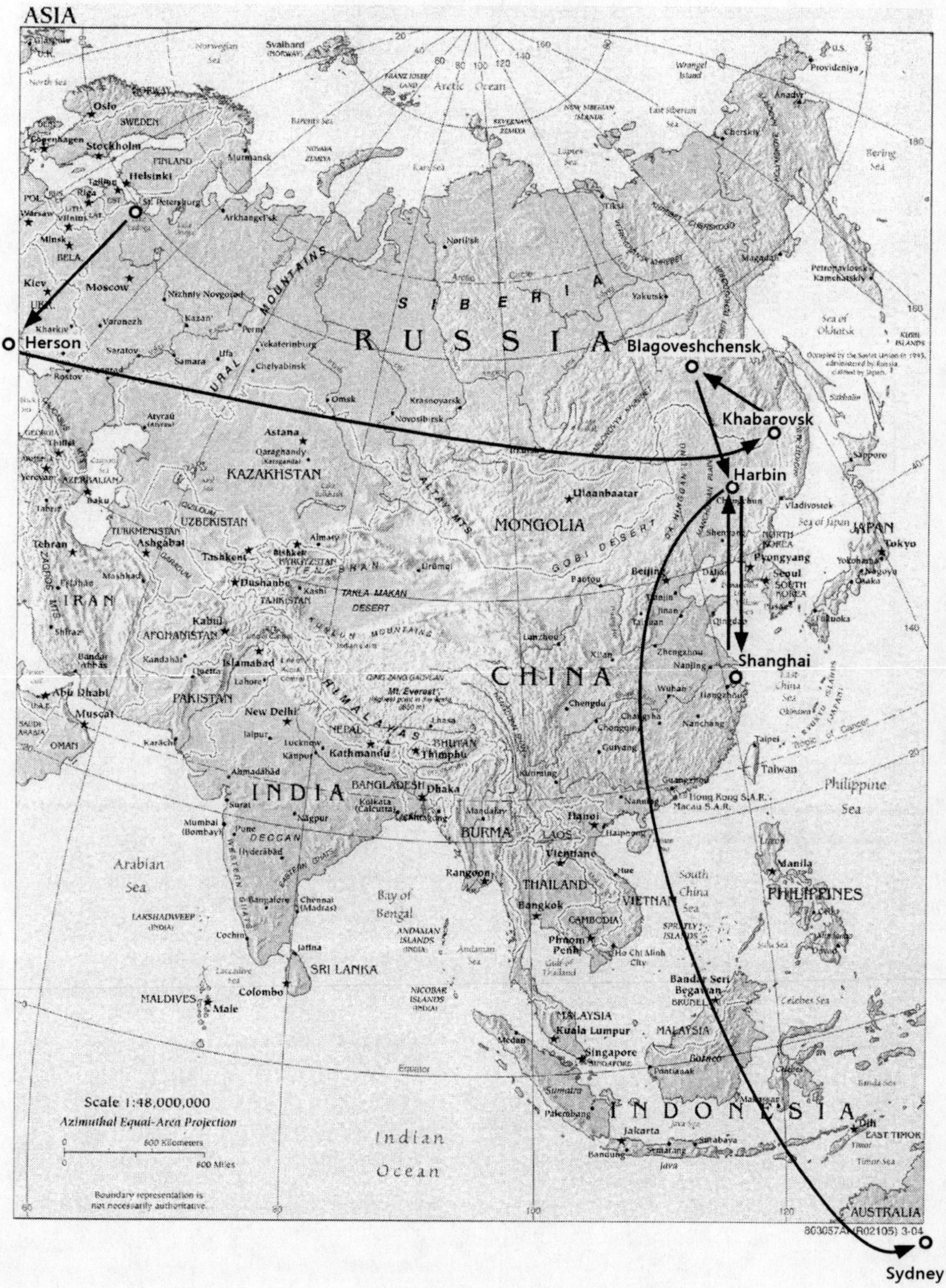

My Ancestry – VASSILIEFF & VAJINSKY

1 **Alexander Vassilieff (III)**
B: 9 Sep 1942
P: Shanghai China
M: 26 Jan 1964
P: ROCC,Sydney Australia
D:
P:

Alexandra Wownenko
(Spouse of no. 1)

2 **Vladimir Vassilieff**
B: 2 Oct 1913
P: Harbin China
M: 27 Feb 1938
P: Shanghai China
D: 3 May 1983
P: Moscow USSR

3 **Klaudia Vajinsky**
B: 13 Feb 1913
P: Blagoveshensk Russia
D: Abt 14 Jan 1977
P: Sydney Australia

4 **Alexander Vassilieff (II)**
B: Abt 1894
P: Russia
M: Abt//1912/1913
P: Harbin China
D: Abt//July1932
P: Harbin China

5 **Alexandra Shuvalov**
B: Abt 1894
P: Russia
D: Abt 1970
P: USSR

6 **Hereditary Noble B Vajinsky**
B: Abt 1883
P: Ananieve (Herson Province) U
M: (23/10/1905 GC) 05/11/05 JC
P: Odessa Ukraine
D: 6/5/1935 (St George's Day)
P: Harbin China

7 **Efrasinia Burdel-Budze**
B: 1887
P: Odessa Ukraine
D: 22 Feb 1973
P: Sydney Australia

8 **Alexander Vassilieff (I)**
B: Abt 1870
P: Russia
M: Abt 1890
P:
D: Abt 1920
P: Harbin China

9
B:
P:
D:
P:

10 **Vladimir Shuvalov?**
B: Abt 1875
P: Russia
M:
P:
D: ?
P: (?)

11
B:
P:
D:
P:

12 **HN Nikita VAJINSKY**
B: Abt 1850
P: Kiev Ukraine
M: Abt//1874
P:
D: Abt 1916
P: Kiev Ukraine

13 **Evdokia**
B: Abt 1850
P: Ukraine/Russia ?
D: Abt 1904
P: Herson - Ukraine

14 **Stepan Burdel-Budze**
B: Abt 1850
P: (?)
M:
P:
D: ?
P: (?)

15 **Daria Orloff**
B: Abt 1855
P: (?)
D: Abt 1920
P: (?)

16
B:
M:
D:

17
B:
D:

18
B:
M:
D:

19
B:
D:

20
B:
M:
D:

21
B:
D:

22
B:
M:
D:

23
B:
D:

24 **H-Noble Ivan Vajinsky**
B: Abt 1825
M:
D: Abt 1885/1905

25
B:
D:

26
B:
M:
D:

27
B:
D:

28 **Andrei Burdel-Budze**
B: Abt 1825
M:
D: ?

29 **Marina**
B: Abt 1825
D: Abt 1919

30
B:
M:
D:

31
B:
D

My Wife's Ancestry

1 **Alexandra Wownenko**
B: 3 Jan 1944
P: Berlin Germany
M: 26 Jan 1964
P: ROCC,Sydney Australia
D:
P:

Alexander Vassilieff (III)
(Spouse of no. 1)

2 **Ivan Wownenko**
B: 24 Sep 1902
P: Ivanovka Dniepropetrovsk Uk
M: 9 Oct 1932
P: Berlin Germany - St Vladimir'
D: 13 Apr 1964
P: Sydney

3 **DC Daria Kolessnikoff**
B: 23 Mar 1912
P: Rostov-Don
D: 4 Jan 1989
P: Sydney

4 **Arhip Wownenko**
B: Abt 1875
P: Ukraine
M:
P:
D: ?
P: (?)

5 **Ecapitolina Hartschenko**
B: Abt 1875
P: Ukraine
D: ?
P: (?)

6 **DC Gregory Kolesnikoff**
B: 1889
P: Dmitryevka (near Rostov-Don
M: Abt 1911
P: Rostov on the Don Russia
D: 1948
P: Oberammergau Germany

7 **DC Elena Bogachev**
B: 1 Jun 1891
P: Rostov-Don
D: 2 Sep 1972
P: Sydney

8
B:
P:
M:
P:
D:
P:

9
B:
P:
D:
P:

10
B:
P:
M:
P:
D:
P:

11
B:
P:
D:
P:

12 **Don Cossack Jacob K**
B: Abt 1860
P: Rostov-Don
M:
P:
D: ?
P: (?)

13 **Olga**
B: Abt 1855
P: Rostov-Don
D: ?
P: (?)

14 **DC Ignatiy Bogachov**
B: Abt 1865
P: Rostov-Don
M:
P:
D: ?
P: (?)

15 **Theodora**
B: Abt 1870
P: Rostov-Don
D: ?
P: (?)

16
B:
M:
D:

17
B:
D:

18
B:
M:
D:

19
B:
D:

20
B:
M:
D:

21
B:
D:

22
B:
M:
D:

23
B:
D:

24
B:
M:
D:

25
B:
D:

26
B:
M:
D:

27
B:
D:

28 **DC Feodor Bogachov**
B: Abt 1840
M:
D: ?

29
B:
D:

30
B:
M:
D:

31
B:
D:

Alexandra's & my Descendents

Alexander Vassilieff (III)
B: 9 Sep 1942
P: Shanghai China
D:
P:

sp: Alexandra Wownenko
B: 3 Jan 1944
P: Berlin Germany
D:
P:

Vladimir Vassilieff
B: 5 Nov 1964
P: Sydney
D:
P:

sp: Nicole Fetingis
B: 18 Sep 1972
P: Sydney
D:
P:

Matthew Vassilieff
B: 2 Nov 2001
P: Sydney
D:
P:

Luka Vassilieff
B: 18 Dec 2003
P: Sydney
D:
P:

Helen Vassilieff
B: 10 Jan 1968
P: Sydney
D:
P:

sp: Gregory Cook{A}
B: 10 Dec 1965
P: Sydney
D:
P:

Benjamin Cook
B: 15 Jan 1999
P: Sydney
D:
P:

Jordan Cook
B: 30 Jun 2000
P: Sydney
D:
P:

ACKNOWLEDGEMENTS

With gratitude and appreciation to:

Archbishop Hilarion	Russian Orthodox Diocese of Australia
D.R. Murray	(Major I.A. Retd.) Preliminary Editor
G.B. Nash	Information Technology and Preparation Assistance
G. Domansky	Librarian Russian Club Limited
G. Kositsin	Australian Representative – Hills of Manchuria Newspaper
J. Hinwood	Information Technology Assistance
T.I. Zolotareva	Librarian Archbishop's Chapel of All Saints of Russia
V. Reetov	Assistant Librarian Russian Club Limited
I. Dunn	Executive Director NSW Writers' Centre Inc

The Church of Jesus Christ of Latter-day Saints (The Mormons) Library have built up in Salt Lake City, Utah, a microfilm library of genealogical records from Britain and continental Europe, which is probably unequalled. Their software was very useful to me for the development of my family tree.

Moscow Administration of the Federal Security Service (FSB)

– Home security police, successor to the KGB and the Interior Ministry. Through an intermediary they provided me with restricted records of my father's case history.

Alexandra Vassilieff, my wife, who encouraged me, reviewed the manuscript and did not give up on me during the lengthy ordeal of research, technical hitches, rewrites and the associated moodiness of writing.

MAIN CHARACTERS

(Refer Appendix for detailed genealogy)

THE RUSSIANS

Vajinskys

Hereditary-Noble Boris, a family man – my maternal grandfather

Efrasinia (Franya) – my maternal grandmother – Babushka

Hereditary-Noble (Captain/Navigator) – Commander Vasily – my grandfather's older brother

Euginia, stage alias Gloria Star – Vasily's eldest daughter

Valentina (Tina), Boris's eldest daughter – my eldest aunt

Maria (Musya), Boris's second daughter – my second aunt

Klaudia (Klava), Boris's youngest daughter – my mother

Vassilieffs

Alexander (II) Engineer/lecturer – my paternal grandfather

Vladimir (Volodya/Vova), Athlete, Business-man a GULAG inmate and escapee – my father

Alexander (III), (Sasha/Shurick/Alex), Engineer/Manager – myself – Odysseya's author

Kolesnikoffs/Bogachevs
Don-Cossack Elena – The searcher – my wife's maternal grandmother – Babushka
Don-Cossack Daria (Dasha), Business and family woman – my wife's mother

THE UKRAINIANS

Wownenkos
Ivan (Iva) Engineer/truck-driver, family man – my wife's father
Alexandra (Shura/Alex), Laboratory technician, Artist and homemaker – my wife, mother and babushka

CONTENTS

PREFACE

Life must be lived forward but it
can only be understood backwards
Soren Kierkegaard 1813-55

In Imperial Russia, there used to be four social classes. As in the West, the main three were the *working class* – peasants and labourers; the *middle class* or *bourgeoisie* – administrative personnel, merchants, clerks, professionals and clergy; and the *aristocracy,* including the nobility (both 'personal' and 'hereditary') and the titular (title-holders), such as princes and counts.

The fourth class, the *Cossacks,* was rather unique. The Cossacks were allotted land, a certain degree of autonomy and self-government. For this semi-autonomy, each man was required to give twenty years of military service to the Tsar, commencing at the age of eighteen. Their services were mainly used for protection against border incursions and during times of war. At birth, the class of an individual was recorded on the birth certificate and in a special 'Book of Births' so there could be no future doubt as to his or her status. To some degree, the Cossack Clans could be said to resemble the Scottish Clans; the Macgregors, MacDonalds, Campbells and so on.

This is a story which covers a period of about 200 years. It is near enough to a biography about my family, or rather a number of families whose roots intertwine all class barriers and stretch across half the globe as they journeyed to new lands to better their lives and sometimes to save them.

The story also covers briefly a period of Russian history from the beginning – the summoning of the Viking warriors to the fall of the Romanov Empire and the resulting Russian Diaspora. It does it in a way to introduce the reader, unfamiliar with the Russian beginnings, to what Russia used to be. The historical information is sourced from Old Russian chronicles, eminent historians, encyclopedias, and word of mouth, from those who lived through some of the more recent horrors of the Russian tragedy. The historic outline covers the development and richness of Russian thought and culture, its never-ending turmoils and some of its contributions to our world.

My family's life is deeply intertwined in Russian history and the resulting Diaspora and typifies to the reader what millions of Russians went through during the turbulent times of the 20th century. Although I was unable to acquire all of my family's history, I filled in the gaps the way it may have happened to the best of my ability through deductive reasoning of events – similar family behavioural patterns of blood relatives, family chitchat and factoring in of surrounding events of the time. As such I take full responsibility for any errors in the story for which I hope my ancestors will forgive me.

My grandparents and parents fled from Russia to China during the Russian Civil War immediately after World War I. Most of my family survived two generations of the worst bloodshed, political and economic upheaval experienced during the 20th century (World War I, the Russian Civil War, Japanese occupation, World War II, Stalin's GULAGS and Political Oppression).

Although my father and two of my uncles survived Stalin's postwar GULAGS, four of my granduncles were killed in the Russian Civil War and one distinguished himself and lived to tell the tale.

Both of my grandfathers died during the Japanese occupation of Manchuria, one as a result of torture, and the other from stress and related physical ailments.

My wife, who brought much love and joy to my development, experienced with her parents and grandparents similar dislocation and turmoil in fleeing from Russia at about the same time as my family, but fleeing in the opposite direction of France and Germany. They experienced life under Hitler, the destruction of Berlin and the postwar Displaced Persons camps prior to coming here to Australia.

1 GHOSTS FROM THE PAST

1 REMINISCENCE

I love you, work of Peter's warrant,
I love your stern and comely face,
The Broad Neva's majestic current,
Her bankments' granite carapace,
The patterns laced by iron railing,
And of your meditative night
The lucent dusk, the moonless paling;
When in my room I read and write...

The Bronze Horseman 1833

A. Pushkin[1]

Now that the future which I used to dream of is in the past, my memories of past and former future have merged in the sea of life gone by. But, *the past is like a ghost it never goes away.* Now in the autumn of my years the question that I most often ask is: What legacy will my generation leave for the next? Closer to the point, will my grandchildren know what we left them and what our grandparents left us?

Life is sweet now and I have experienced great times and met

1 A Yermolinsky – The poems, prose and plays of A. Pushkin – Random House New York 1936

some extraordinary people who by their example influenced my life. In fact, both my wife and I were blessed living in perhaps the best country in the world with a good, healthy, happy and relatively secure life. Yet it was not always like this.

I was too young to remember my birthplace – Shanghai. However, I have some recollection of Harbin, where I went to school for a while. It was a newly built city in Manchuria, where my parents and grandparents lived a significant part of their life. But what were they doing there? They were not Chinese, they were Russians.

I remember the stories my mother and later my aunts and grandmother used to tell me, as well as many other people with a similar background to ours. My paternal grandfather's past is sketchy at best. His father brought his family to Harbin probably to work on the then construction of the China Eastern Railway. My maternal grandparents, who belonged to the aristocracy, were colonists in the Ukraine near the Black Sea and their immediate ancestors were believed to have come from the northern part of Russia. So in effect my family's journey of about 200 years had started in the Russian north, went on to China and ended up in Australia. Hence, our: *Odysseya*[2]– From the Far North via the Middle Kingdom to the Land Down Under or for brevity – An Epic Journey from Russia to Australia.

As my grandchildren, like most people in Australia, do not know much about Russia and the Russians I have decided to devote a brief but concise section to Russian history and the 20th century Russian Diaspora, the largest in its history, as an introduction to the reader to help to understand our ancestry better. In doing so I hope to make my contribution to the history of my family and to the unique cultural and national identity that Australia, like the United States of America, is developing through the assimilation of its indigenous and immigrant populations in *this Southern Land* under one language, one government and one flag.

However, we all have ghosts; English, Irish, Chinese, German, Indian, etc. My Ghosts from the Past are the Russians. So who were they?

2 A Russian term for Odyssey

2 THE RUSSIANS

The Russians, like their cousins, Ukrainians and Belo Russians, belong to the eastern Slavic tribes who in turn emerged from the Indo-European (Arian) white race. The beginning of Russian history (Rus as it was known then), as recorded in the monastic chronicles by Nestor (and later by a Kiev monk Sylvester), reads: Town stood against town until there was no truth left. They decided to find themselves a duke and in the year of 862 sent ambassadors over the sea to the Viking Norman tribe (also known as Varangians) with a message:

Zemlya nasha velika i obilna, a poryadka v nyei net; prihoditye knyazhit i vladyet nami. – Our Land is great and abundant, but without order; come, rule and control us. And so the three brothers with their personal army came to Rus. Their names were Rurik, Sineus and Truvor. Rurik established himself in the city of Novgorod, his brothers in smaller towns. After the death of his brothers, Rurik ruled the whole north. Following Rurik's death, his nephew Oleg moved the capital to the well-established city of Kiev.

THE RURIK DYNASTY lasted 736 years, from 862 until 1598, with the death of a childless Tsar Theodore, the son of Ivan the Terrible. This makes this dynasty one of the longest ruling dynasties of Europe. By comparison the better-known Hapsburg Dynasty lasted 700 years, from 1218 and finally dying out in 1918.

Perhaps the Rurik Dynasty of Viking/Norman origin mixed with Slavic stock produced a type of symbiotic result that is best known for its Democratic Beginnings, Territorial and Trade expansions, Military triumphs and the Introduction of Christianity.

Its Democratic initiations were demonstrated by the election of a national leader and the instrument of collective decision-making known as the *Novgorod Vyeche,* where its town-folk gathered to make a collective decision often rowdy, in which the loudest screams usually led to the accepted choice. If no distinction in volume could be made, the second method required a gathering on the bridge by the opposing sides and similar to the tug of war the winners remained standing on the bridge. The losers were usually in the water below.

In its expansion of territory and trade, Rus progressed along its waterways – *Iz Varyaga v Gryeki* – from Scandinavia to Greece. It also extended these undertakings to the Caspian Sea and Central Asia.

The Military triumphs over neighbouring Slavs, Greeks and Nomads included the siege of Constantinople, first by Oleg and later again by Igor in order to open up trade and cultural ties.

The introduction of Christianity and the conversion of a whole nation from paganism to a spiritually based faith resulted from trade and political ties with Byzantium and Vladimir's deliberations in choosing a faith for his new nation. To this end he entertained the envoys of Islam – the Volga Bulgars, Judaism – the Khazars, Catholicism – Papal emissaries from Rome and finally an Orthodox monk from Constantinople. At last, after 10 Kiev town-folk went to check out the St. Sophia Cathedral in Constantinople, Vladimir made his decision. Their message was – *I ne svemi, na nyebe li yesmi bili li na zyemle – We did not know whether we were in Heaven or on earth.*

The town-folk then told Vladimir: "If the faith of the Greeks was bad your grandmother Olga would have never converted." And so Rus was baptized.

Its weakness was no doubt a curious system of inherited rule in which power as the right of succession, passed to all male heirs rather than to the eldest son, thereby leading to the fragmentation of the Kingdom. Hence, after the earlier rulers unified Rus, their descendents particularly after Yaroslav 1015-1054 began to break it up. This led to destructive competition between the Dukes, which left Rus vulnerable to neighbouring nomads. In particular, the Polovtsi – Turkic tribes – regularly raided the outskirts of the expanded nation. Although the powerful and highly educated Vladimir Monomah 1113-25 temporarily reversed the trend, his children did not follow suit. Therefore, the Polovtsian tribes again commenced their raids.

Compounding this situation a new foe of an apocalyptic magnitude appeared from the east. His name was Temujin – more commonly known as Genghis Khan. A brilliant Mongolian warrior-ruler, he united all the Mongolian tribes and fitted them out for war. His troops were organised; based on the decimal system and rigidly disciplined. They were well equipped and supplied. The generals were his own sons or exceedingly able men, absolutely loyal to him. As a military genius, Genghis Khan was highly flexible and could rapidly adapt himself to changing circumstances. At first, his troops were exclusively cavalry, riding the hardy, grass-fed Mongol pony that needed no fodder. Their manoeuvres included firing arrows at the enemy while riding away. Their reflex-bow had greater velocity than the European bow, which gave them superior advantage over their foe. With such an army, other nomads could be defeated, but cities could not be taken. Before long Genghis's military strategies developed further so that the Mongols were able to undertake the siege of large cities, using mangonels[3], catapults, ladders, burning oil, and so forth and even diverting rivers

In 1223, on the banks of the river Kalka near the Azov Sea, the Mongolian Horde of far superior numbers met and overran the

3 Missile-throwing engines

fragmented Russian army and won a resounding victory. They did not return for 13 years.

In 1236 Batu Khan, Genghis's grandson mercilessly overran the Volga Bulgars near the Urals and in 1237, the Mongols commenced their systematic destruction of Russian cities. Although each city was defended bravely by its inhabitants, there was no unity in the Russian forces overall. Much of Rus was destroyed and Batu went on as far as Hungary and lower parts of Poland where again the Hungarian and German-Polish armies were no match for him. Batu than established the Tartar/Mongol new capital –Sarai-Batu – on the Volga River, near where Volgograd is today. The area became known as the Golden Horde – the centre of the Tartar/Mongol Empire.

Only Novgorod and the nearby lands were spared, thanks to the wise Duke Alexander Nevsky, who paid homage and taxes to the Khans. This ensured the survival of Novgorod and the continuation of Russian culture and the Rurik Dynasty. The severe destruction of much of Rus attracted raiders from Sweden and Germany, the then Teutonic Knights. In both instances, the valiant Alexander fought off the foes. The Swedes were defeated along the banks of the Neva River. Hence, Alexander became known as Nevsky. The Teutonic Knights were defeated on an iced Lake Chudskoye. It gave the Russians a badly needed lift in their morale and hope for a better future. The Orthodox Church canonized the brave and wise Alexander some time after his death for the saving of Rus from total annihilation.

However, Russia was to suffer and endure the Tartar yoke from Batu's established Empire, known as the Golden Horde, for about 250 years.

Unlike the Mongols, Tartars spoke a Turkic language, and they may have been related to the Cuman or Kipchak peoples. After various groups of these Turkic nomads became part of the armies of the Mongol conqueror Genghis Khan in the early 13th century, a fusion of Mongol and Turkic elements took place, and the Mongol invaders of Russia and Hungary became known to Europeans as Tatars or Tartars.

Finally, Ivan III stood up to them in 1480. And the Tartars went home. Russia then began to progressively move southward and eastward.

THE TIME OF TROUBLES – 1598-1613 – was a period in Russia which lasted for 15 years. It was a time between Monarchs where Russia again endured hard times. Historically it is referred to as *Smutnoye Vremya* – Times of Troubles. During that period at least three interesting things happened:

Firstly, Boris Godunov, an uncle of the last Tsar Theodore, ruled for five years for his young and inexperienced nephew. He continued to rule for another seven years after the death of the last Tsar. Godunov was like a de facto Tsar and proved to be very effective.

During his regency, Russia reclaimed lands lost to the Swedes along the coastal strip in the bay of Finland. Moreover, Russia acquired an unprecedented agreement from the Eastern Orthodox Patriarchs (of Constantinople, Antioch, Jerusalem and Alexandria) for the establishment of a Moscow Patriarch. This was an historic agreement as it led to the expansion of the original five sees in the Christian Apostolic Church (prior to the great schism into Orthodoxy and Catholicism, Rome was one of the five sees). Furthermore, Russia expanded the recently obtained lands of inner Siberia, which were acquired by an expedition force, headed by the Cossack Yermak, sent by Ivan the Terrible.

Secondly, the last seven years of the troubled times were the most difficult. Towards the end of Godunov's rule there were three years of crop failure, followed by famine and disease of epidemic proportions. Simultaneously there were Moscow fires. These misfortunes led to lawlessness, disorder pillage and false tsars. Poland and Sweden took advantage of the situation and claimed significant Russian territories. This included much of the land known as Ukraine and Byelorussia today. The Poles got as close as Moscow.

Russia was in ruins, burnt and pillaged and on the brink of

total collapse. Many heroic deeds happened during that time. Many noble and ordinary Russians gave their lives for their country. Memories of the Tartar conquest were still fresh. Russia was not going to be overrun once again by a foreign foe. Russia needed unification under a new brave wise leadership.

The third interesting thing that happened when Russia was on the brink of collapse was a democratically based election of a new Tsar. In 1613 a National Council – *Zemsky Sabor* – was elected from 50 towns/cities. It consisted of the highest clergy, nobility and representatives of Moscow. A lengthy debate followed regarding the election of a new Tsar. Finally, the Cossacks, with the support of two nobles, proposed sixteen-year-old Michael Theodorovitch Romanov, son of the Moscow Metropolitan Theodore. Metropolitan Philaret was a second cousin to the late Tsar Philaret. The Metropolitan himself as a clergyman could not be elected to the throne. Furthermore, he was then incarcerated in a Polish prison. However, once free the respected Metropolitan could bring his influence to bear on the affairs of state through his son.

And so the new Tsar was elected. Behind the scenes, however, there was danger lurking in the woods. The Poles upon hearing of the new Tsar-elect sent a detachment of troops to kill young Michael. The detachment got to the Kostroma woods where Michael was living and asked for direction from a local peasant – Ivan Susanin. Suspecting foul play, Ivan mislead the Poles. He led them into the thick of the woods but paid dearly for it with his life. Nevertheless, the Poles perished as well.

By giving his life for the Tsar, Ivan's heroic deed earned him a place in Russian history. More than 200 years later, a gifted Russian composer Mikhail Ivanovich Glinka (described as a dilettante of genius) composed an opera that won him fame, entitled *Life for the Tsar,* as a lasting tribute to Ivan.

Simultaneously a National Army was established mainly from Nizhny Novgorod, headed by an able administrator, Kuzma Minin, and an experienced general, Prince Dimitry M Pozharsky. This disciplined force succeeded in driving out the Poles from Moscow and stabilizing the land sufficiently to allow the election of the new Tsar.

THE ROMANOV DYNASTY ruled for just over 300 years from 1613 to 1917. The Last Tsar Nicholas II abdicated for himself and his son and heir 16 March 1917 (3 March Julian calendar).

The main achievements of the Romanovs were that they brought Russia out of the dark ages. When Tsar Michael (1613-45) came to power Russia was in ruins and still suffering from the effects of Tartar rule. Owing to his youth and inexperience, he wisely leaned on the National Council for advice. By 1619 his father returned from prison and was made a Patriarch. Together with his son, they both ruled Russia and shared the same title of Mighty Sovereigns.

Similarly, after Michael's death, his son Alexei (1645-76) befriended an outstanding monk by the name of Nikon who became a Patriarch. Together they ruled Russia and bore the same title as their predecessors of the Mighty Sovereigns.

Between Michael and Alexei and their co-sovereigns Russia started to slowly heal. Wars with Poland and Sweden were reduced. Peace treaties signed. Some lands returned. In particular, the great Ukrainian Cossack Hetman Bohdan Khmelnitsky sought and received help from Tsar Alexei. Thus in 1654 most of Ukraine (Little Russia) was liberated from Poland and reunited with Russia. New territories in Siberia were progressively added. With the help of Kiev and Constantinople, Orthodox scriptures – church service books were corrected, which inevitably went astray during the Tartar rule. Widespread corruption and lawlessness were also significantly reduced.

Perhaps none more than the Greats, Peter I and Catherine II, helped to Westernise and develop Russia into a great world power (but at great cost to the people). Achievements were visible practically on all fronts; construction of a new capital, St. Petersburg – Window to the West – sometimes referred to as Venice of the North; a newly-established navy, that became only second to the

British navy (for a while at least); higher education for men and women, particularly of the upper class. During Peter's rule Russia became an Empire stretching from the Baltic and the Black Sea to the Pacific Ocean. Catherine carried on the work begun by Peter. With her ministers, she reorganized the administration and law of the Russian Empire and extended Russian territory, adding the Crimea and much of Poland.

Of course, there was always a price to be paid for rapid development. It took the great reforms of Alexander II (1855-81) to undo and improve many of the ill-effects that resulted from the great changes introduced, in particular those of Peter the Great and Catherine the Great, as well as some out-of-date practices made paramount by the onset of the Industrial Revolution. Major reforms of Alexander II included: Emancipation of the peasant class, although some of his predecessors introduced limited emancipation, notably his grandfather – Paul I. This reform alone earned him the title of Alexander the Liberator. A range of land reforms was also introduced to make it easier for emancipated peasants to own land and landowners to be compensated for any loss of land and labour. However, the full implementation of this reform dragged on until Prime Minister P. Stolypin under Nicholas II had re-ignited the initiative.[4] He introduced a court based on a jury system based on the criteria of accountability, openness, justice and swiftness. National conscription (introduced by Peter the Great) was reduced from 25 years to three to six years with many exemptions and Military service received a general overhaul, which included education of all enlisted ranks. The education system became universal, structured and professional, e.g. middle level schools received a classical program and education for women became more widespread and advanced.

Alexander III (1881-94) only became heir apparent on the death

4 It is interesting to note that regarding the first two reforms, the reformers Alexander II, P. Stolypin as well as Nicholas II at different points in time were assassinated and/or murdered by revolutionaries who allegedly were fighting for the same thing.

of his elder brother Nikolay in 1865. Alexander then began to study the principles of law and administration under the jurist and political philosopher K.P. Pobedonostsev, who influenced the nature of his reign by instilling into his mind a hatred for representative government and the belief that zeal for Orthodoxy ought to be cultivated by every tsar.

One can appreciate the new Tsar's state of mind as he came to the throne after the assassination of his father Alexander II. The murder of his liberal reformer father by a terrorist radical, and the advice of his tutor to maintain autocracy and clamp down on reforms, convinced him that multicultural underdeveloped Russia needed greater uniformity and control. Hence Alexander III became an opponent of representative government, and a supporter of Russian nationalism. He adopted programs based on the concepts of Orthodoxy, autocracy, and *narodnost* (a belief in the Russian people) that included the Russification of national minorities in the Russian Empire as well as discouragement of the non-Orthodox religious groups. These policies clashed with those seeking greater political and religious freedom.

This was the paradox of Alexander's rule – a harsh conservative government. It favoured economic growth and industrial development at the expense of badly needed social and political reforms. It produced strong foreign, monetary and domestic policies resulting in peace and strengthening of Germanic, Austrian and later Franco-Russian ties. Both Alexander III and Nicholas II are credited with the establishment of a new gold standard as a basis of Russia's monetary policy. They also hastened the pace of industrialization – expanding the manufacturing base and public works infrastructure, such as the construction and development of new factories, mining and railroads. However, the attempt to accelerate the badly needed change from agrarian to industrial base, without tempering the change with socio-political reforms, created a large dislocation of labour and an unhappy young intelligentsia.

The legacy that Alexander left his son Nicholas II (1894-1917) was a boiling cauldron with no pressure relief valves. Nicholas, who was probably more like his grandfather than father in character, tried to continue with his father's policies but did not have the same will to enforce them. He was a softer man, more family-oriented and would have preferred implementing the social reforms of his grandfather and world peace to which he strongly subscribed, rather than engaging in the fast pace of industrial development and the developing foreign and domestic conflicts with a dubious successor to the throne – a haemophilic son.

Too often, the negatives of the last Tsar are highlighted and the positives are left out. Yet he was so strongly remembered and missed by much of the Russian Diaspora after the revolution. In 1988 in honour of the celebration of 1000 years of Christianity in Russia, Tsar Nicholas, together with his family and faithful servants (who were all brutally murdered by Lenin's henchmen), were canonised for their martyrdom by the Russian Orthodox Church[5]. In addition, President Yeltsin had the remains of the Romanov family exhumed, verified by DNA testing and brought to St. Petersburg for a requiem mass and Orthodox burial.

The last Tsar's contributions to Russia and the world were impressive. To Russia he brought the intellect of P.I. Stolypin[6], the best Prime Minister (1906-11) it ever had (unfortunately assassinated) who recommended the reinstitution of the unfinished reforms of Alexander II and other initiatives. Nicholas further abolished all traces of Corporal punishment and continued with the mass development of national education at primary, secondary and tertiary levels evidenced by the blossoming of Russia's art and sciences. At the same time, the country enjoyed

5 The Russian Orthodox Church Outside Russia cannonised them earlier – in 1981, together with all the new martyrs and confessors of Russia.

6 A conservative statesman, who during his tenure as Prime Minister initiated extensive agrarian reforms to improve the legal and economic standing of the peasantry as well as the general economy and political stability of Imperial Russia. As a former provincial Governor he demonstrated his concern for improving the welfare of the peasants as well as his firmness and efficiency in subduing their rebellions.

a period of high economic growth that lasted up to 1914. Nevertheless Nicholas's most lasting contribution to Russia (with the aid of another great minister – Witte[7]) was and must be the linking of European and Asiatic Russia by means of the Trans Siberian Railroad – the largest in the world – which was constructed during his reign.

To the world Nicholas brought a number of world-first industrial reforms, such as shorter working hours and the banning of underage employment. At The Hague, he initiated two world Peace Conferences in 1899 and 1907 which were the precursers of the League of Nations/United Nations of today. Sadly for Russia and the world this gentle, humane and well-meaning man was overtaken by a series of events that culminated in the March Revolution of 1917 under the gigantic sham of World War I that was a disaster for Russia. Returning home as the Commander-in-Chief of the Russian Forces, rather than going into exile he and his family were incarcerated and, despite not only his own abdication from the throne but also his son's, the family were later put to death.[8] (In abdicating the Tsar said: "There is nothing I would not do for Russia.") Reproduced below is his last bequest/appeal to the Russian troops.

---

7 He was Finance Minister between 1892 to1903 and first constitutional Prime Minister of Imperial Russia between 1905 to1906. Perhaps his contributions even exceeded that of Stolypin. He endeavoured to join firm authoritarian rule to modernization along Western lines. Witte demonstrated his freedom from bureaucratic prejudice by appointing men on merit of all nationalities – Jews, Poles, Ukrainians etc. as his subordinates and by cultivating favourable relations with the media. His economic wisdom was shown in his collection and use of railway statistics and in the implementation of an effective freight tariff, which through the lowering of freight rates provided increased revenue.

8 It is still a controversial issue today whether a ruling monarch can abdicate on behalf of his heir. Whatever the case the action of the Tsar did not save his son and family from their fate.

The Last Appeal To The Troops: *This is my final appeal to you, my beloved Troops. As a consequence of my and my son's abdication from the Russian Throne, authority is now transferred to the provisional government under the initiative of the Representative Assembly of the State Duma (Nicholas II abdicated the throne in favour of his brother Michael, who refused it the following day).*
May the Lord God help you my valiant Army, to defend and save our homeland from the evil enemy. During the course of two and a half years, you have carried the heavy hourly burden of active battle service. Much blood has been spilt, much effort has been exerted and the hour draws near when Russia and its valiant allies will strive and achieve victory over our foe. This unprecedented war must be brought to a supreme victory.
Those who think of peace now, those who want it now – they will betray us and they are traitors to our homeland. (Tr. Note, peace comes at a price.)
Every true warrior knows this. Perform your duty, defend our valiant homeland, and accept your new provisional government and obey your leaders.
Remember that any deviation from order is to the benefit of the enemy!
My firm belief is that your infinite love for our great homeland still lives. May the Lord God bless you all and may the great martyr and patron, Saint George, lead us to Victory.
NIKOLAS
Stavka. 15 March 1917. (2 March 1917 Julian calendar)

On the negative side, he appeared to be more preoccupied with his family than with the dynamics of running the empire. He was slow to act and often procrastinated in decision-making or made second-rate decisions. (These traits are not that uncommon amongst world monarchs and their side effects are minimal in a well-established constitutional monarchy with a dynamic executive/government.)

Rather than initiate political reform he reluctantly agreed to create a national representative assembly – the Duma. This was a big political reform for Russia, a change from Autocratic to Constitutional Monarchy and late in coming. It was brought on by the people's revolt in 1905.

Through poorly thought through Far East politics, Russia became involved in a Russo-Japanese war. Apart from humiliation, it cost Russia dearly (a modern American/Vietnam involvement).

Russia's desire to help others and be the protector of all Slavic nations (very noble but not always pragmatic) in this case to help Serbia, led Russia to its downfall. The assassination of Arch-Duke Ferdinand – the last remaining Hapsburg heir to the throne in Sarajevo – was the trigger to a number of world changing events. It precipitated World War I and (later) World War II, the end of four dynasties – Austro-Hungarian, German, Turkish and Russian – and the start of a communist state in Russia. It also resulted in the spread of communism to other parts of the world that impacted upon world affairs for the remainder of the 20th century.

Had Nicholas II stayed out of the conflict, which was uncompromisingly pushed ahead by the infuriated Axis powers[9], Russia may not have gone through the horrible turmoil of that period. By avoiding a war, its Tsar at the front line and with continued economic growth Russia would have most likely avoided a revolution and the communist grab of power by deceit. Although eventual war may not have been avoided – as coalition partners, France and Britain had some say in the matter – there may have been a different outcome for everyone, had it occurred years later. Amazing what a cooling off period can do. Even Rasputin advised the Tsar to stay out of the conflict. Thus, Russia would have been spared the mass executions, destruction of the countryside and the exodus

9 Namely Austro-Hungary and the German desire to try out their new high tech war machine.

of its intelligentsia. Had the war been avoided or delayed perhaps the Russian monarchy eventually through evolution could have resembled its related monarchs in Great Britain.

As we come to the end of this review of Russian Monarchy, a reflection on some of the developments of art, literature and science in Russia can only be described as absolutely remarkable. Whatever the downside of some of the Russian monarchs, their overall rule resulted in the exponential development of Russian culture. In particular, the 19th and pre-revolutionary 20th centuries which are classed as the golden and silver periods of Russian literature.

In order to enlighten the reader further and before I introduce my ancestors, I must beg the reader's patience a little longer, while we briefly review Russia's achievements in Science, Literature, Music, Theatre and Art during the Romanov dynasty, for only then can the reader be in a better position to make a relatively astute judgement of what Russia lost and/or gained by becoming a communist state.

Science, Literature, Music, Theatre and Art in Russia made their greatest leap forward between the late 18th to the early 20th centuries. These were the results of rapid growth and transformation of Russia from an old feudal state to a modern first class empire. Following are some of the more prominent thinkers and innovators of that time.

The greatest Russian scientist of that time was Michael V Lomonosov 1711-65 – poet, scientist, and grammarian. He is considered the first Great Russian linguistic reformer. His substantial contributions to the natural sciences include: works on Origin of Light and Colours, creation of the first coloured glass mosaics in Russia, theoretical works on electricity, reorganization of the St. Petersburg Imperial Academy of Sciences and the Establishment of Moscow University that today bears his name.

Lomonosov was the son of a poor fisherman. He too took up that line of work at the age of 10. At the age of 19, after he read the few books he was able to obtain and they could no longer satisfy his growing thirst for knowledge, he left his native village, penniless and on foot, for Moscow. He answered the legacy of Tsar Peter's call to the learned to transform Russia into a modern nation. But first he had to educate himself.

He eventually became a member of three Academies of Science: Stockholm, Bologna and St. Petersburg. His theories concerning heat and the constitution of matter were analysed with interest in European scientific journals although at that time the empiricist scientists of Germany opposed them. Some of his contributions were only fully realized in the 20th century.

Dmitry I Mendeleyev 1834-1907 – Russian chemist who developed the periodic classification of the elements. His legacy included the final version (1871) of the periodic chart (also referred to as Mendeleyev's Table) in which he left gaps, foretelling that they would be filled by elements not then known as well as predicting the properties of three of those elements.

Nikolai I Lobachevsky 1792-1856 – Russian mathematician, he independently discovered non-Euclidean geometry. He did this at about the same time as Carl Gauss, a German scientist, and János Bolyai, a Hungarian mathematician. His work was not widely recognized until Einstein's general theory of relativity became known as it revealed the non-Euclidean nature of space-time.

Vasily O Klyuchevsky 1841-1911 – Russian historian whose sociological approach to the study of Russia's past and lively writing as well as his lecturing style made him one of the foremost scholars of his time.

Klyuchevsky was a son of a poor village priest. He attended a seminary school before transferring to the University of Moscow (1861). Klyuchevsky wrote a series of theses, including his doctoral dissertation on the Boyar Duma (council of the upper nobility) of Muscovite Russia. The dissertation won him immediate professional recognition and several appointments at the Alexandrian

Military School, the University for Women at Moscow and the Moscow Theological Academy. In 1879, he became Professor of History at the University of Moscow, where he taught until 1910.

The publication of his lectures on *Kurs Russkoy Istorii* – A History of Russia – brought him worldwide renown. It was originally published in four volumes (1904-10). The fifth volume was published posthumously in 1921. This great literary work (probably the best-recorded history of Russia to date) described as a *magnum opus,* traced Russian history in a logical, systematic, and highly readable form. Klyuchevsky wrote from a 19th century liberal perspective and gave a broad but vivid socio-economic analysis of the processes of Russian history. He emphasized such aspects as the succession of social classes and the spread of colonization, as well as painting some of the most memorable images of leading figures (such as Peter the Great, Catherine the Great and Alexander II) in Russian historiography. His closest contemporary was Sergey F Platonov (1860-1933) also regarded as a leading historian of his time who was eventually exiled by the Soviet government for his alleged anti-Stalinist views.

Alexander S. Pushkin 1799-1837 – Russian poet, novelist, dramatist, and short story writer, considered as Russia's greatest poet and the founder of modern Russian literature. Like Alexandre Dumas, he was partly African. Like Shakespeare was to England, Pushkin was to Russia. His best-known works include; *Eugene Onegin, The Bronze Horseman, Ruslan and Lyudmilla, The Captain's Daughter, Mozart and Salieri* and *The Queen of Spades.* His works make up several volumes of publication. He was killed in a duel in his prime.

Mikhail Lermontov 1814-41 – considered a successor to Pushkin and like his idol he, too, was killed in a duel. He was a leading Russian Romantic poet and author of the novel *A Hero of Our Time,* which was to have a profound influence on later Russian writers.

Other works include; *Prisoner of the Caucasus, Masquerade, The Tambov, Paymaster's Wife, Sashka* and many more.

Nikolai V. Gogol 1809-52 – Russian/Ukrainian novelist, dramatist, and short story writer, born in the Ukraine. He captivated the Russian literary world with the Ukrainian countryside, with its colourful peasantry, its Cossack traditions, its rich folklore and numerous Ukrainian words and phrases. His writings are satirical, often exploring themes of fantasy and the supernatural. His notable works include: *The Government Inspector, Notes of a Madman, Dead Souls, The Overcoat, Evenings on a Farm near Dikanka,* and the best known in the West, *Taras Bulba.*

Fyodor M Dostoyevsky 1821-81 – internationally regarded as one of the finest novelists who ever lived. His thoughts and ideas have profoundly shaped literary modernism, existentialism, and various schools of psychology, theology, and literary criticism. Dostoyevsky's works are often regarded as prophetic, such as in his novel *The Possessed* in which he so accurately predicted how Russia's revolutionaries – the communist successors – would behave if they came to power. During his time, he was also renowned for his activity as a journalist. His best-known works include: *Crime and Punishment, Brothers Karamazov, The Possessed, The Idiot, Notes from the Underground, The Double* and *White Nights.*

Leo N Tolstoy 1828-1910 – perhaps even more than Dostoyevsky, Tolstoy is praised as being the greatest novelist in world literature. The 19th century English critic and poet Matthew Arnold famously expressed the common view in saying that a work by Tolstoy is not a piece of art but a piece of life: Tolstoy's novels read as if life itself was writing directly, without an intervening medium. His tone and style reflect his belief that theory is inadequate in explaining the world's complexity, which evolves by tiny grain-like and almost pattern-less change. He contended that True life, is lived not at moments of grand crisis but at countless ordinary and prosaic moments, which human beings usually do not notice. Tolstoy illustrates his ideas and explicitly expresses them in *War and Peace,* covering the period during the Napoleonic wars, and in *Anna Karenina,* which applies this unromantic view of life to marriage, the family, and work. *Anna Karenina* also contrasts romantic love, which is based on intense moments of passion and infidelity, with the prosaic love of the family, based on intimacy. Other works include; *Resurrection, The Cossacks, Childhood, Boyhood, and Youth.*

Anton P Chekhov 1860-1904 – like Tolstoy he was an unusually fertile writer, but unlike Tolstoy, he has not written a single novel. He was a literary artist of laconic precision. He probed below the surface of life, laying bare the secret motives of his characters. Although, he did not attempt to analyse his characters in the way Tolstoy and Dostoyevsky did, like delving to great depths in psychoanalysis, and linking the destinies of their heroes through the thinnest psychological threads. Instead, he wrote about the humdrum existence of ordinary people and their daily happenings.

Chekhov's best plays and short stories are not based on complex plots and neat solutions. Appearing trivial, they tend to create a special kind of atmosphere, at times haunting or lyrical. Devoid of obtrusive literary devices, he describes the Russian life of his time in a deceptively simple way. Chekhov is regarded as the outstanding representative of the late 19th century Russian realist school. Along with Gogol's *The Inspector General,* Chekhov's plays are the high point of Russian drama. His works include the four great plays, *The Seagull, Uncle Vanya, Three Sisters,* and *The Cherry Orchard,* along with many others.

Other writers of that period include: Nikolay Turgenev, Ivan Krylov, Nikolay Nekrasov and scores of others. As mentioned earlier, the 19th century was considered as the Golden Era and the pre revolutionary 20th century as the Silver Era of Russian literature. These periods produced an almost unmatched and unending string of brilliant writers and only the Russian revolution reduced this flow of talent to no more then a trickle by comparison for the rest of the 20th century. Some of the better known modernists and postmodernists, having departed from the style of their predecessors but not lacking in creativity and heroics, include Alexander Block, Anna Ahmatova, Nikolay Gumilev, Maxim Gorky, Vladimir Mayakovski, Yevgeny Evtushenko, Boris Pasternak and Alexander Solzhenitsyn.

Apart from spiritual music, the Western model of music appeared later than did Westernised literature in Russia. However, some works of interest have survived from the 18th century. The Father of modern Russian classical music, Mikhail Glinka (1804-57), worked in the second quarter of the 19th century. In his youth, he already believed that music was his soul. Glinka also loved literature and associated with writers like Pushkin, Gogol and Joukovsky. Joukovsky, who was close to the court of Nicholas I, inspired Glinka to write his first and best masterpiece opera *A Life for the Tsar* (1836). Later he was inspired by Pushkin to write *Ruslan and Lyudmilla* (1842). These two are the oldest Russian operas that remain in the standard repertoire. His series of romantic melodies, in particular one based on Pushkin's poetry, *Ya Pomnu Chudnoye Mgnoveniye* (The Magic Moment I Remember) is regarded as one of the masterpieces of Russian lyrical music. Glinka through his innovative composition created a Russian national music in which he grafted Russian melodies onto European harmonies.

After the death of Glinka and by the second half of the 19th century, active Russian musical life took hold. Like much of Russian culture, music was split into Westernised and *Slavophil* (nationalist) camps. The principal composer of the Westernised camp was Peter Tchaikovsky, whose symphonies, overtures, ballets, and operas combined a careful European craftsmanship with a judicious use of native melodies. The Slavophil camp called for a more national form of music that would be based not merely on native melodies but also on the harmonic system of the Russian folk song. Although to the musical Westernised ears the work of the nationalists sounded primitive, the major compositions of the Slavophil composers Aleksandr Borodin, Modest Mussorgsky and Nikolay Rimsky-Korsakov have become staples of the international repertoire, just as have those of Tchaikovsky.

The Mighty Five (Moguchaya Kuchka), a group of five composers who, in about 1875, united in their efforts to create a truly national school of Russian music, were César Cui, Aleksandr Borodin, Mily Balakirev, Modest Mussorgsky, and Nikolay Rimsky-Korsakov. They bore the name *Moguchaya Kuchka*, coined by the critic Stasov in his newspaper article in 1867. They were St. Petersburg-based and are often considered to have been a rival faction to the more cosmopolitan Moscow-based composers such as Peter Ilich Tchaikovsky, who often used actual folk songs in his music, and Borodin and Rimsky-Korsakov, who emphasized traditional European training in their work.

Precursors of the Five were, of course, Mikhail Glinka and Aleksandr Dargomyzhsky. These two were, in turn, succeeded by a less-energetic generation, including Anatoly Lyadov, Sergey Taneyev and Aleksandr Glazunov.

Prior to Peter the Great, Russian theatre resembled European plays during the early Middle Ages. As early as the 10th century there were mimicking performers, called *skomorokhi* (buffoonery), probably itinerant comedians who performed in small towns and villages. However, Russian theatre can be traced back even further: as far back as the pagan rituals of the ancient Slavs and the later Christian festivals, through to the middle ages, displaying the mixed rituals of these two influences. At the beginning of the 17th century, the only theatre using a literary text and a trained company was the drama brought from Poland to the Ukraine.

In 1672, the first public performance of a play was offered in Moscow. A special theatre was built at Tsar Alexis's residence. There seems to have been no scenery other than a fir tree on either side of the stage, although there was a sliding curtain. The Tsar was so excited that he sat in the theatre for 10 hours on the day of the first performance,

During the time of Peter the Great, the theatre became more refined and began to include French plays by Pierre Corneille – the founder of classical French tragedy – and his rival Jean Racine – French dramatist – the principal tragedian of the French classical period.

By 1730, change was on the way, when an Italian group brought the commedia dell'arte, elaborate sets, and machinery to Moscow. Over the next 10 years, Italian opera and ballet were also introduced to Russia. Westernisation was probably a catalyst in the birth of the Russian national theatre in 1749, making the theatre more open to the public.

Catherine the Great also contributed to the theatre by writing a number of witty plays herself. She initially promoted the nation's foremost dramatist playwright Denis Fonvizin, who satirized the cultural pretensions and privileged coarseness of the nobility. He of course overstepped the boundaries and fell out of favour with Catherine. Thereafter, his works were banned, and his last years were spent in travel.

By the end of the 18th century, staging spread throughout most major cities and many private theatres were being opened. Most of the staging of their productions was imitative of French and Italian theatre.

Russian drama in the early 19th century was similar to that of Germany and was conducive to the flowering of Romanticism, often manifested in patriotic spectacles. The theatre often comprised of melodrama, Shakespeare, and musical plays. However, from about the 1830s the new realistic school emerged and some of the best-known plays began to include Aleksandr Ostrovsky, Nikolay Gogol, and Ivan Turgenev.

Until 1883, under strict government controls Russia's two major cities, Moscow and St. Petersburg, had a monopoly on productions in The Imperial Theatres. After monopolies were revoked the public theatre expanded. However, the state troupes, such as the Bolshoi in Moscow, continued to offer the most professional productions.

However, from an international perspective, it was in the area of *classical ballet* that the Russian theatre had its greatest success. Since the 1820s, Russian dancers have reigned supreme on the ballet stage. Many great choreographers, both of Russian and non-Russian origin, worked for the Russian Imperial Theatres, including Marius Petipa, who choreographed Tchaikovsky's ballets *Swan Lake* and *The Sleeping Beauty.*

Unlike literature but like music, the visual arts in Russia were slower to develop along European lines. Great works, with the exception of the portraitist Dmitry Levitsky, mainly began to appear after the 1830s. In the 1830s, the Russian Academy of Arts – founded in 1757 – began sending Russian painters abroad for training. Among the most gifted were Aleksandr Ivanov and Karl Bryullov: Both are known for Romantic historical canvases. However, a truly national tradition did not begin until the 1870s with the appearance of the Itinerants – trained craftsmen for whom portrait-painting was a natural extension of their work as house painters or as coach and sign painters.

Although their work is not well known outside Russia, the serene landscapes of Isaac Levitan, the expressive portraits of Ivan Kramskoy and Ilya Repin, and the socially-oriented genre paintings – scenes from ordinary life – of Vladimir Makovsky, Vasily Perov, and Repin, are internationally acclaimed.

Peredvizhniki – The Wanderers (somewhat like the Mighty Five composers) – a group of essentially romantic painters in the second half of the 19th century, rejected the restrictive and foreign-inspired classicism of the Russian Academy. They formed a new realist and nationalist art that would serve the common man. They believed that art should be useful – like an instrument of expression of humanitarian and social ideals. They produced realistic portrayals of inspiring or pathetic subjects from Russian middle-class and peasant life in a literal, easily understood style. In 1870, they formed a Society of Wandering Exhibitions organizing mobile exhibitions of their works in an effort to bring serious art to the people.

Some of the greatest museums in the world can be found in the cities of Moscow and St. Petersburg.

In Moscow, the Pushkin Fine Arts Museum houses treasures of Western European art; whereas the Tretyakov Gallery has the largest collection of Russian art in the world (about 100,000 paintings in all). Similarly, in St. Petersburg the Hermitage is one of the world's truly great art museums. The Hermitage has a rich collection of Western European paintings since the Middle Ages, including many masterpieces by Renaissance Italian and Baroque Dutch, Flemish, and French painters, Russian Art, extensive holdings of Oriental Art and a noteworthy collection of Central Asian Art.

The city's superb collection of Russian art is housed in the Gosudarstvenny Russky Muzey – Russian State Museum – opened in St. Petersburg in 1898 and is comparable with the Tretyakov Gallery in Moscow. It is the central museum of Russian art and life and houses art from the 10th century to the revolution. In addition, in the suburbs outside St. Petersburg, the former Imperial palaces at Pavlovsk, Pushkin, and Petrodvorets have been restored as museums and are popular destinations for both Russian citizens and foreign tourists.

Similar developments took place in other crafts: architecture, icon painting and frescoes – paintings done in watercolours on a wall or ceiling while the plaster was still wet.

From the time of Christianity, in Kiev and Novgorod Byzantine craftsmen, artists and artisans worked intermittently on churches, monuments, mosaics, icons and frescoes. Architecture and icon painting grew up as important independent arts, both having their beginnings during this period. This Byzantine-style of architecture soon spread throughout the principalities of Novgorod and Vladimir-Suzdal and later to Moscow, St. Petersburg and throughout the land.

However, transformation from the Byzantine style to a developing Russian style of art and architecture began to take place gradually. The most noted change was that of the Byzantine cupolas to the so-called onion dome.

A significant contribution to Russian architecture came from Pskov (located at the end of Russia's northwest border near Estonia) a feature that became known as the *kokoshnik* – resembling a peasant woman's headdress, it was to become a favourite Russian structural and decorative element. It encompassed the church porches, the exterior walled-in galleries, and the arcaded bell towers.

A further modification of the earlier Byzantine style came from the region of Vladimir-Suzdal (now part of the Moscow's Golden Circle and another former centre of early Russian culture). This area produced a creative fusion of Byzantine, Romanesque, and Caucasian influences, the Romanesque being seen as the post Roman style appearing in Western Europe and the Caucasian influence appearing in the churches to the south. Among the outstanding monuments of Vladimir-Suzdal are the Church of the Assumption (1158-89), which was to serve as a model for its namesake in the Moscow Kremlin; the Church of the Intercession of the Virgin on the Nerl, one of the loveliest creations of medieval Russia (1165); and the Church of St. Dmitry (1194-97). The Suzdalians made a number of other innovations such as cut stone instead of brick, carved-stone embroideries instead of polychrome wall facings and the organization and arrangement of the forms and patterns. This period of Russian art, which lasted until the adoption of Western European culture in the 18th century, is also known as the Moscow or National period.

Synonymous with the new Russian capital Moscow is the Kremlin. The first documentary reference to Moscow is found in the early monastic chronicles under the year 1147, when a Suzdalian prince Yuri Vladimirovich Dolgoruky, was host at a great banquet for his ally the Prince of Novgorod-Seversky in *Moscow.* This is the traditional date of Moscow's foundation. Although the invading Tartars burned Moscow it was soon rebuilt. Its authority was greatly enhanced when in 1326 the metropolitan of the Russian Orthodox Church transferred his seat from Vladimir to Moscow. From then on the town remained as the centre of Russian Orthodoxy. After the fall of Constantinople to the Turks (1453), Moscow claimed the title of the Third Rome. Under Ivan Kalita, the principality of Vladimir was incorporated into that of Moscow. Gradually the princes of Moscow extended their rule over the other surrounding Russian princedoms. Finally, Moscow became recognized as the new capital of Russia and in particular with the end of the Tartar yoke over Russia by 1480 largely due to the Moscow Prince Ivan III. During this time, Moscow's title changed from a princedom to a capital of a sovereign state. Also, after the death of Ivan's first wife he married Sophia Paleologus, the niece of the last Byzantine Emperor. With the marriage to Sophia, Ivan took from Byzantium the double-headed eagle as the new national emblem. He also progressively became known as a tsar and imitated many of the Byzantium customs, mannerisms and procedures.

During Ivan III's reign, the St. Basil's Cathedral was built in red Square and the modest Moscow Kremlin was further enhanced with turrets, and a luxurious stone palace. Part of the Palace, like the Armoury Museum, still remains today. The Kremlin lost its importance as a fortress in the 1620s but continued its use as the centre of Russian government until 1712 and again after 1918.

After the Bolshevik seizure of power in October 1917, the Moscow Kremlin became the headquarters of the Communist Soviet government and the symbol of its dictatorship. Since the collapse of the Soviet Union in 1991, it has now become the executive headquarters of the Russian federation. Over the years, the Kremlin has developed into a city within a city radiating Europe's most concentrated expression of art, architecture and history.

Novgorod and Moscow are closely linked in artistic terms and in particular, the introduction to Moscow features characteristics of the Byzantine and Novgorodian traditions. That is because many of the great icon and fresco painters of the 16th century worked first at Novgorod and later at Moscow. The literary movement of the 16th century strongly influenced contemporary painting, and artists looked to new subjects. Some illustrated church preoccupations and prayers or expressed the rites of the church in symbolic images; others represented parables and legends.

At the end of the 16th century, the Stroganov School made its appearance in Moscow, introducing a small-scale manner of icon painting. The masters of the Stroganov School became famous for the elegant attitudes of their figures, their choice of Eastern colours, and their elaborate detail. Some of them; Prokopy Chirin, Nikifor, and Istoma Savin, were later to join the icon-painting studios in the Kremlin armoury in Moscow.

Moscow icons of the 17th century constitute the last authentically Russian (character) painting. As early as 1650, much of their Russian character had disappeared. From the end of the century, Western European influences spread rapidly.

The most renowned Russian icon painter was Andrey Rublyov (1360-1470), best known for his magnificent masterpiece, an icon of the Old Testament Trinity, portraying the three visiting angels to Abraham. It is now exhibited in the Tretyakov Gallery in Moscow.

Little is known of his life except that he was the assistant of another great painter of murals, icons, and miniatures called Theophanes the Greek, who came to Russia from Constantinople. Fairly late in life, Rublyov became a monk, first officiating at the Trinity-St. Sergius monastery at Sergiyev Posad and then at the Andronikov monastery in Moscow. As Russian painters did not sign their works until the 17th century, their paintings can only be assigned to them on the basis of written evidence or of style.

With the fall of Constantinople to the Turks in 1453, Moscow, already being the centre of the Russian Orthodox Church, became the virtual centre of Eastern Orthodoxy. An artist whose career reflected the new sophistication was the major painter Dionisy, a layman. Dionisy's compositions, based more on intellect than on an instinctive expression of spirituality, are considered more eye-catching than either Theophanes's or Rublyov's.

The new prestige of the Russian Orthodox Church led to an unprecedented seriousness in the mystical interpretation of traditional subject matter. By the mid 16th century, there were specific directives from the Church based on a new didactic iconography that expounded mysteries, rites and dogmas. The general stylistic traditions already established were followed throughout the 16th and 17th centuries, but icons became smaller and crowded in composition and steadily declined in quality. By the late 16th century, much of the former spirituality had been lost, replaced by decorative enrichment and often less tasteful elegance.

At the beginning of the 17th century, the so-called Stroganov School of accomplished Moscow artists assumed the leadership of the last phase of Russian medieval art.

2 THE BEGINNING

LATE 18TH CENTURY - EARLY 20TH CENTURY

3 THE NOBILITY

My maternal ancestors probably owe their noble beginning to the Petrine modern system of administration. I have been unsuccessful in penetrating the current Russian bureaucracy to access information about the beginning of my ancestral noble heritage. However, through family members' word of mouth and genealogical analysis I have been able to go back to at least my great, great grandfather who was born about 1825. Anything earlier is based on my assumptions of what may have happened when integrating a few known family key events with the historical events of the time. Hence it becomes important to familiarize the reader with the historical events preceeding and leading into the early days of my pioneering ancestors.

Under Peter I the Great the internal policy served to protect the interest of Russia's ruling class – the landowners and the nascent *bourgeoisie*. The material position of the landed nobility was strengthened considerably under Peter. Almost 100,000 acres of land and 175,000 serfs were allotted to it in the first half of the reign alone. Moreover, a decree of 1714 instituted succession; belonging to the first-born and so prevented the breaking up of large properties. It also removed the old distinction between *pomestya* (lands granted by the tsar to the nobility in return for service) and *votchiny* (patrimonial or allodial lands) so that all such property became hereditary.

Moreover, Peter modified the status of the nobility by introducing his Table of Ranks (1722). One of promotion replaced the old system of promotion in the state services, based on ancestry, by merit according to services actually rendered. It classified all functionaries – military, naval, and civilian alike – in 14 categories, the fourteenth being the lowest and the first the highest; and admission to the eighth category conferred hereditary nobility. Thus, factory owners and others who had risen to officer's rank could accede to the nobility, which hence received new blood and thereby, ending the predominance of the boyars. The ancient boyar families in any case were dying out: and the few that remained were in economic decline. In their place arose a new upper class, the *dvoryantstvo* – nobility/aristocracy – and of its own accord, removed all existing political restraints on the power of the sovereign. The Code of Laws of the Russian Empire defined the nobility as follows:

> *The appellation of nobility is the result of the qualities and virtues of men who having been foremost in the past, distinguished themselves by their services and turning their services into merit, acquired for their descendents the distinction of noble birth; are treated as noble all those who either descended from noble ancestors or having received the title from the Monarch in recognition of their deserts.*

Catherine II the Great undertook some of the work left unfinished by Peter. Notably, the reform of local government was undertaken but not completed and remained with some contradictions. However, in response to the needs of the lower classes voiced by the Pugachov rebellion, Catherine shaped the local administration into a structure that remained in force until the reforms of Alexander II about half a century later and also served as a foundation for the *zemstvos* (local elected councils), established in 1864.

The basic pattern was established by the statute on the provinces of 1775 and complemented by the organization of corporate self-administration contained in the Charters to the Nobility and the Towns (1785). Essentially, the reforms divided the empire's territory into provinces of roughly equal population, subject to military considerations. Each of these units (*guberniya*) was put under the supervision and responsibility of a governor or governor-general acting in the name of the ruler, with the right of direct communication with him. A governor's chancery was set up along functional lines (paralleling the system of colleges), subordinated to, and supervised by, the Senate. The regular provincial administration was assisted by officials who were elected from amongst the nobility for the countryside and from the higher ranks of townspeople for the cities. These elected officials took care of routine police matters in their jurisdictions, helped to enforce orders received from the central authorities, and assisted in the maintenance of law and the collection of taxes. Other elected personalities (marshals of the nobility and heads of city councils) protected the interests of their respective classes and helped to settle minor conflicts without recourse to regular tribunals.

This delegation of some administrative functions to the local level multiplied the number of state agents on the local level, but also fostered a sense of responsibility among the active and cultured members of the local upper classes. On the other hand, the serfs and the lower classes in the towns found themselves without anyone to protect their interests. Public Administration Reform was urgently needed.

The major institutional weakness of the Petrine system remained – namely, the lack of a coordinating body, for the jurisdictions and resolution of conflicts of the colleges and for policy planning and control and its implementation. A ruler as energetic, hardworking, and intelligent as Catherine could perform these tasks almost single-handedly, as had Peter I. However, with the growing complexity of public administration even Catherine felt the need for such a body, if only to reduce her involvement in every small detail or contested matter and to provide a wider scope for government by permanent laws and uniform regulations.

Catherine's attempt to update the Code of Laws was unsuccessful, but the unimplemented instructions prepared under her guidance stimulated the modernization of Russian political and legal thought in the early 19th century.

Catherine's social policy aimed at steering the nobility towards cultural interests and economic activity so as to reduce their dependence upon state services. (Peter III, her late husband, had already freed the nobles from compulsory service in 1762.) To this end, she attempted to stimulate agricultural expansion and its modernization by providing easy credit and by disseminating the latest techniques and achievements of Western agriculture through the Free Economic Society, founded in 1765, and ordered a general land survey that fixed clearly and permanently the boundaries of individual estates. She also granted the nobility the exclusive right to exploit their land resources and to market the products of their estates and of their serfs' labour. The nobles thereby obtained a monopoly of ownership of inhabited estates, which in practice restricted ownership of agricultural serfs to the noble class.

Catherine also fostered the nobility's corporate organization. The Charter to the Nobility (*Gramota Na Prava, Volnosty, I Preimushchestva Blagorodnogo Rossiyskogo Dvoryantstvo* – 1785) gave the body of nobility in every province the status of a legal entity (except in northern European Russia and Siberia). The corporation's members gathered periodically in the provincial and district capitals to elect a marshal, who represented their interests before the governor and the ruler himself. They also elected a number of officials to administer welfare institutions for the nobility (schools, orphanages, and so on), to help settle disputes, and to provide guardianships for orphans.

The charter, however, by accentuating dissimilarity among certain elements of the nobility, actually fostered bad feeling between the old aristocracy (descendants of princes and boyars) and the new gentry (which acquired its status as reward for service to the state). Nonetheless, by its recognition of the nobility as an elite class, the charter ensured that the gentry would support and maintain the autocratic form of government in Russia.

However, the corporate life of the nobility did not develop as well as expected. The nobility never became the class it was in Prussia or England, but the charter did foster a sense of class-consciousness and afforded legal security to the members and their property. The periodic electoral meetings stimulated social intercourse, led to a livelier cultural life in the provinces, and helped to involve the nobility in local concerns. The charter provided both a framework and the stage for the gradual formation of a *civil society* whose members cultivated interests, activities, and values independent of the state's – a trend that would come to full bloom and manifest itself in the first half of the 19th century.

Turning the nobility's attention towards economic activity saw the return home of many landowners to supervise the operation of their estates. Interested in obtaining greater income, they not only intensified the exploitation of serf labour but also interfered in the traditional routine of the village by attempting to introduce new agricultural techniques. In most cases, this meant increased regimentation of the serfs. At the same time, the secularissation of monastic and episcopal estates in 1764 had brought a considerable amount of land into the possession of the state. Some of this land Catherine then gave to her favourites. In order to encourage economic activity, most of the remaining large tracts of land passed to the nobles, whereby many peasants now had to work for ambitious and capricious masters.

The reader is reminded that during the period from about the middle of the 13th–17th century Russia was subjected to the Tatar and Polish/Lithuanian invasions. This divided the country into Great Russia and Little Russia and subsequently each acquired a different history. The early Romanovs were determined to re-establish the political and national unity of all Russian Lands. The gathering of Russian lands began in the 15th century, gathering momentum by Catherine's reign.

4 VAJINSKYS THE COLONISTS

A sneeze by Catherine during
A Royal visit to the new
Province received a blessing
from a local peasant woman:
Have the good health of a cow
Be as fertile as a sow
And have the riches of the
Good earth that we sow
The Blessing of Catherine

In the late 18th century, between the time when the Colony of New South Wales (NSW) was discovered by Cook and the arrival of the first settlers in Sydney, another colonization was taking place in the old world of New Russia. It was when Gregory Potemkin – Catherine's favourite – promoted large-scale foreign colonization and peasant resettlement in New Russia (now Ukraine). These new lands became the new southern extremity of the Russian Empire. Great success can be attributed to the visionary Potemkin in a number of newly created towns and, later, cities. Two in particular were common to my ancestors, the ports of Odessa and Herson. Eventually,

Sydney in NSW would also, one day, become a home to some of the descendents of these colonists who will become a link to this coincidental beginning of the two colonies half a world away.

Potemkin invited Russian and foreign colonists with the aim of advancing economic development of the area. He brought out specialists from parts of Europe such as Germany, Italy, Rumania and Scotland and with their assistance began the cultivation of vineyards, fruit orchards, silkworm breeding and so forth.

It was not difficult to find willing immigrants. The Russians from the colder regions of St. Petersburg and Moscow, even the Ukrainians from moderately cold Kiev, welcomed the prospects of new land offers, the prestige from large land ownership and the accompanying imperial *blessing.* The Scots, for example, who lost so much during and after the Jacobite uprising, with their memories still fresh from Culloden were eager to respond to new land grant offers. They were willing to travel as far away as the Carolinas in North America, New South Wales in Australia and even New Russia in the Russian Empire. Also, as the Empress was German born she did favour and encourage immigrant specialists particularly from nobility from her former homeland and other European neighbouring states.

Within the next two generations, the ports of Odessa and Herson became lively cultural centres and major commercial cities for all of southern Russia. This contributed to the restructure of Russia's pattern of trade with the development of agricultural exports from Ukraine. The new society of Southern Russia was transformed on the existing Russian pattern; the landlords became imperial service nobles with the usual control over their peasants; vast new lands were parcelled out to prominent officials and made available for purchase by wealthy Russian nobles, who also received the right to resettle their own serfs from the central regions.

It was somewhere about this time that a relatively wealthy Yaninov family of noble birth, very likely from St. Petersburg, decided to take advantage of this offer. Apart from the economic benefits offered to the new settlers, the climate was less harsh than that of the north and with it came the excitement of new horizons.

Yaninov, who was obviously concerned for the well-being of his family, decided to make some further enquiries about the new Promised Land. Although most things appeared as good as they were presented to the new pioneers, some negatives were also to be encountered; the area was far and remote from any Russian civilised town or city such as St. Petersburg or Moscow or even smaller settlements on the fringe of these two great cities.

Herson had by far the greatest promise and appeal to the Yaninovs. Herson *oblast* (province), named after its capital, is neatly tucked away on the Dnieper, which flows into the Black Sea down stream. Herson town (now a city) is in close proximity of the Crimea and the ports of Odessa and Nikolayev. It lies on the right bank of the lower Dnieper River, about 25 kilometres from the latter's mouth. In more recent times[10] it was founded in 1778 by that same military leader and statesman Gregory Potemkin and became a fortress and an arsenal to protect the newly acquired Black Sea frontage of Russia. Furthermore, Herson became the first Russian naval base and shipyard on the Black Sea. It was sufficiently out of harm's way. Unlike potentially Odessa and Sebastopol – built in 1784 and well known for its prolonged siege during the Crimean War about half a century later.

As we now know the whole area of these new lands and beyond is in the steppes, like the American prairies. It stretches from the plains of Bessarabia and extends all the way to the lower Volga being

---

10 The original site located near the city of Sebastopol is attributed to at least the 10th century when it was known as Hersones, a rich Greek city which Grand Duke Vladimir the Red Sun subjugated. With an army of 6,000 Vikings, Vladimir protected Constantinople from the attack by the barbarians. Initially the Byzantine Emperor reneged on his agreement to Vladimir for his help. Hence Vladimir took Hersones and threatened to sack Constantinople. Basil II finally conceded and rewarded Vladimir with the hand of his sister Anna. That same year Vladimir and all of Rus were baptized. Byzantium and Rus from then on formed a strong alliance.

part of the Eurasian grassland belt devoid of forests and extending some 8,000 kilometres from Hungary in the west through Ukraine and Central Asia to Manchuria in the east. Only the sketchiest information was known back then. However, the visionaries of the time had a good feeling about the place and that feeling proved them right.

Bessarabia [11] within close proximity of Herson showed evidence of archaeological remains of interest to students of history, including mounds and barrows of early epochs, the remains of a wall built by the Roman emperor Trajan, some traces of Greek and Roman towns, and some forts along the Dniester built by the Genoese in the 14th century. Bessarabia was a favoured area for agriculture, chiefly for cereals, fruit, and wine. The Yaninovs were overjoyed with what the future had in store for them.

However, because it would take many years to set themselves up in Herson as it was so remote, they would need to spend a great deal of time in some other place that offered the amenities of civilised life, such as basic and higher education for the children, a church, a hospital and library facilities. If their descendents are an example, the Yaninovs probably would have loved to read. Some of their interests may have been in Russian and European history, local news and popular reading. They would need regular access to building and farming materials and other supplies for their new establishment. The only place that had all these facilities was Kiev – the ancient Russian capital. It was about one to two weeks travel upstream along the historical river route of the wide picturesque Dnieper. The much-loved river is often described in an old Ukrainian river song that moves both its performers and listeners – *Reve ta Stogne Dnieper Shiroky* – The Wide Dnieper Moans and Weeps. Kiev by that time was the capital of the Ukraine, recently annexed from the Poles. Although Poland was once a mighty empire, more recently it had its wings clipped by the current powerful empires

11 Bessarabia was later divided mainly between Ukraine, Moldova and Rumania.

of Russia, Prussia and Austria. These political changes did not endear the Russians to the local Polish population, particularly the Pans[12] in the Ukraine. Because of this Polish influence in the area, newly arrived Russian nobles could expect resentment and non-cooperation from the locals.

A Russian diplomat in St. Petersburg suggested to the Yaninovs the simplest solution to this dilemma was a change of name as they had their heart set on going. And so Yaninovs became Vajinskys[13] prior to their move to Kiev and Herson, which became their residence for over a hundred years.

12 Polish and Ukrainian Gentry

13 Vajinsky an Anglicised version alternative spelling Vazhinsky a Polish name.

5 WHO WAS IVAN

A generation or two after the Yaninovs resettled in about 1825, one of their descendents, the noble Ivan Vajinsky, was born in either Kiev or Herson. He was my great-great (maternal) grandfather. But in the hiatus of the Revolution regional records were either lost or misplaced, so Ivan the personality must remain obscure until fortune facilitates further social identification. However, the following is known.

Ivan begat at least one son, Nikita, who was born in about 1850, also either in Kiev or Herson. Nikita married Evdokia about 1874. She, like Nikita's ancestors, was thought to have come from St. Petersburg. They had three sons. All were likely born in Ananieve – Herson Province.

The first son Vasily was born in 1875. He completed Odessa (Realnoye) High School in 1895. He immediately chose a naval career and completed the Herson Naval School concurrent with seven years navigational sailing experience (including a period on the Royal Yacht – *Standardt*). In 1897, he was sent to the Far Eastern Island of Sakhalin where he built barges for the Department of Corrective Services. In 1898, he became involved in the investigation of the proposed China Eastern Railway in Manchuria. By 1899, he received his first command of a small ship the *SS China* with the China Eastern Railway (CER).

In 1901, during the Boxer Rebellion, Vasily as an experienced young officer was given the task of moving Russian troops from Khabarovsk to Harbin for its liberation from the Boxers. From 1898-1916, Vasily was repeatedly given command of the best shipping vessels in the Amur and Sungari River basins (*SS: Lukes, Kanavino, Votkinsky* and others).

As Vasily often commenced his shipping runs from Sretensk on the River Shilka in Siberia, there, he inevitably became acquainted with the community leaders and businessmen. One prominent family, the Ivanovs, quickly noticed the handsome young nobleman who was a Commercial Navy officer with a promising career. They were originally from St. Petersburg and were posted for what seemed like forever to the outback with little prospect of meeting an appropriate suitor for their daughter. Ivanov, himself a semi-retired General, offered frequent hospitality to young Vasily whenever he was in town. Consequently, by the early 1900s, Vasily and Pavlina were married. Vasily was often at sea, therefore the Ivanovs suggested the newly-weds share their own residence for as long as they wished, ensuring their daughter would not be lonely during her husband's frequent absences.

The second son Eugene was born about 1880; he was probably the most academically gifted of the three brothers. However, during his university studies, at about the age of 20, he died from consumption/tuberculosis.

The youngest son Boris (my grandfather) was born in about 1884. Like his older brothers, he probably completed Odessa (Realnoye) High School by about 1900, then acquired accounting/commercial qualifications and pursued a career in management.

In his middle age, Nikita would often sit on the steps with his neighbour – Stepan Andreyevich Burdel-Budze. Stepan was originally from Rumania near Moldavia (formerly Bessarabia). The

Burdel-Budzes, like the Vajinskys, settled in Herson some time ago and they brought their winemaking skills with them. One day in the summer of 1905, Nikita shared his intimate thoughts with Stepan over a glass of red wine:

"Stepan, my dear friend, look at all these beautiful vineyards around us. Your skills are responsible for this fine wine. It is one of the best in this South Russian region. Wouldn't it be nice if some of it remained in both of our families?" He went on, "You know my elder son Vasily has recently married. Zhenichka (term of endearment for Eugene) passed away almost five years ago. However, my younger son Boris, who has already turned 21, has not gone unnoticed by your eldest daughter Efrasinia. I think they are keen on one another".

Stepan and his wife Daria (born Orloff) had five sons and five daughters, and were only too happy to join their families through the betrothal of their much-loved Efrasinia (Franya – diminutive) to young Boris. They looked at one another, embraced and sealed their agreement with another glass of wine.

The agreement did result in a life long marriage of Boris to Efrasinia, but fate had a different future awaiting both of their families.

6 TIME TRAVEL - THE MARRIAGE

I recall a quote that goes something like this: When we are young we dream of the future. At what point in time do we begin to dream of the past? Perhaps when the future that we were dreaming of becomes the past. Put another way: We look forward to the future and then the future becomes the past. This theme of time is associated with the most widely admired and highly honoured American poet, Robert Lee Frost (1874-1963).

For as long as I remember, I have been fascinated with time travel. If we could time travel, there is so much history that we could substantiate. Without time travel, to learn how people lived throughout history we must rely on written testimony, man-made objects of the period, and living remains. However, the best witness to history is speaking to the person who lived it. In trying to fill the missing pieces of my family history, I have had to rely on all three methods and have often still come up against a blank wall. One such dead end was Ivan. Until one night something happened to me, which even now is hazy and perplexing to me. So this section I leave to you the reader to judge for yourself.

It was about midnight on 5 November. My wife and I returned from an outing – our son's birthday. Trying to unwind, I went to my study and sat down at my desk. After a night of discussion about our ancestors I was still attempting in my own mind to define or bring into coherence my grandparents' experience and my still unproductive research into my great-great grandfather Ivan. Who the heck was he? I loosened my coat and tie and was about to take off my cuff-links to place them in my trinket box on my table – as I often did – when I picked out of the box a ten rouble gold coin, some other smaller coins, my grandfather's gold pocket watch and my grandmother's gold wedding ring. Recently, I had toyed with these things to help me collect my thoughts when writing my family history. On this occasion, however, I was drawn to them like to a magnet and an eerie and buzzing feeling went through me. I felt hot, cold and dizzy; my immediate thoughts were that I should have avoided that last glass of vodka. As if this was not bad enough, I then began to feel as if I was being drawn through a funnel and fell to the floor.

I came to, not on our floor, but on a grass patch alongside a pavement next to a wide stone cobbled street across which I saw a beautiful Orthodox timber-built church with couples silhouetted against a bright blue sky. It was broad daylight.

"Good Lord," I said. "This must be heaven and I didn't even realize that a bus had come for me."

Suddenly from behind, a voice said to me: "Are you all right, sir? That was a nasty trip. I did not even see you fall. Here, let me help you on your feet, Your Honour, I will help you across the street. You look a little shaky. You don't want to miss the wedding do you?"

As my eyesight cleared, I noted that the man who was helping me was dressed as a coachman and the ringing in my ears was in fact the church bells chiming. I realized that he was speaking to me in Russian. Turning to him I said: "Where am I and what wedding are you talking about?"

"Oh, you have been celebrating, Your Honour. Are you from out of town? This is the Vajinsky wedding. It's the biggest wedding of the month here in Odessa, particularly since peace was declared in the Far East; it's even mentioned in today's Odessa-News. Here, look, Your Honour." The coachman saw that I was still dazed and said "Oh! That must have been a really bad fall, Your Honour. Here, you better sit on a seat inside the church courtyard and collect yourself before you go inside, the wedding is still only half way through."

I thanked him and gave him the smaller coin of 20 kopeyeks that I found in my pocket beside the ten rouble coin. He graciously accepted the silver coin and hurried back to his coach. I quickly looked at the front page of the Odessa newspaper and saw the date – 23 October 1905. One of the front-page headlines read: "Travel to the Far East has resumed once again and passengers can proceed in all safety and comfort as far as Harbin in Manchuria since the signing of the Portsmouth peace treaty in the United States of America."

As I was still not sure what was happening to me – it was like a dream but seemed so real that I did not think I was dreaming – I thought I might as well go along with the situation and see where it took me.

On entering the church, by habit I crossed myself and at that moment I saw the archpriest walking the newly married couple on their final circle around the wedding altar with the gold wedding crowns[14] held above their heads by the two groomsmen. Soon after, the couple was taken to the steps in front of the Iconostasis[15]. The archpriest announced to the congregation that they were welcome

---

14 In Russian Orthodoxy the second part of the Marriage Service culminates in the ceremony of coronation; the crowns signify an outward and visible sign of the sacrament, the special grace that the couple receive from the Holy Spirit, before they set out to found a new family or domestic Church. The crowns are crowns of joy, but they are also crowns of martyrdom, since every true marriage involves an immeasurable self-sacrifice on both sides. At the end of the service the couple drink from the same cup of wine, which recalls the miracle at the marriage feast of Cana in Galilee: this common cup is a symbol of the fact that henceforward they will share a common life with one another.

15 An icon covered screen that separates the sanctuary-altar from the body of the building.

to approach and congratulate the newly-weds – Boris Nikitich Vajinsky and his new bride Efrasinia Stepanovna Vajinsky. As is the custom, the first two couples who approached were the parents of the bride, then the groom, followed by the rest of the congregation joyously congratulating the newly married couple.

Still partly stunned, I too approached the couple, kissed them warmly and expressed my delight on this important occasion. As I began to walk away, mesmerised by their youthful beauty and happiness, an old man asked me to help him out down the steps. Once outside we began a conversation.

"My name is Ivan Vassiliyich. You look as though you are on your own, can I offer you a lift to the reception?"

Still taken back by the events I gladly accepted, giving him my full name and patronymic. We chatted on about the wedding, the lovely day. He asked me if I was related to the couple. Before I could answer, the carriage pulled up in front of an attractive sandstone building where the reception was being held. As we got out of the carriage, I helped the old man up the short wide stone stairway and past the beautiful Greco-Roman columns, then through a lobby into a reception room where the guests were gathering and champagne was being offered. The old man introduced me to a couple of guests and excused himself. The middle-aged couple, Mr. and Mrs. Orloff, with whom I exchanged formalities, pointed me into the direction of the large French windows, through which I saw the most spectacular view.

"A sunset over the Black Sea is absolutely divine, would you not agree Alexander Vladimirovich?"

"Absolutely spectacular, Mrs. Orloff," I answered.

"Call me Gutya," Mrs. Orloff responded. "After all we are practically all related here."

Before Gutya could ask me how I was related, I led the conversation into a different direction.

"The sunset is rather early, is it not?" I asked.

"Oh no! I would say it's right on time." She pointed in the

direction of the clock on the wall, which showed five o'clock. I then remembered my grandfather's gold pocket watch and took it out of my pocket, setting the right time. Gutya immediately remarked, "There are very few of these around. It bears the imperial trademark of Pavel Bure, the supplier of His Majesty's clocks and watches. It is usually presented to people of distinction."

I was getting deeper into hot water and looking for a way out.

"Ah my dear chap, there you are."

Saved by the bell, I thought, as Ivan Vassiliyich reappeared.

"I think we are just about to be seated. Look, the bride and groom are being greeted with bread and salt by the parents," said Ivan Vassiliyich excitedly. "Yes God bless them," he murmured. "Come along, Alexander Vladimirovich, and sit next to me. You seem to be an interesting companion."

"But ... " I said.

"No buts, I know we have much in common to discuss." Ivan Vassiliyich began our conversation almost immediately after we were seated and the archpriest blessed all present and said a brief prayer for the coming meal.

"You must be related to us, I can see it in your face, your ears and your chin but you must be from some distant land. Your accent appears to be a mixture of St. Petersburger and something foreign, not French or German, maybe English. Your clothing is different to everyone else's. A good quality suit and tie, your shirt looks as though you have been travelling in it all day in a hurry to get here. Am I right so far?"

"You are very observant and quite right on every count, Ivan Vassiliyich, almost as though you are a detective."

"Thank you for the compliment, Alexander Vladimirovich, but no I am no detective. However, I do believe that a gift of memory is what makes us truly human! I have lived a long time – 80 years you know, travelled somewhat, I participated in the Crimean Campaign as a supply officer and I love to read foreign and local news, novels, science and politics." He then looked at me for a response.

"You are right, Ivan Vassiliyich; we do have a lot in common. I am a distant relative of yours and I have lived in a far away land for a long time. It's a relatively new country called Australia."

"Ah! That explains the unrecognisable accent. English? And yet not quite English! You are now a Federation of States and no longer a colony. I think your Prime Minister is Alfred Deakin? You export merino wool and you have interesting animals like kangaroos and koalas." (He pronounced the last two words with a strong Russian accent.)

"I am becoming more impressed with your knowledge, Ivan Vassiliyich." I personally had to think back a hundred years to who was the then Prime Minister and had he asked me I may have given the wrong one like Barton, Reid or Fisher, but Deakin sounded more correct when he said it. "Yes I also like to read similar topics to yours."

Then he further amazed me by saying: "You know,Alexander Vladimirovich, by the turn of the 19th century and at least by the end of this year so many new discoveries were made that they are now revolutionizing our age in so many different areas such as: Telephone and Telegraph, Electricity and Electromagnetism. They are already talking of lighting up all of St. Petersburg and connecting by telephone Moscow to St. Petersburg and maybe later down here to Odessa. Mendeleev's Chemical Periodic Chart and his prediction of future elements are making considerable breakthroughs in chemistry and photography. The recent Wright Brothers Flight suggests we will have flying ships in the not too distant future and just a few months ago, I read in a scientific journal that a new Swiss scientist, Albert Einstein, discovered a relationship between energy, matter and light and he called it the Theory of Relativity. So possibly, in the near future Jules Verne and H G Well's fantasies might become a reality of under water ships, flights to the moon and maybe even time machines. So people will be able to be transported underwater, through air, outer space and maybe even through time itself. Maybe these people – Jules Verne, H G Wells, Mendeleyev and now Einstein – are time travellers. For that matter you too could be a time traveller."

"You know, dear Ivan Vassiliyich, you are more right than anyone could possibly know." During our conversation, time was flying and the bride and groom were being continually toasted. The atmosphere was jovial – love, kisses, food, wine and song overflowed in abundance at times making it difficult for us to stick to our conversation. On a couple of occasions we did tear away from our conversation and joined the rest in a couple of Russian and Ukrainian songs. A Russian wedding without singing is incomplete and no participant can remain immune to the atmosphere and/or abstain from joining it.

"This has been a most splendid evening, Alexander Vladimirovich. I have enjoyed myself thoroughly," said my companion. "Do you think our young couple will have a long and happy future with many children?"

"I am sure they will on all three counts," I responded without hesitation. Then as if by habit I placed my right hand into my coat pocket and took out the pocket-watch to check the time, which was about 11.00 p.m., not noticing that my grandmother's wedding ring had slipped on to my little finger. As I read the time, my companion observantly asked, "You have a second wedding ring on your right hand."

"That was my grandmother's," I replied.

"May I see it?" he said.

Uncomfortably, I gave it to him. He rolled it and read the inscription on the inside: 23 October 1905.

"But that's today's date!" He looked at me astonished. "How can this be?"

He gave me back the ring and said: "That Pavel Bure gold watch you are holding, I have an exact one in my pocket that I am going to give my grandson tonight when they depart on their honeymoon."

As astonished and bewildered as he, I said, "Then you are Ivan!"

"But of course, my dear fellow. Who else did you think I was?"

"I have been searching for you a long time."

"Well now you found me, what are you going to do?"

As if in response, we both embraced and then reached out to shake each other's hand. But as our hands met with the pocket watches still in each other's hand I felt the same funny sensation that earlier on came over me. I once again felt dizzy and began to be drawn through a funnel until I finally fell to the floor. As I tried to get up and get myself together, something wet was slobbering my face. On opening my eyes I saw my cocker spaniel, Toffee, next to me in my study where I was lying on my carpet with my grandmother's wedding ring and my grandfather's pocket watch in my right hand showing about 11.05 p.m. I then looked at my wall clock and it read five minutes after midnight. The wall calendar next to it still showed yesterday's date – 5 November 2005 (23 October old style).

7 THE FAR EAST

The approval of the Great Siberian way in 1892 and its planned extension of the Transbaikalian line parallel to the Amur River from Sretensk to Khabarovsk gave rise to a further development, namely connecting the Siberian and the Ussurian rail by a shortcut running via Manchuria. This shortcut would reduce the overall rail length by 514 versts.[16] It would also provide a strategic southward connection to Port Arthur. A triangulation of the three lines intersected at a central junction of a small fishing village on the Sungari River – Harbin.

In 1895 after some preliminary planning and the conclusion of the Shimonoseki Treaty[17], Russia forced Japan to give up the main trophy to China – the Liaotung Peninsula held by Japan from

---

16 An old Russian measurement, one verst is approx. equivalent to 1.06 kilometers.

17 An agreement (17 April, 1895), that concluded the first Sino-Japanese War (1894-95), which ended in China's defeat. China was obliged to recognize the independence of Korea, over which it had traditionally held suzerainty; to cede Taiwan, the Pescadores Islands, and the Liaotung (south Manchurian) Peninsula to Japan; to pay an indemnity of 200,000,000 taels to Japan; and to open the ports of Sha-shih, Ch'ung-ch'ing, Soochow, and K'ang-chow to Japanese trade. The Triple Intervention (1895), secured by Russia, France, and Germany, subsequently required Japan to retrocede the Liaotung Peninsula to China in return for an additional indemnity of 30,000,000 taels.

the Sino-Japanese war of 1894-95, which Japan never forgot and reclaimed back in 1905 after its triumph in the Russo-Japanese war of 1904-05.

Meanwhile, the Treaty gave way for Russia and China to organise a contractual arrangement for Russia to finance, build, own and operate the China Eastern Line (CEL)[18]for about 80 years.

In 1896, Russia and China concluded a military alliance and construction of the railway commenced. For that purpose a private bank, later known as Russian-Asian Bank, was set up in Khabarovsk.

The newly-appointed Chairman of the CEL Board, A.I. Yugovich, was one of the most experienced civil engineers at that time. He was a specialist in constructing railways in the desert and highlands. Some of the more progressive construction methods of the time were implemented in the construction of this line. Minimum radius of curves made up 440 metres. Only in the mountain conditions were they reduced to 250 metres, maximum incline was 0.015, and thickness of ballast layer was 45 centimetres for 24-pound rails. 1,464 bridges were constructed, including the biggest one over the Sungari River; nine tunnels were cut with the two longest over three kilometres. The two-way Khingaskiy tunnel engineered by Chief Engineer N.N. Bocharov was unique at that time.

Nearly 200,000 Chinese construction workers were employed by the CEL. Several thousand Russian engineers, technicians, administrative and other support staff were also brought in from various parts of Russia. The Vajinskys and the Vassilieffs were among those pioneers. The board of administration of the company rendered free medical service to builders and paid a temporary disability allowance as well as a grant for a family in case of the death of a worker.

The railway line was completed in record time. On 1 July 1903 the line was opened to the first commodity traffic. In 1903 the

18 CEL became known as China Eastern Rail (CER) after the Russo-Japanese (1904-05) war where Russia amongst other things had to cede to Japan the South Manchurian Line.

company owned a flotilla of 20 steamships. Captain Vasily Vajinsky, my grand uncle, from the time of his youth at the turn of the century to the time of his death in 1944 when he was almost seventy, spent most of his time navigating company vessels through those waters. The company also operated telegraph communications and prospected minerals in Manchuria. The large number of railway line towns operated maintenance depots, hospitals, schools, shops and libraries.

In 1903, a new Managing Director Lieutenant General D.L. Khorvat further contributed to the development of the CEL/CER with technical rigging, new station buildings, dwellings for railway men, organisation of local production and new branches of industry plant. A variety of food factories arose to serve the demands of the communities that supported and were supported by the railway. At the same time the hinterland of the Sungari was opened up to gold and coal mining and forestry, which in turn increased the volume of river and sea-going traffic. In a more personal way, these developments promoted the wellbeing of my family as my great-grandfather Nikita Vajinsky and grandfather Boris Vajinsky operated and managed some of these goldfields, including a branch in Blagoveshensk.

Although very little is known about the Vassilieffs other than their pioneering spirit at that time, the Vajinskys, however, left a wider trail.

8 VAJINSKYS GO EAST

"Now that you are married and the war is over in the Far East," said Vasily to Boris and Franya, "here is my wedding gift to you. Two first class tickets with private sleeping quarters to the Far East next spring, when the weather will be much nicer in Sretensk where I live. You can stay with us at my wife's parents' place now that you have met them at your wedding. They have already said they would be delighted to have your company. *Papasha* (a rough term of endearment for dad) also agreed to come and familiarise himself with the Siberian way of life. You will have the time of your life, as I will personally escort you on my ship along a well-established route of the three rivers, when I make my run from the Shilka, to the Amur and finally the Sungari to Harbin – the Moscow of the East as our Russian Harbinites call it. You will see the Far East in all its glory and wilderness where Russia and China meet. Perhaps we will even have time for a brief hunt for pheasant or quail when we pull in to Khabarovsk. Pity Mama is not alive to see this new land and Grandpa looks so frail that he is unlikely to see the winter through."

"I think you are right about *Dedushka* (Grandpa)," responded Boris. "At the wedding, he looked so happy and energetic at first, but then suddenly he appeared to run out of steam and looked exhausted. He said to Papa that he enjoyed himself thoroughly, that he met some interesting people and believes that we will have a long and happy future together, but he feels that his time is almost up." Two weeks later, Ivan passed away.

Efrasinia looked on as the brothers became more involved in their rare but frank discussion and she had a hunch that something very profound and personal was about to be said.

Boris announced, "I think we should pay our respects to *Dedushka*, Mama and Zhenya and the rest of our departed kin, before we leave".

"You always think of the important things, Boris. That's why I love you so much, little brother," replied Vasily.

"You know, Vasily, let's have a smoke, before I go on," interrupted Boris. "I may not have mentioned it to you before, but one of the reasons why Mama died so early, I believe, is because of us – her children. When Zhenya died, I thought she would never get over it. When they gave you leave and you came back for a while from the Far East it helped her so much. Then as she started getting better and the Boxer Rebellion erupted, you were sent to transport our troops to the unstable Harbin at that time. Her nerves began to get worse again. Later, the war in the Far East began and she was certain you would be called up. As you recall, shortly after that she died. Papa too has not been the same since. I think the move East will be good for him and all of us as well. We will be closer together again and it will enable our new families to have a new start and settle down".

"We should have more of these heart to heart discussions, Borya, for we are family. Even though I am away so often, I always look forward to seeing you and the rest of the family. Now I have something to tell you," Vasily, went on. "Pauline and I have not told anyone yet except her parents. We are expecting our first child and it is due just before you come to visit us."

"What are you hoping for?" asked Franya.

"A son of course," replied Vasily. "I have already selected a name for him – Eugene – in honour of our dearly departed brother."

"I suppose Pauline is overjoyed with the coming event and the name that you have selected Vasily?" asked Franya.

"Oh yes!" said Vasily. "She teases me by asking 'what if it's a girl?' So I told her that in that case Eugene could always be changed to Eugenia. But I am pretty sure that we will have a boy."

9 FROM THE STEPPES TO TAIGA

Boris and Franya were mesmerised. They watched the Siberian landscape from the ship's deck. The shoreline changed from the small town settlement of Sretensk as they steamed along the Shilka, until it met the Amur River and the forest setting of the Taiga, displaying a variety of conifers – pines, spruces, firs and larches – as well as birch and other Siberian species. The woodpecker and the squirrel reflected the abundance of bird and animal life. Gradually the scenery shifted as they went through a gorge and then more of the Taiga. It is something that they would soon get used to after the steppes of Southern Russia to the Far Eastern Taiga.

During dinner that night, the Vajinskys excitedly conversed at the Captain's table. Vasiliy's family was impressed with his knowledge of wildlife in Siberia and Northern Manchuria.

"In time you will see the brown bear, the Amur tiger, wolf, glutton (a kind of wolverine), otter, ermine, sable, lynx, elk, forest reindeer, hare, and several kinds of squirrel. Our birds include species of grouse and woodpecker and the pine grosbeak, crossbill, siskin, redpoll, red-spotted bluethroat, rubythroat, redwing, fieldfare (a medium-sized thrush), nutcracker, and Siberian jay. The wading birds even include the terek sandpiper, which frequents marshes and pools and much, much, more." Vasily could not stop talking for some time in sharing his love of the Far East.

"I am proud of you, son, you have done well. Look at you, a Captain at 31," said Nikita, gleaming with pride at his son Vasily. At his father's praise, a feeling of humility and embarrassment came over Vasily. To divert his father's attention, he attempted to explain the peculiarity of naval ranks.

"Thank you for the compliment, Papa, but I am not a real Captain yet. You see, in the navy they call you a Captain if you are in command of a boat even if one is only a Lieutenant like me. You are only a true Captain when you have four stripes on your sleeve and usually in charge of a big boat. In our Russian navy we refer to that level as Captain 1st rank. The three stripes on your sleeve that the British refer to as Commander we call Captain 2nd rank. The 2½ stripes that the British call Lieutenant Commander we refer to that level as Captain 3rd Rank. Then, of course, in both navies the 2 stripers are Lieutenants but if in command of even a small vessel are also referred to as Captains. As you can see I am but a humble Lieutenant, momentarily a ship's Captain".

"Oh! You are too modest Vasily," said Efrasinia. "I did not understand any of that mumbo jumbo. To us you are a ship's Captain of whatever class or rank".

"Anyway I am proud of both of you boys and your wives," went on Nikita. "It's a pity Paullina had to stay home with your new daughter Eugenia, but I think her parents will be of better help to her than you could be on this trip. Besides, she does not look as though she has recovered fully from the birth yet. And, my dear Franya, I think it will not be long before you and Borya will become parents too. I am also very grateful to your new father-in-law for giving Borya and me a letter of introduction to General Khorvat in Harbin for when we meet."

Upon arrival in Harbin, the Vajinskys presented the letter to the Managing Director of the CER. The letter of introduction was only a formality. When General Khorvat appointed people to new positions he did so based on his own assessment, which included shrewdness and insight into people's character, and he was rarely wrong. Besides, Vasily had already proved himself as a worthy young junior officer, with a potential to go higher. The Russian proverb says an apple does not fall far from the tree. Conversely, a good apple is an indicator of a good tree and the rest of the fruit. His father and younger brother should make worthy managers of the new goldfields near Khabarovsk, which also required frequent liaison with the goldfields in Manchuria and the banking and/or movement of gold from one location to another. Having a son who had to frequently transport goods and services along the waterways of the Amur and Sungari would ensure efficient networking, honesty and security, which these positions required. Khorvat was very pleased to offer positions of Manager and Assistant Manager to the new Vajinskys – father and son.

Nikita and Boris familiarised themselves with the new town/city of Harbin and the neighbouring railway and river towns. They briefly went back to finalise their affairs in Herson and came back to the Far East before fall to settle in Khabarovsk and start their new careers.

10 THE NEW SIBERIANS

The Far East, as part of East Siberia, shares in its riches. The mineral resources of Siberia are enormous; particularly notable are its deposits of coal, petroleum, natural gas, diamonds, iron ore, and gold. Life in the Far East was not all rosy; severe long winters, brief hot summers and few civilized facilities. These negatives were however, offset by the richness of the local flora and fauna. It was a hunter-gatherer paradise: pheasant, quail, elk-deer-moose, a variety of furry creatures, plenty of fish such as the sturgeon known for its caviar, with a large variety of berries and mushrooms. Siberia offered land in abundance and prospects of good pay. What more could one want?

In the next three years, Vasily and Paullina had one more daughter, Natalia, but still no son. Franya and Boris were not as fortunate. All their three babies; Michael, Maria and Gleb, did not survive beyond their first year. Devastated, Franya was ready to give up and return to their familiar and beloved Herson. However, Boris persuaded her to try once more before giving up. Franya never forgot the loss of her first three children, mentioning them in her nightly prayers for the rest of her life.

Finally, in March 1909, they were blessed; Franya gave birth to Valentina[19] (Tina). The following year Boris took on a change in

19 Recent information suggests that Valentina was also born in

career – Deputy Warden of a Corrective Detention Centre in Blagoveshchensk. The city is about 600 kilometres westward (as the crow flies) from Khabarovsk, also along the Amur River and was founded in 1856, two years earlier than Khabarovsk. At that time, they were similar in size and development and slightly more urbanized than the new city of Harbin in Manchuria. As Nikita wanted to be close to his son's family, he was able to obtain a transfer to the Blagoveshchensk goldfields. As Blagoveshchensk was on the river route between Sretensk and Harbin, Vasily was able to visit his father and brother frequently.

The young Vajinsky family began to grow. In July 1911, Franya and Boris were blessed with the birth of their second daughter, Maria (Musya), and in February 1913 with their third daughter, Klaudia (Klava). These were some of the Vajinsky family's happiest times. Franya learned a lot about the local forest. She put into practice many secrets learned earlier from her mother, Daria, and grandmother, Marina, such as cooking and preserving summer garden fruit, herbs and vegetables as well as berries and mushrooms gathered in the forest. She made jams, liquors and wines from the same berries and preserved meats and fowl from the regular catch that Boris, his father, Nikita, and Vasily – when around – brought from a hunt.

When Boris went on a hunt, he took his dogs with him but he always left one with Franya for protection, usually Duke. On one occasion, recalled Franya: "I opened the door to a perfect stranger who looked like a Siberian derelict with overgrown hair and beard and ragged clothes. He asked: 'Can you spare me some bread and water, mum?'

"Come in and rest your feet, while I will fix you a sandwich and something to drink."

As Franya came out with the food and hot tea the derelict pulled

Blagoveshchensk. If that is correct than the move away from Khabarovsk would have occurred one or two years earlier i.e. about 1908.

out a knife and said, “Forget the food, you silly cow, and give me your money and valuables.”

Within a split second Duke, seeing his mistress being threatened, jumped on the derelict who, not expecting any opposition, lost his balance and fell to the floor where Duke held him by the throat.

“Mercy, mum!” he cried. “Please let me go and I won’t bother you again.”

“You’d better not, as next time the dog will tear you apart.” Franya was quite proud when she relived the story to Boris when he returned that evening and asked if she had had an interesting day.

11 NIKITA RETURNS HOME

As a goldfield manager, Nikita regularly had to move gold bullion to a safe location for banking. Very few people could be entrusted with the movement of the bullion. Initially the task of moving bullion alternated between father and son. When Boris moved on to a different position, Nikita usually looked after the task himself. He found it difficult to delegate this task to anyone else. However, as time went by a young Chinese man, who had been with him a few years, now progressively assisted Nikita with the task.

It was about the early part of 1912 as Nikita and his trusted Chinese associate were loading their first bullion of the year onto a carriage, after the snow had melted. Then quite unexpectedly Nikita's associate pulled out an axe and struck him on the head, leaving him unconscious for some time. Fortunately, another co-worker found Nikita in time before he bled to death. Possibly the cold ground acted as a soothing compress on the wound, assisting in the coagulation of the hemorrhage and the retention of fluid. Nikita promptly received medical attention, but never fully recovered. He became moody, much more irritable than he used to be in recent years and began to suffer from frequent headaches and reportedly asthma. Needless to say, he was offered early retirement due to ill health.

By the following year, the doctors suggested that Nikita move to a more moderate climate, which might ease his continual discomfort. Consequently, Nikita sat down with his two sons and laid it on the line.

"I could not stand another winter of painful headaches; in fact I do not know how much longer I will last. I am sure you boys understand that this is not easy for me. I am not good company for myself or anyone else. Even my oldest granddaughter Eugenia when she was here last said: 'Why are you always so cranky, *Dedushka*?' So I have made up my mind. I am going back to Herson to spend my last days there. I still have plenty of friends and relatives there, so I will not be lonely and we will only be about two weeks away by train. You might even be able to visit me on occasion. I also want to settle any outstanding property matters and update my will so your families can be looked after."

"Papa," Boris began, "Vasily and I both understand the agony you have been through this last year and we do not want to see you suffer. If going back home to Herson will help, then of course you must go. We will certainly visit you. But, for goodness sake, do not worry about us. We are well and financially secure."

"Boris is absolutely right, Papa, just as I believe that I speak for both of us too. Right now, your health is more important to us than your occasional grumpiness. I am sure as Eugenia grows older she will understand that when a person does not have his health his spirit is depressed and he can not be expected to be charming all the time, as well as respond in a jovial way to children's tomfoolery, in particular to a high-spirited girl like our Eugenia. Boris is quite right. Do not worry about us. As you are aware we are doing well and are financially secure."

"Thank you boys for being so understanding. I will leave before this summer ends here. It will be strange to see the old house again, and I think I will move into something smaller. Anyway, I look forward to visiting my old friend Stepan and being close to my departed Evdokia, my parents and the rest of the clan. By the way, on a brighter note I heard that in view of this year's 300-year celebration of the Romanov dynasty, there are special celebrations in the south in early autumn. I heard that The Royal Family is coming for a visit, and will stay at their usual retreat in Yalta. There will be a special evening when members of the local nobility will be invited to meet the Family. I look forward to such an event as it has been some time since any of us met the Family personally."

12 OF THINGS TO COME

Meanwhile the storm clouds were gathering over the horizon. The closing stages of *La Belle Epoch*[20] would end unexpectedly in August 1914 the following year. For almost 20 years from 1895, nearly the entire West experienced prosperous times. Russia in particular went through a very high growth rate throughout that period. The next 30 or more years, the so-called *La Deuxieme Epoch* however, would be the worst the 20th century had to offer humankind: two World Wars separated by the worst influenza epidemic of the century, the great stock-market crash followed by the Great Depression, the fall of several great empires and reconfiguration of a number of nations. All this would be accompanied by the loss of much individual freedom and some of the worst atrocities and genocide experienced by humankind; namely, Jews, Russians, Ukrainians, Byelorussians, Poles, Armenians, and Chinese.

---

20 An attempt by some strategic thinkers to divide the 20th century into four periods; 1st (1895-1914) as the most beautiful, the 2nd (1915-45) as the worst, the 3rd (1946-1980) not quite as good as the first and the 4th (1981-2001) between the second and the third.

13 THE VASSILIEFFS

I had to do a lot of deductive reasoning in trying to build a picture of my paternal great-grandfather, Alexander Vassilieff (I), about whom information is now almost non-existent, like for my distant Vajinsky ancestors. In genealogical research, if exact information is difficult to obtain you either give the game away or develop new skills to help with the detective work. Here I was progressively developing a skill somewhat akin to a cross between a forensic detective and an anthropologist.

By piecing together a number of known factors and integrating them together with known events of the time, the following picture emerged. He was born about 1870 in Russia. His time and place of death and the name of his spouse are unknown. It is very likely that he arrived in Harbin at the time of the construction of the China Eastern Railway (CER) – 1897-1903. From the genetic disposition of his offspring it is very likely that he was of a lively nature – mentally and physically energetic, physically fit and self-motivated. Like the Vajinskys, he had a pioneering spirit and probably associated with the CER. He had at least[21] the following four children:

---

21 A review of my father's KGB-rehabilitation file – initiated at the time of the arrest in 1933: Registered Case No 44249 shows that there could

Lidia, the eldest, was born in about 1891 in Russia. She married a manual trade teacher, Nikolai Vishnevsky, in Harbin, China. They had three children – Lev, who later died in the USSR, Lidia (Jnr.), and Galina, believed to have died in Canada. I met Aunt Lidia only once back in Harbin when I was about seven or eight years old. All that I remember was that she was very overweight and sick in bed. It is very likely that she died between 1955-70, probably in the USSR (or possibly in France or Canada).

Alexander (II), my grandfather, was born in about 1894 in Russia. He died about June 1932 in Harbin, China. I was fortunate enough to find more information about his career in other publications, which I have been able to integrate with the information I already had from my mother and other relatives into chapter 16 and Part IV of this book. As there are three Alexanders in my paternal lineage I numbered us accordingly by seniority and for ease of recognition.

Sergiey was born in about 1897, either in Russia or Manchuria. He worked in the Administration of the CER, later becoming a Russian/Japanese translator during the Japanese occupation. By about the mid 1930s he moved to San Francisco, USA. He married either in China or the USA and fathered two children, Nickolai and Nina. He died in the 1970s, most likely in San Francisco, USA.

Nickolai was born in about 1901, either in Russia or Manchuria. Like all the Vassilieff boys he loved sport and became a teacher in physical education. He probably moved to the USSR in the mid 1920s and lived in Stalingrad – now Volgograd – where he died during the World War II siege of Stalingrad. He had at least one son, Nickolai. It is unknown whether his son survived the offensive or not.

---

have been two more daughters – my father's aunts – with my great-grandfather's patronymic; Podkamenskaya Pod. Alexandravna, age 38 Pensioner in Harbin and Kazanskaya Elena Alexandravna, age 32, factory worker in Moscow. That would make Elena and Sergey born in the same year if all the dates of birth are correct somewhat unlikely but not impossible, particularly if they were twins or if they were spaced less than 12 months apart.

14 THE COSSACKS

A Cossack's Wish in Exile
(In memory of Ataman Platov)
Be brave my friends the hour is near
The victory over our foe
We have not long to wait for now
To see our old abandoned home.
Fall down in tears on our bare earth
And our own homeland soil
Again embrace our own folk,
And all remaining friends.
Unknown Poet

Even as a young boy I was already fascinated with the tales about the Cossacks. My favourite was the one about the Cossack warrior, *Taras Bulba* by Gogol. I also met many Cossacks, one of whom especially was a great influence in my life and would become a father figure to me (his name was P.R. Sokolov, a British ex serviceman. He told me much about the Cossack past, much of which is now only a memory. What's more I fell in love with a ... oops! I am getting ahead of myself and am yet to be born. Perhaps I should give the reader some background first of where this is leading to.

The origin of the Cossacks is foggy. Some historians and anthropologists are of the view that the Cossacks were a race dwelling in the Northern hinterlands of the Black Sea. Others disagree. The uncertainty arises from the generous and fiercely independent Cossack nature that admitted to their ranks all who came to them for assistance or protection. A review of their family names suggests that they are now a grand amalgam of several races. For instance, the family name Grekov from the Greeks, Gruzinov from the Georgians, Millerov from the Germans, Tatarinov from the Tartars, and Polyakov from the Poles. Later Cossack units also admitted Buddhists (Lamaists of Tibetan tradition) and Moslems, which further compounds the problem of historical ethnic identification. For this reason, the clans became denominated geographically (as shown in the appendix). Therefore, simply their ethnic or religious background cannot define Cossacks.

By the 19th century and certainly well before the 1917 revolution the Cossacks coalesced into 12 tribes[22] who, though predominantly Slavic, were Cossacks first with a distinctive Cossack tradition which they passed on to their children.

However, this much is known: The Russian word *Kazak* derives from Turkic, meaning adventurer or free man, and that Cossack communes were formed and shaped by never-ending wars and their generous independent nature that absorbed all who came to them for protection. Because of these factors, the Cossacks acquired some distinctive traits, despite being historically connected to Russia, the Ukraine and even Poland.

In folklore, the Cossacks are related to the Eastern Slavs and their heroes can be traced to the oldest Russian *Bylina* – traditional heroic narrative poetry – about the hero Cossack *Ilya of Murom*[23]

---

22 Refer Appendices 2.1 at the end of the book.

23 His legend was the basis of the Symphony No. 3 (1909-11; Ilya Muromets) by Reinhold Glière.

who defended Rus from the nomads. He is the best of the best, he is the bravest and the strongest and in the *bylina,* he is referred to as an independent Bogatyr of peasant origin, a sort of a cross between a Knight and a Cossack. There is also some mention of the Cossacks who fought on the Russian side in the Battle of Kulikovo (1380), in which Dmitry Donskoy, Prince of Moscow, defeated the army of the Golden Horde. From the 1400s, the history of the Cossacks is more distinct as they are frequently referred to in records as units engaged in border defence or as mounted troops patrolling the territory between the *stanitsas* – forts/settlements in which they were stationed.

In the 15th century, the term Cossack referred to semi-independent Tartar groups, which formed in the Dnieper region and by the end of the century, the term also applied to peasants who had fled from serfdom in Poland, Lithuania and Muscovy to the Dnieper and the Don Regions. There they established free, self-governing military Communes. In the Ukraine's southern steppe frontier, their centre was the Sich – an armed camp in the lands of the lower Dnieper beyond the rapids – *za porohii* – hence, Zaporozhye. In the early 16th century, the Polish kings began to organize the Cossacks into military colonies to protect Poland's borders. It was largely due to the participation of some 40,000 of these Zaporozhian Cossacks, under the leadership of Petro Konashevych-Zahaydachny, that the Poles were able to defeat the Turks in the Battle of Chocim in the Polish-Turkish war of 1620-21.

Throughout the 16th century and the first half of the 17th, these Cossacks retained their political autonomy, briefly forming a semi-independent state under Bohdan Khmelnitsky. But in 1654, threatened by Polish domination, the Zaporozhian Cossacks signed a treaty with Russia at Pereyaslav and formally submitted to the Tsar's hand under which their autonomy was to be respected. Thereby they initially regained to a large degree their cherished liberties under the Russians that they had lost under the Poles. The Russians likewise used the Cossacks first as defenders of the

Russian frontier and later as advance guards for the territorial extension of the Russian Empire.

Accordingly, the Russian throne reserved the right to approve Cossacks' negotiations with the Poles and the Turks, as Russia's relations with both these nations were very sensitive. Nevertheless, the chief, the Hetman or Ataman of the Cossack army, had a free hand in foreign policy in exchange for some military obligations, and had restored to them some of their autonomy in the short term. Over the years, however, Russia increasingly came to dominate the Cossacks.

Owing to the Cossack independent nature and their adventurous and pioneering spirit, they were often at the forefront of exploration and the development of new territories. Usually with the support of Tsars, the Cossacks expanded southward and eastward from their home in the Don and were the early colonists of Siberia. In fact, most Siberian cities and towns were founded and developed as Cossack settlements. In 1582, Ataman Yermak, the conqueror of Siberia, established Kashlyk – the capital Sibir – on Irtysh River (an old Cossack song carries his name – *On the wild banks of the Irtysh, Yermak stood embraced in contemplation*). In 1648 the Cossack – Semion Dezhnev – rounded the northeastern tip of Asia – way before Vitus Bering (the recognised founder of Bering Strait), who only in 1728 announced that Asia and America were separate. Perhaps the passage should be known as the Dezhnev Strait.

The Cossack relationship with the Russian State was unique. It was based upon two creeds: *S Donu vydachi net*! – There is no extradition from the Don and *Mi ne klanyaemsya nikomu, kromye Gosudarya* – We do not bow to anybody, other than the Tsar. Although the Cossacks recognised the sovereignty of the Tsar, their strong tradition of independence would not let government officials arrest runaway serfs accepted into their communities. Nevertheless, their allegiance to the Tsar was strong. They believed that God anointed the Tsar, and as – *otets-batiushka* – a father he took care of his people, including the Cossacks. Furthermore as a father and their supreme benefactor, he can also punish them for disobedience. No doubt, it was this understanding that inspired the Don Cossacks under Ataman Mezhakov to assist (or intervene) in the election of Michael, the first Romanov Tsar – who also became known as The Cossack Tsar. Thus, the Cossacks were effectively attached to the Russian Crown by a bond of loyalty that was qualified by their fierce sense of freedom and independence. So when their privileges were threatened they rebelled.

During the Romanov reign, the Cossacks began their military service at the age of 18. Every physically capable man usually enrolled. They provided their own uniform, horse, riding gear and weapons (although the cost of the rifle could be split between the government and the Cossack, the ammunition, without limitation was provided by the state). The term of service initially was from 18 to 25 years but progressively reduced to about six years in line with the rest of the military. The percentage of the Cossack male population that served in the army was usually twice as high as that of the rest of Russian population. A similar trend is evident even now with a higher percentage of army recruits appearing to come from the traditional Cossack areas.

It is evident that the relationship between the state and the free Cossacks was not always amicable; in fact it was often quite turbulent and enigmatic. The State and the Cossacks shared a common culture, language, religion, and the same rivals but the Cossacks openly disliked state bureaucracy and only respected the authority of the Russian Tsar and the Russian Patriarch. However, when they felt that the Tsars were unjust and/or did wrong, they did not hesitate to rebel. Equally, they were the most vigorous defenders of Russia under the Romanov dynasty in all the external wars. An analogy can be drawn between the Great Wall of China as a protection from the nomads, and a mobile Cossack Great Wall of Russia as they protected the borderlands where they lived and where they served.

The Cossacks never became serfs like other Russians and Ukrainians. They were always free. Also, in the army, guilty Cossacks could not be punished in the same way as other soldiers; their punishment system was similar to the one for officers.

The complexity of the relationship between the Russian State and the Cossacks is even more evident when it is realized that although the Cossacks defended the borders, and provided excellent light cavalry for Russia's wars with her enemies, in contrast, they were also involved in practically all peasant wars against the throne. However, while a large number of Cossacks participated in both the Razin and Pugachov revolts, most of the Cossacks chose not to support the rebellions. Beginning with Peter the Great, the Russian government made strong efforts to suppress the anti-state moods in the Cossack communities. Under Catherine the Great, the Zaporozhian Cossack Host was disbanded, the Cossacks were moved closer to the new borders, and later the Zaporozhian Cossacks together with some of the Don Cossacks became the basis of the new Kuban Cossack clan. The Yaik Cossacks were renamed as Ural Cossacks and resettled as the name Yaik had too many negative anti-government connotations after the Pugachov rebellion.

After the execution of the last Tsar and his family the relationship between the Soviet leadership and the Cossacks was never the same. The link between the Russian State and the Cossack Dom was broken and the special relationship with the Romanov dynasty was gone. The Cossacks who left their homeland and fought on the side of the Germans under General Krasnov during World War II believed that they would free Russia from the *Evil Communist Empire.*

The Cossacks did not fit any bureaucratic mould. They were certainly highly principled, free spirited and free thinkers. Their loyalty to the higher being and/or principle could override their traditional loyalty to their chief – Ataman or even the Tsar.

Cossack insurrections include their most famous rebel leaders of the 17th and 18th centuries – Stenka Razin, Kondraty Bulavin, and Yemelyan Pugachov. The better-known Stenka Razin is mainly remembered for his armed insurrection along the Volga River, which eventually turned into drunken orgies with the perpetration of savage atrocities against the nobility and the military. In Russian folklore, Razin (somewhat like but more brutal than the Australian Ned Kelly) became a popular hero, the incarnation of a free man who triumphs alike over society and nature. His exploits have been immortalized in numerous folk songs and legends (*The Carnival Is Over* by the Seekers is based on the theme song of Stenka Razin). Equally remembered is Yemelyan Pugachov. He was more idealistic than Razin with romantic visions of grandeur. (The poet A. Pushkin depicts this era in his famous novel *Captain's Daughter,* also depicted in the Hollywood interpretation of the film *The Tempest.)* Pugachov claimed to be Emperor Peter III, the late husband of Catherine II. He decreed the abolition of serfdom and gathered a substantial following, including the Yaik Cossacks, peasant workers in the mines and factories of the Urals, agricultural peasants, clergymen, and the Bashkirs[24]. Planning ultimately to depose Catherine, Pugachov stormed and laid siege to Orenburg, an important commercial and industrial centre of the Ural region. After a number of fierce battles he was eventually defeated at Tsaritsyn (now Volgograd) by General A.V. Suvorov. After still another escape and then a betrayal by some Yaik Cossacks, he was sent to Moscow and executed.

As a result, the Cossacks gradually lost their autonomous status. By the late 18th century, all Cossack males were required to serve in the Russian army for 20 years; and although each Cossack village (*stanitsa*) continued to elect its own assembly, the hetman[25] was appointed by the central government. The Cossacks'

24 Their language is Turkic but their culture is mixed; some ethnographers believe that they were originally Hungarian.

25 At different times had a different connotation – principally either a military Chief or Head of the Ukrainian state.

social structure, which had traditionally been based on equality and communal landholding, deteriorated, particularly after 1869, when Cossack officers and civil servants were allowed to own land privately and rent it to outsiders.

In the 19th and 20th centuries, the Russians used Cossacks extensively to suppress revolutionary activities. During the Russian Civil War (1918-22), the Cossacks were divided. Cossack lands became a cradle for the White Movement and the main centres of resistance against the Bolsheviks. However, a significant minority of Cossacks did join the Red Army. It was a very bloody war and the Cossacks, who fought in the most active units on both sides, experienced particularly heavy losses. For example, the Ural Cossack Host lost most of its male population during the Civil War. Tens of thousands of Cossacks and their families left Russia and the Ukraine with the White armies. Their descendents, like the rest of the Russian Diaspora, settled around the globe but primarily in the US, Germany, Canada and Australia. During the Russian Civil War (1918-22), those in southern Russia formed the core of the White armies there, and about 30,000 fled Russia with the White armies. Under Soviet rule, Cossack communities ceased to function as administrative units.

15 AND QUIETLY FLOWS THE DON

Our story picks up about 500 kilometres as the crow flies in the easterly direction from Vajinsky's residence in Herson along the Dnieper River to where another great river – Don – flows and which is almost parallel to the Dnieper. The Don is one of the great rivers of the European part of Russia. By the 2nd century BC, tribes of herdsmen occupied the valley of the Don and they built-up agriculture and livestock along the river. During the 13th century AD the Tatars conquered the region. By the middle of the 15th and 16th centuries the Russian state, expanding southward incorporated the Don River basin. The Great Don Cossack Clan shortly before the demise of the Zaporoztsi established themselves in independent military settlements along the middle and lower Don. By the 16th century they came under the Imperial control.

The river is associated with images of the turbulent and colourful Don Cossacks – romanticized in a famous series of novels, in particular in the 20th century by the Russian writer Mikhail Sholokhov.

Nowadays the Volga-Don Ship Canal stretches from the upper part of the now Tsimlyansk reservoir to the Volga, which at that point is a mere 80 kilometres distant.

From its source in the Tula oblast, the Don crosses the Lipetsk,

Voronezh, Volgograd, and Rostov oblasts, through the forest steppe and renowned steppe zones of southwestern Russia. Along the way it collects the waters of numerous tributaries. The river winds throughout its course in the southerly direction like the Dnieper, dropping about 620 feet (190 metres) along its length and like the Dnieper flows out to the sea. Rostov on the Don is an ancient Cossack capital. Although it is relatively close to Herson the Vajinskys are unlikely to have ever travelled there. However, an interesting fate awaited one of the Vajinsky descendents and a future descendent of our newly to be introduced characters.

Two Cossack families lived nearby Rostov on the Don, the Bogachovs and the Kolesnikoffs. Both families came from a line of Don Cossacks. The Bogachovs could recall that by about the end of the Napoleonic Wars, young Taras was born who begat Feodor and he in turn fathered Ignaty, who in 1911 with his wife Theodora were now ready to marry off one of their daughters, Elena, to another young Cossack, Grigory Kolesnikoff, son of Jacob and Olga who lived nearby in Dmytrievka. Grigory, only six years older than his wife-to-be Elena, was very happy with the arrangements made by their parrents. She was a good looking young Cossack maiden, a fair catch by any set of imagination. Elena on the other hand was reluctant to go into this marriage as her heart was set upon another. But she was only 20 and could not disagree with her parents' wishes. Young daughters at that time rarely questioned the wisdom of their parents. In time maybe she could learn to love him.

When the time came for Sotnik[26] Grigory to go and defend their motherland in 1914, young Elena was left at home to raise their 18-month-old Daria (Dasha). With bitter memory, Elena recalls when Grigory came home on furlough he stole the housekeeping money which she kept behind a portrait. She only realised it after he was gone.

During the heated battles of the Brusilov Offensive in 1916 with

---

26 A junior officer: Cossack rank. It is approximately equivalent to a senior lieutenant or a captain.

the improved Russian counter offensive from the disastrous losses of the previous two years, Elena received a letter from the war office that her husband was wounded and taken prisoner on the Eastern-Austro/Hungarian Front. By the time the Imperial Government fell the following year and just prior to the Socialist Government taking over, Elena with her four-year-old daughter went in search of her husband.

She bid farewell to her loved ones. She patted her favourite horse that she and already young Dasha used to ride. She took one last look at the serene and beautiful countryside through which flowed her beloved Don, and then commenced her journey from Rostov to Poland. At some ill-fated station in Poland awaiting a connecting train, she left her daughter Dasha holding onto their suitcases while she went to make an enquiry. When she returned Dasha was asleep holding the handles, the only remains of their suitcases as someone had cut them off and stolen them.

After the Brest Litovsk Treaty in 1918, she made her way through Germany and eventually after the Armistice she found Grigory in Oberammergau living with frau Pavit Krach and their one-year-old daughter – Olga. Pavit was the nurse that cared for Grigory during his stay in hospital. Another war story outcome. How could a man that supposedly loved her, so easily take up with someone else whereas she who was not in love with him stayed faithful and awaited his return. After many tears and disenchantment, she thought how can life be so cruel and unfair. During this war she lost her husband and her homeland but she had her daughter and she would do whatever it took to bring her up in the right way.

16 ALEXANDER A VASSILIEFF (II) - MY GRANDFATHER

In 1912, the Harbin Vestnik No. 1 newspaper marked the hundred year anniversary commemoration since the Great Patriotic War with Napoleon. Many memorable events were highlighted such as Kutuzov's strategies at Borodino, the burning of Moscow and the Cossack raids on the retreating armies of Napoleon and his ultimate defeat. The readers were once more reminded of the heroism displayed by their ancestors in the saving of their empire from a foreign foe. In honour of that great event, the year would be marked by a number of celebrations. Many would coincide with those held throughout Russia. As such, a number of the best performing gymnasts/athletes were selected from the sporting carnival of all Harbin Commercial High Schools held on 9 May at a sports field in Harbin.

The 18-year-old Alexander, the oldest of the Vassilieff brothers, was already showing great promise. He had a scholarly and a sporting potential. His ambition was to become an academic or an engineer but there were no universities in Harbin at that time. So he thought that over the next few years he would save and with a good reference from his school and a potential scholarship he could go to Russia and study. As a quality High School graduate he was able to attain a position as a teaching coach in one of the Harbin Commercial High Schools.

That year he was honoured with being selected to attend an all-Russian youth sporting festival (the Sokols) at the Field of Mars – Imperial Parade Ground – next to the Summer Palace overlooking the Neva River in St. Petersburg, together with other school senior staff and a contingent of 53 students representing all of the Harbin Commercial High Schools. This was the highlight of Alexander's youth. With this honour came a free 16-day return passage on the luxurious China Eastern Rail and the Trans Siberian Rail. The total period of the sporting festival and transportation was about a month (10 July 1912 – 13 August1912).

In St. Petersburg on 1 August 1912, a total of 9000 young Russian sportsmen with their coaches were presented to His Royal Highness Tsar Nicholas II and members of His Royal Family, who honoured the visitors with an exclamation of "Greetings, Harbinites!" The Harbinite contingent were overwhelmed when they received a telegram while on the way back home by train that they were awarded a second place at the Sporting Festival.

After the contingent returned home, the participants were the envy of Harbin. A great future opened up to many, dating was assured. By early 1913 Alexander's namesake sweetheart Alexandra announced to him that they would need to get married as she was expecting their child. Alexander's wish for an academic future was suddenly shattered. The hope of acquiring it in Russia was now no longer possible. He could hardly support himself as a student even on a scholarship let alone a wife and a baby. What had he done? He confided to one of his teaching mentors who replied, "My dear fellow, it's not the end of the world, in fact that's how the world was procreated. You should have waited but you did not, now you have to pay the price. You know the saying, love is not a potato you cannot throw it out the window, well marry your girl, have the child, you will be able to support them. I may as well tell you now; you are on a promotion list here and should get a promotion soon with an increase in salary. There is also talk that sooner or later Harbin will have a university and/or at least a technicum (technical college). As an indirect employee of the CER you will have a good chance to be accepted into part-time studies based on your past scholastics. Alexander, you may still become an engineer, but you will have to become a father first. Besides I understand young Alexandra is nice looking and I don't know how true, but I heard that her father Vladimir Shuvalov is a descendent of some count Shuvalov and although they do not have much money you could have done far worse."

On 2 October 1913, Alexander and Alexandra were blessed with a baby boy whom they named after her father, Vladimir.

In 1919, just after World War I and at the height of the Russian Civil War, owing to the influx of Russian refugees there was a further stimulus to economic activity in Harbin and the need for more educational institutions. Alexander's academic career was on the verge of taking off. Alexander Alexandrovich was admitted as a Member of the Board of Management and the Teaching Council at the first Harbin Russian (Realist)[27] High School, a post that he held until 1924.

27 Realist High Schools excluded Greek and Latin taught in Classical High Schools, instead concentrated more on maths and science as well as modern languages such as French, English or German.

3 EXODUS

1905-1920-1930

17 THE TUNGUSKA INCIDENT

An oak-tree greening by the ocean:
A golden chain about it wound:
Where on a learned cat , in motion:
Both day and night will walk around:
On walking right, he sings a ditty:
On walking left, he tells a lay:

A magic place: there wends his way
The wood sprite, there's a mermaid sitting
In branches, they're on trails past knowing
Are tracks of beasts you never met
On chicken feet a hut is set
With neither door nor window showing.
There wood and dale with wonders teem;
An excerpt from "Ruslan and Lyudmilla" 1820
A. Pushkin (Trans. by Walter Arndt)

It came out of nowhere one midsummer morning in 1908. It was to become known as The Tunguska Incident. Vasily was finishing off a navigational run on the Shilka, about half way between

Chita and where Shilka joins the Amur River. He wanted to get home in time for the arrival of their second child. Just after 7.30 a.m. Vasily was taking a bearing, checking the horizon under the morning sky when something that looked like a fireball lit up the northwestern sky – the spectacular view defied his comprehension. Vasily was so mesmerised by the event that some moments later he almost did not notice the warm wind from that direction and how his boat began to shake in the still waters of the Shilka. An uneasy feeling overcame him. As a sailor he unwittingly was a touch superstitious. Was this an omen of things to come? Even for several nights afterwards, when he arrived home the event haunted him with the night-time sky being unusually bright.

It was only over a period of 30 years that Vasily gradually became aware of what happened on that day. An enormous aerial explosion, at about 7.40 a.m. on 30 June 1908, flattened approximately 2000 square kilometres of pine forest near the Podkamennaya Tunguska River, in central Siberia (60 57' E). It is difficult to describe a phenomenon at that time for which the language had not yet been invented. Some 37 years later, scientists would describe the aftermath at Hiroshima and Nagasaki as somewhat similar and befitting the Tunguska event. The energy of the explosion at Tunguska was probably equivalent to that of 10 to 15 megatons of TNT, which is similar to the generating power of the early atomic bombs. Uncertain evidence of various kinds suggests that a comet fragment colliding with the Earth perhaps caused the explosion. Such an object would be composed mainly of ice and dust and would disintegrate in the atmosphere high above the Earth's surface, creating a fireball and blast wave but no crater. One estimate suggests that the object encountered the Earth at about 100,000 kilometres per hour (62,000 miles per hour) and weighed anywhere from 100,000 to more than 1,000,000 tons.

Vasily never found out whether it was this incident or the difficult childbirth or some other reason but from then on the health of his wife slowly deteriorated. Paulina died about three years after giving birth to their second daughter Natalia.

18 THE CAUCASUS 1914-1917

August 1914 will always be remembered for the start of hostilities between the Central Powers (mainly Germany, Austro-Hungary and Turkey) and the allies (mainly France, Russia, Great Britain and its Empire countries, Italy, Japan, and, from 1917, the United States). It was considered one of the bloodiest and probably the most stupid modern warfare in our history.

The Caucasian front between Russia and Turkey comprised two battlegrounds: Armenia in the west, Azerbaijan in the east. The ultimate strategic objectives for the Turks were to capture the Baku oilfields in Azerbaijan and to penetrate Central Asia and Afghanistan so that they could threaten British India. However, they first needed to capture the Armenian fortress of Kars, which, together with that of Ardahan, had been a Russian possession since 1878.

A Russian advance from Sarkamṣ (Sarykamysh, south of Kars) toward Erzurum in Turkish Armenia in November 1914 was countered in December when the Turkish Third Army, under General Enver Pasha himself, launched a three-pronged offensive against the Kars-Ardahan position. This offensive was catastrophic for the Turks. The combination of battle casualties and cold weather reduced the Turkish Third Army in one month from 190,000 to 12,400 men.

During this campaign the Armenians, in support of the Russians, created a commotion behind the Turkish lines and had threatened the already arduous Turkish communications. The Turkish Government, on 11 June 1915, decided to deport the Armenians. During this process of deportation, the Turkish authorities committed atrocities on a vast scale: amounting to 600,000 Armenian deaths. In retaliation the Armenians perpetrated similar atrocities against the Turkish population of the Armenian country, but on a smaller scale.

In September 1915 Tsar Nicholas himself as the Commander-in-Chief of all Russia's armies superseded Grand Duke Nicholas, whereupon the Grand Duke was then sent to command in the Caucasus. He and General N.N. Yudenich, the victor of Sarkams, started a major assault on Turkish Armenia in January 1916; Erzurum was taken on 16 February, Trabzon on 18 April and Erzncan on 2 August. The drawn-out Turkish counterattack was repelled at Ognut, and stabilized to Russia's great advantage in the autumn; the new front in Armenia was thereafter affected less by Russo-Turkish warfare than by the consequences of revolution in Russia.

The early part of 1916 was that time of the Great War when the protagonists on both fronts stood still, facing each other, having failed to break through the continuous lines of fortifications, and were building up awesome resources of modern warfare in preparation for new bloody encounters.

Russian front lines extended from the Baltic Sea to the Black Sea and from the Black Sea to Persia (Iran). This unbelievably long front line had at its right flank a maritime theatre of operations, the Baltic Sea. Here the struggle was carried out by the submarines and by means of mine warfare. The extreme left flank by contrast was up against the arid deserts of Persia, devoid of even the most basic modern technology. This is where the Terek and Kuban Cossacks of General Baratov's valiant Independent Force performed feats of courage.

It was at this time in 1916 that Commander V.N. Vajinsky was called up to the Caucasus Theatre of War where he was appointed Commanding Officer (under the direct command of Admiral Verderevsky) of the Batumi-Trebizond Railway – Naval Fleet (Northeastern Turkey on the southeastern shore of the Black Sea between Ankara and Erzurum). There he successfully applied his naval and transport skills acquired in the CER to the war effort.

In June 1916 Admiral A Kolchak, after a number of successful operations in the Baltic Theatre, was appointed Admiral Commander-in-Chief of the Black Sea Fleet. Under his command, the front lines were pushed out as far as the Dardanelles with a direct attack on Constantinople (Istanbul). To Commander V.N. Vajinsky, success appeared imminent. The southern flank, Caucasus and the Black Sea were firmly under Russian control. The partial success along the Rumanian and Bulgarian front and in the Baltics was progressively developing a spearhead attack formation and in February the Russian General Staff set the date for a punch-line assault for 25 April (12 April Julian Calendar).

19 BETRAYAL FROM WITHIN

The Germans, fearing an inevitable defeat, placed extra pressure on the Russian revolutionary committee to destabilize Russia from within, with strikes and political unrest. Way back in 1915 at Zimmerwald, and in 1916 at Kiental Switzerland, Lenin organized two international socialist conferences to fight against the war. There a resolution was passed for an unconditional immediate peace. At that time Lenin also received two million marks as a first instalment from the German High command in order to destabilize Russia from within (41,000,000 marks were spent by Germany on secret subversion in Russia).

By 28 February 1917, the revolutionary backed mighty National Rail union stopped all rail movement within Russia. Several newly trained reserve guard battalions, almost entirely members of the socialist revolutionary movement, were put into play by knocking out the St. Petersburg police, arresting most pro-Tsarist ministers and taking control of most government buildings. On advice from a number of remaining ministers and general staff officers, the Tsar abdicated while in transit between Stavka (Central Front Line Command) and St. Petersburg for the good of the nation. The temporary coalition Government that was formed comprised mainly conservative socialists and a minority of pro communist elements.

During the next six months, the government was ineffective at home and on the front line.

October 1917 led to the overthrow of the socialist government by the communist elements and with Lenin's return from exile the overthrow was all but complete.

On 3 March 1918 the new Soviet government accepted a Peace Treaty at Brest-Litovsk (now in Belarus) on German terms forced on it by the Central Powers. The Treaty made Russia lose Ukraine, its Polish and Baltic territories, and Finland. However, in 1919, during the Russian Civil War, Ukraine was recovered once again. On 15 March the Congress of Soviets ratified the treaty. Both the Ukrainian and Russian treaties were annulled by the Armistice on 11 November 1918, which marked the Allied defeat of Germany.

After the humiliating withdrawal of the Russian forces from the front line Commander V. Vajinsky like most of his comrades in arms went home. Like many of his comrades after finding out the intrigues and the dirty politics that led to the abdication and the bloody takeover by a murderous communist regime he joined countless thousands of returned servicemen to overthrow the new Soviet Red Army[28] and fought them as a gun-boat commander on the Amur River in the Far East until 1919. However, one major principle of combat that applied then was that centralized control was by far superior by contrast to a decentralized foe. By having this strategic advantage over the returned servicemen, who were decentralized and did not have a unified command structure and were scattered all over the country with poor communications,

28 The most likely explanation of colour differentiation between two opposing Russian Armies is that: During the Russian civil war two contrasting forces were represented by their ideologies; Lenin's philosophy was that a revolution can not be carried out in white gloves. The new communist Government chose the colour of blood as their banner and their motto for change – hence the Red Army. The anti-communists who opposed them had their allegiance to the former National tri-coloured – white, blue and red flag. They chose the top colour of the flag to represent their ideals – purity, cleanliness and anti bloody upheavals – hence the White Army.

the Reds prevailed. Ultimately it was due mainly to the insurmountable advantages that the Reds enjoyed. They controlled the heartland of what had been the Russian Empire, inhabited by some 70 million Russians, while their rivals operated on the periphery, where the population was sparser and ethnically mixed. In most engagements the Red Army benefited from great preponderance in numbers. It had, also, superiority in military hardware: as most of Russia's defence industries and arsenals of vast stores, weapons and ammunition were located in the centre of the country, which they inherited from the Tsarist army. The Whites, by contrast, were almost wholly dependent on foreign aid. The results were a foregone conclusion and are now history and so started the dreadful 70-year experiment of a new communist state.

The communists' victory cannot be attributed to the higher spirit of their troops. The rate of desertions in the Red Army was unusually high: Trotsky, the Red Army Commander, instituted an utter reign of terror to prevent defections, including placing in the rear of the troops machine-gun detachments with instructions to shoot retreating units. Despite that, desertions continued: at various times nearly one-half of the Red Army's effectives (1.9 million men) were absent from the ranks. Comparatively the Bolshevik triumph can be attributed to superior organization and better understanding of the political dimensions of the Civil War.

20 A MIRACLE

During the great iced retreat[29] (Ledovoy Pohod) by the remnants of the Eastern Front White Army across the vast Siberian plains in the winter of 1919-20 up to one third of the troops went down with typhoid. The temperature plummeted to between –20° to –40° Centigrade. As no mercy would be shown by the Reds to any sick left behind, the sick were clothed warmly, wrapped as well as possible and were dragged along in sleds in which they stayed for weeks at a time. However, they still breathed in the extra cold Siberian air. The high command was expecting the worst. After about a month the Army command noticed that a miracle occurred. The sick in all Regiments and both constitutionally strong and generally weak individuals all began to get better. It was a new miracle cure that the military doctors believed they had discovered. Keeping the typhoid patient with a high temperature in a well below freezing condition of –20° and greater for several days at a time helped to cure the patient. This course of action would be confirmed in years to come. It was precisely the below freezing

29 The incredible four-month retreat eastward of the White Army of the Eastern Front across the great divide during extremely cold and harsh conditions of the Siberian winter was in itself miraculous that anyone had survived. In decades to come, survivors of this ordeal were looked upon as heroes who had survived the *frozen hell*.

conditions including the extra cold air that the patients breathed in that saved their lives. The continual freezing air helped to fight off the patient's high temperature and kill off the bacterium that had infected the host.

21 RETURN TO THE AMUR

In 1918, Vasily returned to the Amur Region. For the next two years, the Amur Region like most of Siberia was under the Administrative control of Admiral A.V. Kolchak – The Supreme Regent of Russia. After the February revolution in June 1917, Kolchak resigned under pressure and went to the United States. He then returned and tried, unsuccessfully, to coordinate the White Russian forces in Manchuria. In October 1918 he went to Omsk, where he became war minister in the non-Bolshevik government and on 18 November 1918, a military coup d'état at Omsk brought him absolute power there.

Initially his armies were successful, but eventually they were routed. At the fall of Omsk to the Red Army on 14 November 1919, Kolchak transferred his headquarters to Irkutsk, but by 4 January 1920, he was forced to resign when a Socialist Revolutionary-Menshevik group seized power in that city. Following his resignation, he placed himself under Allied protection, but the Czechs (under the command of General Janin) who were supposedly helping him, sold him out to the Irkutsk authorities, from whom the Bolsheviks took him. He was instantly executed and his body thrown into the Angara River through an ice-hole.

It was reported along the grapevine later that Kolchak commanded his own execution since the commissar from the Irkutsk

Cheka in charge of Kolchak's execution was a political appointee and did not hold a recognised military or naval rank. However, the code of rules in the then Imperial Russian Army required an officer commanding the execution to be at least of equal rank to the person being executed. Owing to Kolchak's status, he was able to request that the rules be adhered to even without a mockery of a proper trial in order to maintain some decency. As no senior ranking officer of Kolchak's status was available, the commissar mockingly offered Kolchak to command his own execution, which Kolchak accepted. That afforded him the opportunity to take one last parting swipe at his bitter enemy. Rumour had it that the Admiral shouted out the order: *"Krasnaya svoloch po Byelomu Ofitseru pli!* (Red bastards on a White Russian Officer, fire!)"

Kolchak was highly admired and respected even by his enemies for his professionalism and his success against the enemy during World War I. As well as his devotion to his men, dedication to Russia and his former naval and scientific contributions to his country were widely acknowledged. Vasily was proud to serve his country under the command of such an outstanding officer. But when the end was in sight, Vasily endeavoured to save his family.

22 FAREWELL OUR RUSSIAN LAND

Firstly, Vasily organised to move his two daughters to Harbin. Although the details are unknown, it was possibly with the carer's help – his new wife Natalia (Tasya) Ivanovna – whom he married at about that time in 1919 and in that same year he finally got his wish, a son Valentin.

Secondly, he organised the escape of his brother's family after he received an urgent message from them, which read: 'SOS by tonight – Boris'.

Preceding the message, Boris's situation was getting worse each day. By 1919, with the continually changing conditions in the Far East, Boris was arrested and interrogated twice by the local Soviet. However, they failed to pin anything on him. Even the released convicts when questioned considered that they were usually treated fairly by Boris Vajinsky. This time the local Soviet gave the orders to a new Commissar to get this white Bourgeois sacked[30] as a Deputy Warden and his belongings to be confiscated after a fair trial by the local troika. That morning a number of chekists[31] entered the Vajinsky home and were about to provoke him in order to make

30 A nobleman appointed by the previous Imperial Government could not remain in such an important and sensitive position.

31 Early Soviet secret police agency and a forerunner of the KGB.

an arrest more viable. At that moment, through the door came a commissar in the usual black leather jacket and black leather boots with a firearm at his side. He carried quite an aura of authority and signalled his men to wait outside.

"Comrade Vajinsky, I am authorised by the new local Soviet to take you in for further questioning," said the commissar.

"Why don't you just shoot me and get it over with," Boris answered back. By this stage, he was at the end of his tether.

"Don't you remember me, comrade, I was one of your prisoners. A filthy Jew, a zhid,[32] as some called me." The commissar replied, "Yet you always treated me decently. Why?"

"Because we are all equal in the eyes of our Lord and it's not up to me to humiliate others for their beliefs, let alone a prisoner down on his luck."

"Vajinsky, you just bought yourself extra time. I will return with my men after midnight to take you in if you are still around. Here is a pass for you and your family to get you over the border to Manchuria. It expires at midnight tonight. Go across and visit your family. Take only what you can easily carry. And don't come back."

Boris knew how to contact his brother in an emergency. This was a life and death emergency. He sent an SOS. If only Vasily could come through, before midnight. Franya dressed all the girls extra well. Likewise, she and Boris put on extra clothes. In Klava's coat, Franya hid some valuables and jewellery. Boris filled his fine hide *port mannaie* (wallet) with whatever money he had and put it into his inside coat pocket, his gold pocket watch into another. Franya, too, took some money and a little brown chequered bag that could easily fit into the palm of her hand, filled with some gold and silver coins. Boris took his favourite golden retriever – Duke – on a leash and the family went on a late afternoon walk to the promenade. As darkness fell, Franya and Boris were becoming more tense and

32 An offensive term for a Jew.

their girls more restless. Only the faithful Duke walked closely by his master's side as though without a care in the world.

The contact came unexpectedly. A man brushed past them ahead and said, "Do not respond, just keep on walking and turn at the next corner to your right."

As they turned the next corner, they were told to quickly mount the nearby carriage that would take them to a quayside. At about 10.00 p.m., they pulled up near a ramp where two men made them swiftly board a small rowboat, which the same two men rowed for what seemed to be at least an hour. The pier lights could just be seen in the dark as they came up to a motorised passenger ferry.

They quickly climbed up a gangplank and got inside a cabin as the boat's motors kicked in and they slowly moved away from the Russian Mainland and towards China. After a couple of moments inside Captain Vasily Vajinsky appeared. All the Vajinskys immediately embraced and began to laugh and cry at the same time.

"Vasily, I must put the girls to bed as soon as possible. They are exhausted," said Franya.

"There is a cabin already allocated to you," Vasily replied. A Chinese deck hand took Franya, the girls and Duke to their sleeping berths.

Vasily began explaining to his brother that they were still not safe and that an inspecting Soviet gunboat checking for any unauthorised passengers, that is escapees from their motherland, could board them at any time. No sooner did Vasily inform his brother when an approaching powerful torch light from a gunboat letting out foghorn sounds lit up the ferry.

"Prepare to be boarded for inspection," a voice resonated from the approaching gunboat.

"Vasily, you old sea dog, didn't the Turks kill you?" came the words from the boarding gunboat captain.

"Well, Mitka, I see you have come up in the world," responded Vasily.

"It's Dimitry Ivanovich. If you please, comrade, we are now

equals, except some of us are more equal than others, or you may address me simply as comrade captain," caustically retorted the red captain.

"I hope you are not too important to join your old comrade-in-arms with some vodka and *zakuski* (appetisers), together with some of my passengers." Knowing Dimitry's weakness Vasily tempted him with vodka.

"You wouldn't be trying to bribe me, you old sea-dog, hoping that I won't find any contraband or comrades that you may be smuggling out?"

"Ah you are a suspicious soul but I do enjoy seeing you. Let's talk over some of our good times together in the Trebizond and after you have eaten go ahead and search my boat. I have nothing to hide and listen, give your boys a drink too, so they don't feel left out."

Boris, with a couple of crewmen, joined Vasily and Dimitry in the dining area where some light snacks were laid out and vodka was poured in large quantities. After a while, Dimitry's *polytrook* – political officer – joined them and privately whispered something to the red captain. A large glass of vodka was also poured for him which he immediately downed and received another refill.

"My *polytrook,* who is very diligent, tells me your brother here has his family on board and that you are taking them across to Manchuria and onward to Harbin."

"That's correct, comrade captain. As you can see they have signed papers."

"Well how come they have hardly any baggage with them? Where are they running to in such a hurry?"

"I am sorry, comrade, I should have explained earlier. Our father died recently in Harbin and his inheritance is going to be read out by the end of the week. So my brother with his family sought permission from the local commissar and left in a hurry for the reading of the will. They did not take anything because I will be bringing them back as soon as all the formalities are over. Good Lord! You don't think they would leave all their possessions and their beautiful cottage and stay in some outback Chinese village of Harbin. You probably haven't ever been to Harbin or you would not be so suspicious. It's just a backwater village. No way would any of us stay there permanently. I tell you by the end of next week we should be back. Come on, comrades, let's drink to the revolution."

After another round of many Dimitry exclaimed, "Hey, since when have you changed your colours, you old sea-dog? You were so pro God, Tsar, and fatherland back in Turkey."

"So were you then, comrade, when we fought the Turks," Vasily interrupted. "To the days of war and glory when we beat the Turkish foe … ." He commenced an old naval war song and the others joined in as more vodka flowed until only the two captains remained seated as everyone else passed out. Finally, the red captain stood up and said: "There is something fishy here which I can't put my finger on. Just as well I can hold my drink," he said slurring his words. "I have to go now and check if there are any counter revolutionaries in our waterways. I will be looking out for you specifically next week. God will not be able to help you if you put one over on me." The two captains on to the gunboat helped out the staggering *polytrook* as the engines were revved up and the boats went all ahead full, in the opposite directions.

"*Proshay Nash Rusky Kray* (farewell our Russian Land)," said both Vasily and Boris, looking out on the distant Russian shoreline.

23 WHEN TWO SAILORS MEET

Sometimes in life, coincidences occur when we least expect them or for that matter are even aware of them. And so it was after Vasily was called up – on the night of 12 April 1916 (30 March Julian calendar). He was waiting to board the outgoing train from Harbin to Chelyabinsk and thence through a number of interconnections to eventually make his way to the Caucuses. As he stood on the platform, an incoming train pulled in from St. Petersburg, bound for Vladivostok. The stationmaster yelled out: "Five minutes after midnight, Harbin Station, 35 minutes stop-over!"

Vasily looked at the train and noticed two naval officers in one of the compartments half asleep and thought to himself why are they going east when the war is out west? The face of the older one, who was about his age, for some unknown reason imprinted itself in his memory bank – to be made known about thirteen years later. He then shrugged it off and went to the opposite side of the platform to await his coming train.

Now in 1929, on a quiet afternoon, at his modest cottage in Zatonsk on the other side of the Sungari River, Vasily was introduced to a fellow officer. The officer was a former commander of the Russian Imperial Navy, who was travelling en route to Shanghai from Paris and stopped over for a few days in Harbin.

"Commander Vajinsky, meet Commander Aprelev," a voice sounded from a friendly guide who was escorting Boris Aprelev around Harbin.

"To what do I owe this pleasure?" Vasily responded inquisitively.

"I wanted to meet you while I was here," Aprelev replied. "When my guide Nikolai told me that there was a former naval veteran still working as a ship's captain on the Sungari River here in Harbin, I said I knew the name but could not recall from where."

"Well why don't you come and join my wife and me for some afternoon tea and we will talk over old times. Come to think of it, you do look slightly familiar. Tasya, we have a guest for tea, will you bring us some with lemon and honey and that lovely berry jam that you made the other day in my favourite glass with the silver holder and the same for our guest. I was on the Caucasian-Front between 1916 and 1917 until the betrayal of our Government," Vasily went on.

"Ah but of course I remember reading the orders. Late in 1916 I was assigned to the French Admiralty as a Russo-French Liaison Officer and recall reading your name when you were under Admiral Verderevsky in Turkey."

"Where were you from originally?" asked Vasily.

"I too was called out and left St. Petersburg early April (Gregorian calendar) and arrived in Vladivostok on the evening of 12 April. Earlier on that night we passed through Harbin and I was too sleepy to even stretch my feet on the station platform."

"My God!" exclaimed Vasily. "That's where I saw you with another young officer lad in a private compartment."

"Yes that's right, there were two of us, but where were you?"

"I was awaiting my train to travel west while you were asleep travelling east," Vasily answered excitedly. They both laughed and tears appeared in their eyes at the memory of the past.

"So what are you doing now, Borya, may I call you Borya? It's my brother's name you know and I feel now as though I have known you for a long time".

"Of course you may call me Borya and I would like to call you Vasya."

"Well we will have to drink *bruthershaft* to that." On that note Vasily poured a large portion of vodka in both glasses and after downing them in a typical Russian style they both embraced and kissed each other on the cheeks three times as is customary for newly acquainted Russian friends.

"But, I just brought you some tea," cried out Tasya walking in through the door.

"And we will have that too, dearest," said Vasily.

"You asked me what I am doing, Vasya, well I decided to write down some of my memoirs and experiences for posterity. I have kept a diary for much of my active service and I have a few ideas. I have already written one chapter of my proposed book – *Aboard the Viking* – and when I get to Shanghai I hope to write the rest of it and God willing some more afterwards."

"I would love to read your first chapter," said Vasily.

"And so you shall, my new friend. I will leave you chapter one before I depart Harbin as it may take me a few years to finish it off, since I am actually in the process of putting some ideas down for another book, which I hope to name *Sea Spray.*" So the two new friends continued to chat until midnight, long after the host's wife went to bed.

Boris Aprelev did end up writing several books but his best known amongst the Russian immigrants was probably *Aboard the Viking.* Chapter one of that book follows under the heading of The Viking Incident in our story, as it was in a way relevant to the time of my family. It was also a story that I would read in years to come and never forget.

24 THE VIKING INCIDENT

The roaring seas crash into awesome bluffs
And draw back foaming,
The grey rocks that endure this onslaught...
Presented Vikings with their bones,
And gave them blood from the roaring seas
Viking's Song, from Rimsky Korsakov's opera Sadko[33]

In 1899, a ship was launched at Cramp Shipyard in Philadelphia, USA. She was a cruiser ordered by the Government of Russia; under the classification of the times she was referred to as the Cruiser, First Rate, *Varyag* (Viking). She had the following statistics: displacement: 6,500 tons, armament: 12 – 6" guns, 12 – 75 mm guns, 8 – 47 mm guns, 5 torpedo tubes, speed 24.5 knots, with a *combat co-efficient* – an awareness of armament, speed, armour etc. of 14.2.

In the summer of 1902, *Varyag* arrived in Kronstadt from America. She was exceptionally beautiful. As she was due to sail for the Far East, she was painted according to "Overseas" service rules: the hull, the superstructure and the boats were painted white

33 Translated by Commander G. Nekrasov OAM, RAN (Retd.)

and the funnels and the ventilators buff. Every day passenger ships from St. Petersburg and Oranienbaum – the Russian Royal Family's summer retreat in the Gulf of Finland – brought numerous visitors who wanted to have a glimpse of this beautiful ship, a marvel of the naval architects' skill.

A cruel fate awaited this ship and this is what I want to tell my readers.

Varyag sailed for the Far East, where she arrived in due course and joined our Pacific Squadron[34]. This squadron was then under the flag of Vice Admiral Stark, with Rear Admiral Prince Ukhtomsky and Captain First Rank [Captain, Tr.] Rentsenshtein as Junior Flag Officers. [Translator's note: there was no rank of Commodore in the Russian Navy at that time, but certain Captains were authorised to command ship formations under a Broad Pennant.]

As formidable as the decentralised Russian squadron was, the Japanese Fleet (see appendices) comprised of three squadrons with a significantly greater combat co-efficient and united under one command was noticeably superior to the Russian Squadron, particularly in the number of armoured cruisers; this advantage was further increased when two more cruisers – *Nishin* and *Kasuga* – joined the Japanese Fleet.

By January 1904, the political situation in the Far East had become very tense and a clash between Japan and Russia could be expected. On 24 January 1904, the Japanese Fleet sailed from their base at Sasebo. [Translator's note: All dates are given according to the Julian calendar; to convert to Gregorian, add 13 days.] On 25 January, off Mokpo, the 4th Combat Squadron under Rear Admiral Uryu, reinforced by the armoured cruiser *Asama* was detached

---

34 The Pacific Squadron was disbursed over three sub-areas of operation: The armoured cruisers Rossiya (broad pennant of Captain Rentsenshtein), Gromoboi, Rurik, the cruiser Bogatyr and 10 torpedo boats were stationed at Vladivostock.The cruiser Varyag and the gunboat Koreyets were at the disposal of the Russian Ambassador at Seoul in Korea. All remaining ships (see Appendices) were concentrated in the fortress of Port Arthur.

and commenced escorting troop transports heading for Chemulpo, where *Varyag* and *Koreyets* were anchored.

The cruiser *Chioda* was already at Chemulpo, where she was observing our ships. In addition, present at Chemulpo were the French cruiser *Pascal*, the British *Talbot* the Italian *Elba* as well as several foreign merchant ships and transports. Let us remember that the strength of the Japanese force approaching Chemulpo was considerably superior to that of *Varyag* and *Koreyets*. As it was pointed out earlier, the Combat co-efficient of *Varyag* was 14.2 that of the gunboat only 0.05, whilst the cruisers of Admiral Uryu's force had a sum total of 52.84, of which *Asama* alone accounted for 37.6. Such was the ratio of strength.

At midnight on 26 January the cruiser, *Chioda* weighed anchor and departed Chemulpo. Earlier the same day, the Japanese ashore had cut the telegraph line between Chemulpo and Port Arthur. Thus the Commanding Officers of the *Varyag* and *Koreyets*, as well as the Russian Ambassador in Seoul, had no knowledge of what was happening outside Korea.

On 26 January, *Varyag* Commanding Officer, Captain Rudnev, with the approval of the Russian Ambassador in Seoul, despatched the gunboat *Koreyets* to Port Arthur for a situation report. No sooner had the *Koreyets* left the confined waters than she had encountered four Japanese torpedo boats, which attacked her by firing three torpedoes, two of which missed, whilst the third one bottomed after launch. During this incident, one of the Japanese torpedo boats ran aground.

One should point out that the harbour entrance to Chemulpo is a typical skerries-type channel, so narrow that it is impossible to manoeuvre in it. *Koreyets* did not respond to the hostile action of the Japanese and returned to Chemulpo harbour.

Commanding Officers of *Varyag* and *Koreyets* protested to the Japanese Consul through the Commanding Officers of other warships present, about the inexcusable actions of the Japanese torpedo boats.

On the same day, 26 January 1904, at about 5.00 p.m. Admiral Uryu's force appeared off Chemulpo. Japanese transports entered harbour and immediately began to disembark troops. Several Japanese cruisers also entered harbour and anchored between their transports and our ships.

Both *Varyag* and *Koreyets* were still unaware of commencement of hostilities, and being in a neutral harbour (for Korea was technically a neutral state) were observing scrupulously International Maritime Law in detail, and took no hostile action against the Japanese.

On 27 January at 6 a.m., the Japanese cruisers and transports, having completed the disembarkation, put to sea. At 8 a.m., the captains of *Talbot, Pascal,* and *Elba* gathered in *HMS Talbot.* The Commanding Officer of *Varyag,* Captain Rudnev, was also invited to this meeting. Upon opening the meeting, the senior of the foreign Commanding Officers, the Captain of *HMS Talbot,* handed Captain Rudnev a letter from Rear Admiral Uryu.

The Japanese Admiral was informing the Captain of *Varyag* of the commencement of hostilities between Russia and Japan, and invited *Varyag* and *Koreyets* to leave harbour and fight his squadron. In case they should decline, the Japanese Admiral informed them that he would disregard the provisions of the International Law, enter Chemulpo, and attack them in the neutral harbour.

After handing this letter to Captain Rudnev, the foreign Captains, visibly upset by all this, said that they would leave Captain Rudnev alone for a while to allow him to consider the situation. As it became known later, the Captains of the *Talbot, Pascal* and *Elba,* having come to the conclusion that their protest to the Japanese would be unsuccessful, decided amongst themselves that in the case *Varyag* and *Koreyets* should decline to leave harbour, they themselves would sail from Chemulpo and allow the Japanese to destroy the Russian ships at anchor.

When the Captains of *Talbot, Pascal* and *Elba* returned to the cabin, where the Captain of *Varyag* had been left alone, they found him completely calm. After a minute Captain Rudnev said in a firm and dignified voice that he still protested against the Japanese violation of the International Law, that he now knew war was declared, that ships of the Russian Imperial Navy never declined battle, and therefore he requested the Japanese Admiral be informed that *Varyag* and *Koreyets* were sailing to meet him in battle.

The words and resolve of Captain Rudnev impressed the foreign Captains. They shook his hand expressing admiration for his gallantry. A letter of reply to the Japanese was immediately written and signed. Captain Rudnev returned to *Varyag.* A few minutes later thick black smoke began to pour from all four funnels of the valiant Russian cruiser. Smoke also began to pour from the funnel of the diminutive *Koreyets.* Russian ships were flashing up all their boilers. At 11.20 Action Stations were sounded in both ships. A huge ceremonial silk St. Andrew Ensign was unfurled at the gaff of *Varyag.* St. Andrew Ensigns were also hoisted at the mastheads of both ships. The handsome cruiser weighed anchor and proceeded towards the sea; *Koreyets* followed astern of her. As they passed the anchored *Talbot, Pascal* and *Elba*, hundreds of voices shouted excitedly: "*Vive la Russie*", "*Eviva Russia!*" "*Bravo!*" "*Hurrah*". The bands in the foreign ships played the Russian Anthem "God protect the Tsar".

Varyag and *Koreyets* disappeared beyond the islands in the skerries. Dozens of binoculars followed them. Admiral Uryu's squadron was waiting beyond the Yodolmi Island. It was not long before the ships in harbour heard the thunder of gunfire.

The battle had commenced – it was a short one. Powerful explosions of *Asama's* heavy, 250 lbs 8-inch shells were tearing apart the sides and the superstructures of the *Varyag.* [Translator's note: *Varyag*, although a "protected cruiser", was designed primarily for commerce raiding and had minimal armour protection; her upper deck 6-inch guns were completely exposed.] Dozens of 6-inch and 120-mm shells from other Japanese cruisers were falling around her and onto her. Sub-Lieutenant Count Nirod was killed by the first hit. *Varyag* furiously returned enemy fire. *Koreyets*, being out of range because of her obsolete guns, was unable to bring them into action. The confined waters of the channel hindered *Varyag's* ability to manoeuver. Any damage to her steering could result in her running aground and becoming an easy prize for the enemy. By contrast, the Japanese Squadron, apart from enjoying an overwhelming superiority in guns and armament, could easily continue to straddle *Varyag*, as they had plenty of sea room to manoeuvre and unsettle the Russian gunners' aim.

After 20 minutes of action *Varyag* was holed five times below the water line, over half of her guns were put out of action, of her crew of 573, 115 were either killed or seriously wounded and a further 100 with lesser wounds. Finally an enemy shell cut her steering cable. The loss of the cruiser became inevitable. To press forward meant an almost certain grounding or foundering in shallow water. So it was now imperative to find a spot deep enough for the ship to sink without becoming an enemy prize. Only in Chemulpo harbour were there areas that more or less satisfied this requirement.

With a heavy heart Captain Rudnev turned the ship around by means of her engines and headed back to Chemulpo, fighting back with all the still functioning guns. A thunderous "hurrah" from the foreign ships met *Varyag*. She was now an image of destruction. Only one hour before, she was a lean and immaculate ship. Now she was unrecognisable. She had shattered funnels, wrecked guns, and huge jagged holes in her sides, mutilated superstructures and puddles of blood on her decks.

Slowly she approached the deepest spot in the harbour. Boats with doctors and sick berth personnel headed towards her from the foreign cruisers. The wounded were the first to be brought off. A workboat filled with bodies, covered by the St. Andrew flag, left her side; and then followed by the boats taking off sailors, followed by the officers. The last one to leave the ship was her Commanding Officer, Captain Rudnev. There was a dull thud as the demolition charges, which were placed under the ship's condensers, detonated.

The ship began to settle. The upper deck went under, and then the cruiser began to list. Finally only the torn funnels and one surviving mast were left above the water. The depth was insufficient for the ship to go under completely. A minute later a thunderous explosion shook Chemulpo harbour. The Captain of *Koreyets*, having moved his crew to the foreign ships, blew up her magazines. The ship broke in two and went down forever. She could do no more. So ended this, valiant but sad battle. The Tsar appointed the Commanding Officer of *Varyag* his ADC. The Commanding Officer and all officers were awarded the Order of St. George, 4th class, and the sailors the Military Order.

Russian intellectual society was at that time spineless and unpatriotic, but even it was moved by the heroic action of *Varyag*. The whole country was soon singing a song written by an unknown author and put to music by the celebrated composer Cesar Cui ...

Up top, gallant fellows!
Battle stations are on!
Our last parade will follow!
Our proud Varyag –
Will not, give in to our foe
And no one will beg for Mercy[35]

Varyag, however, did not perish: she was destined to fly the St. Andrew Ensign once again.

The Japanese re-floated and repaired the ship after the war. Together with a few other ships, they sold them back to the Russian Government during World War I.

Commander B. Aprelev, who sailed on the *Varyag* in 1916 from Vladivostock to the then Battle zone surrounding the European Theatre of War, later wrote and published a book in Russian *Na Varyage* (Aboard the Viking) in 1934 in Shanghai, about that journey and the telling of the battle recounted above with a colourful, and absorbing story of the crew's voyage and their encounters

35 Translated by Commander G. Nekrasov OAM, RAN (Retd.)

during World War I on the way to the Theatre of War. A friend of mine, Commander G. Nekrasov OAM, RAN (Retd.), translated the book into English recently. As yet we have been unsuccessful in re-publishing it.

In retrospect decades later, it became clear to military strategists and chess players alike that the opening gambit by the Japanese in their attack on the Russian Far Eastern Fleet was a prelude to Pearl Harbour on 7 December 1941.

25 THE RUSSIAN DIASPORA

After the 1917 Russian Revolution, as the Russians dispersed to the four corners of the globe, most initially settled in China, Europe or the Middle East. The eight major destinations then were Harbin, Shanghai and Tientsin in China and Berlin, Prague, Belgrade, and Paris in Europe and Constantinople (now Istanbul) in Turkey. Perhaps the best example that I can share with the reader is where my immediate family spent most of their time in China – Harbin and Shanghai. My wife's family, of which my information is limited, went to Europe – mainly to Paris, Prague and Berlin. As Berlin and Shanghai became the birthplaces of my wife and me, I will give an appropriate account of both places respectively later in the book.

The Russian Diaspora had some of the best minds that Imperial Russia had produced and, added to the millions that died prematurely under different circumstances, stripped post revolutionary Russia of its most important resource for decades to come. Hence, Russia's economy and lifestyle is even now suffering from the after effects of the communist regime.

Most people are aware that communism has brought much death, despair and destruction to the people and their possessions around the world of the 20th century but none more so than to its own land and its population.

A number of Russian historians, including the novelist and one time dissident A. Solzhenitsyn, put the human cost to Russia and its former territories in excess of fifty million people. This loss of life was the result of the Russian civil war and its aftermath – famine, forced restructuring with its executions, GULAGS, and unpreparedness for the Second World War. Even after, Hitler had taken most of Europe. Stalin's continual executions of the *cream* of its population, including in 1938 on the brink of Hitler's commencement of hostilities, Stalin had executed or sent to the GULAG the majority of his most experienced senior general and officer staff. That mistake alone contributed to a large loss of Russian life at the beginning of the war as well as affecting military morale and was just another factor in helping to persuade Soviet prisoner of war officers to ally themselves with the Germans against Stalin's regime. Russia paid a high price for its remaining senior officers such as Zhukov to gain their needed field experience and eventually repel the invader.

For the West, the Russian revolution was of mixed blessing. On the down side, there was the domino effect from the spread of communism, the hot wars of Korea and Vietnam and the Cold War, which eventually brought the Soviet economy to its knees. On the upside, there was the inflow of highly talented people fleeing from the post revolutionary Russia as well as the Soviet dissidents further down the track – in both cases the intelligentsia. The early flow of immigrants from Russia perhaps resulted in some significant contributions to the West.

In the next chapter, I mention a few of these renowned immigrants and leave to the reader's imagination the benefits that would have flowed to the respective adopted countries from their distinguished careers.

26 RENOWNED RUSSIAN IMMIGRANTS

Vladimir K. Zworykin – born in 1889, Murom, Russia, died in 1982 Princeton, New Jersey, USA. Russian-born American physicist, electronics engineer, inventor, and the father of modern television. He invented a precursor of the television camera, the first to scan the image electronically.

Georgy A. Gamov – born in 1904, 1968 Russian-born American nuclear physicist and cosmologist who was one of the foremost advocates of the big-bang theory, according to which the universe was formed in a colossal explosion that took place billions of years ago. In addition, his work on deoxyribonucleic acid (DNA) made a basic contribution to the modern genetic theory.

Igor I. Sikorsky – born in 1889, 1972 – born American and a pioneer in aircraft design who is best known for his successful development of the helicopter.

Sergei P. Diaghilev – born in 1872, Novgorod Province, Russia, died in 1929 Venice, Italy. Russian ballet impresario and promoter of the arts who revitalized ballet by integrating the ideals of other art forms – music, painting, and drama – with those of the dance. From 1906 he lived in Paris where, in 1909, he founded the Ballets Russes. Thereafter he toured Europe and the Americas with his ballet company, and produced three masterpieces by Igor Stravinsky:

The Firebird (1910), *Petrushka* (1911), and *The Rite of Spring* (1913). He directed the Company until his death in 1929.

Anna P. Pavlova – born in 1881, St. Petersburg, Russia, died in 1931 The Hague, Netherlands. Russian ballerina and the most celebrated dancer of her time. She was a British resident from 1912. Her highly acclaimed solo dance *The Dying Swan* was created for her by Michel Fokine in 1905. On settling in Britain, she formed her own company.

Fyodor I. Shalyapin – born in 1873 near Kazan, Russia, died in1938 Paris, France. Probably the most distinguished Russian operatic bass. His vivid declamation, great resonance, and dynamic acting, made him the best-known singer-actor of his time. In 1984, his remains were disinterred from Batignolles Cemetery in Paris and reburied in the Novodevichy Cemetery in Moscow (against his requested will).

Sergey Jaroff – born in 1896, Russia, died in 1985 USA. He was a Choirmaster of the Don Cossack Choir for more than 50 years. Jaroff graduated from the Moscow Synodal College in 1917. During the Russian civil war although not a born Cossack he served in the shock battalion of the 3rd Don Cossack Division under General Kornilov. Afterwards in exile he became a Choirmaster to the remnants of the Don Cossack group that he was inseparable from for the rest of his life. His performances were unique and innovative at the time: an all male singing and dancing cast of Cossacks performing repertoires from the deepest bass to the highest tenors/falsetto, producing a variety of Russian national, military and spiritual songs. The replenished American-based Choir became renowned around the world, toured all continents of the globe and gave in excess of 8,000 performances in over 50 years.

Leonid N. Andreyev – born in 1871, Oryol, Russia, died in 1919 Kuokkala, Finland. Russian novelist, whose best work, has a place in Russian literature for its evocation of a mood of despair and absolute pessimism, he was a passionate anti-revolutionary. After the Bolsheviks came to power he moved to Finland; his last work, *S.O.S.* (1919), was an appeal to the Allies to save Russia.

Ivan A. Bunin – born in 1870, Voronezh, Russia, died in 1953 Paris, France. He was probably the last surviving poet and prose writer from the Russian silver period. Bunin was an opponent of modernism and concentrated on the themes of peasant life and love. He was the first Russian to receive the Nobel Prize for Literature (1933) and one of the best Russian stylists.

Dmitry S. Merezhkovsky – born in 1865, St. Petersburg, Russia, died in 1941 Paris, France. Russian poet, novelist, critic, and thinker, he played an important role in the revival of religious-philosophical interests among the Russian intelligentsia.

Alexander A. Alekhine – born in 1892, Moscow, Russia, died in 1946 Estoril, Portugal. After the Russian Revolution of 1917, Alekhine became a naturalized French citizen and studied law at the University of Paris. He became a world-champion chess player from 1927 to 1935 and from 1937 until his death, noted for using a great variety of attacks. Among his books is My Best Games of Chess 1908-1923 (1927).

Mikhail F. Larionov – born in 1881, Tiraspol, near Odessa, Russia, died 1964 Paris, France. Another Russian-born French painter and stage designer, he was a pioneer of pure abstraction in painting. In particular he was noted for his founding, with Natalya Goncharova, his future wife, of the Rayonist36 movement (circa. 1910). In 1914 they moved to Paris, where both achieved renown as designers for Sergey Diaghilev's Ballets Russes.

St. John – Ioann of Shanghai and San Francisco – born in 1896 in the Harkov province Ukraine, died in 1966 San Francisco, USA. He was born of a noble family of Maximovich's and christened Michael at birth. He graduated in law at the Harkov Imperial University in 1918. After evacuation to Yugoslavia he studied theology and in 1926 took his vows and the name Ioann. In 1934, he was

36 Ray-like lines concerned with spatial forms – Cubism, Futurism, and Orphism.

made a bishop of Shanghai. In 1949, over 12,000 Russian refugees fled Shanghai. About 6,000 of them had temporary sanctuary on the Island of Tubabao in the Philippines. Bishop John made successful representation to the UN in New York and the American Government in Washington for the resettlement of the refugees, mainly in the USA, Australia and France. He served as an Archbishop of the Russian Orthodox Church abroad both in Western Europe and on the west coast of the USA.

In 1988, he was canonized for his extraordinary spiritual work and for his devotion to his flock and humanity in general. From the day he took his vows, he never slept in a bed. He fell asleep at times in a chair or was found in the morning asleep on his knees after night prayers. He ate only once a day and walked either barefoot or in sandals. He helped, visited and cared for the young and old, the incarcerated, the sick and needy at any time of the day or night and is believed by some to have had extra sensory perception and a highly developed gift to see and heal.

Erté ne Romain De Tirtoff, b 1892, Russia, died in Paris, France. Became known for his artistic talent as a fashion illustrator and visual artist of the 1920s and creator of visual displays for French music hall revues. His designs included dresses and accessories for women; costumes and sets for opera, ballet, and dramatic productions – posters and prints.

He was the son of a Russian Admiral, brought up in St. Petersburg, and moved to Paris in 1912. He originally studied architecture but then switched to costume and fashion design. He briefly collaborated with Parisian couturier Paul Poiret and then began selling his pen-and-ink and gouache fashion illustrations to American fashion houses, in particular to the American fashion magazine *Harper's Bazaar*, from which a collection of illustrations was published in *Designs by Erté* 1976, with text by Stella Blum. His highly lavish style of graphic images depicted models in mannered poses draped in luxurious jewels, feathers, and soft, flowing materials against a background of interiors in the Art Deco style.

The same lush style marked Erté's theatrical designs. For 35 years he designed ornately structured opening and closing scenes, with costumes for the French theatre. He worked for the Folies-Bergère in Paris from 1919 to 1930. During the 1920s he costumed the performers appearing in such American musical revues as the *Ziegfeld Follies* and *George White's Scandals.* In the 1960s, Erté produced lithographs, serigraphs, and sheet-metal sculptures. His autobiography, *Things I Remember,* was published in 1975.

27 HARBIN

Harbin today is the second largest city of Northeast China and is the capital of Heilungkiang Province. It is situated in the middle of the central Manchurian plain, and grew up on the right bank of the Sungari River as an accumulation of Chinese hamlets and a Russian railroad settlement. The city owes its origin to the construction of the Chinese Eastern Railway (CER) by the Russians at the end of the 19th and beginning of the 20th century. Thus the Railway City provided benefits to almost all walks of life. To most Russians during the next half a century, it was known as a Russian city in Manchuria and to some as Moscow of the East.

Before 1896 it was a small fishing village. Thereafter it became the construction centre for the railway. By 1904, it radiated in three directions: northwest to Manchouli and the Trans-Siberian Railway, east to the port of Vladivostok and south to Changchun, Mukden, Dairen and Port Arthur – strategically located to the Sea of Japan. Harbin was a base for Russian military operations in Manchuria during the Russo-Japanese War (1904-5). After its defeat, Russia ceded to Japan all its interests in southern Manchuria. Harbin temporarily came under joint Chinese-Japanese administration.

After the Chinese Revolution of 1911, Manchuria came under the nominal control of the local warlord Chang Tso-lin, who was forced to grant the Japanese vast concessions in the region in return for their tacit military support. The notorious 21 Demands that Japan presented to China in 1915 compelled the Chinese to extend Japan's lease on the territory of Kwantung (at the tip of the Liaotung Peninsula) for 99 years and to grant the Japanese far-reaching civil and commercial privileges in Manchuria. During the Chinese civil war, Japan exercised a controlling influence in south Manchuria with the support of its Kwantung Army.

On 9 March 1932, the Japanese created the puppet state of Manchukuo out of the three historic Manchurian provinces. The last Ch'ing (Manchu) emperor, P'u-i, was brought to Manchuria from his retirement in Tientsin and made chief executive, and later emperor, of the new state. The Manchukuo government, though nominally in Chinese hands, was in fact rigidly controlled and supervised by the Japanese, who proceeded to transform Manchuria into an industrial and military base for Japan's expansion into Asia. The Japanese took over the direction, financing, and development of all the important Manchurian industries, making Manchuria the most industrialized region in China by the end of World War II. With the fall of Manchuria after the War, many Manchurian soldiers, aided by armed civilians, cooperated with the Chinese Communist underground in organizing a vast anti-Japanese guerrilla movement.

During the period of 1932-45 in the Japanese-dominated state of Manchukuo, Harbin was known as Pin kiang. Soviet troops occupied the city in 1945, and a year later Chinese Communist forces took it over and from it directed their conquest of Manchuria. Since 1949 Harbin has become the chief industrial base of Northeast China.

Today, however, at the beginning of the 21st century, the city continues to have a Russian air about it, although many of the Russian-built or Russian-influenced buildings are progressively being replaced with contemporary Ferro-concrete structures. The greater city population is about five million. There is some talk, however, that the beloved Sabor – the Russian Orthodox Cathedral of St. Nicholas in the city centre that was demolished by the Red Guards during Mao's Cultural Revolution – is being considered to be re-constructed by the local authorities. Perhaps the spirit of St. Nicholas is still there like a guardian angel protecting that special place that once gave refuge to so many. It was all so long, long ago ... The spirit of the pioneers is all but gone and only the memories remain.

The Russian Harbin, blessed with excellent rail and river transport, prospered after 1900 as a distribution centre for grain, cotton and soybeans. By 1916, it had a residential Russian population of over 34,000. After the Revolution of 1917, Harbin was inundated with refugees from Siberia and for a time had the largest Russian population of any city outside the Soviet Union (for a brief while Berlin may have been an exception).

Although Harbin was called a city, it came closer to a mélange of seven towns, each with its own ambience and in some cases with its own administration. The two biggest and more affluent – Pristan and Novy Gorod – spring to mind. In the 1920s flanking the Sungari River lay Pristan (literally pier), a port and a commercial hub with the city's principal stores, banks, theatres and cafes as well as an Orthodox church, a synagogue, and a mosque. Novy Gorod (New Town) was perched on a hill to the south and separated from Pristan by a wide network of CER tracks, spanned by a single viaduct. It exuded a stately atmosphere, with its tree-lined avenues such as Bolshoi Prospect, Novotorgovaya Ulitsa and Sungari Prospect sheltering elegant residences, foreign consulates and the CER Club. Handsome squares opened on vistas of parks and the Sabor – The Russian Orthodox Cathedral of St. Nicholas – entirely constructed of timber without the use of a single nail. Another square contained the Harbin Railway Station, in which hung a huge Icon of St. Nicholas later transferred to the Sabor.

Less picturesque were the five remaining sectors of Harbin. To the East of Pristan lay the eighth Section, an industrial morass of bean-oil mills, factories and rail yards. Beyond that sprawled Fudzidian, the Chinese quarter, whose river wharves protruded into the Sungari from a labyrinth of cramped dwellings in which nestled the red light district. Southeast of Novy Gorod was Stary Gorod (Old Town) and Madiugou. Stary Gorod was once Harbin's business centre but after 1905 lost its prominence to Pristan, and by the 1920s it consisted mainly of flourmills and garrison barracks. Madiugou had been built largely by Russian émigrés after the October Revolution and continued to serve as a modest residential quarter, its squat wooden houses decorated with ornately carved eaves. To the southwest of Pristan crouched Nakhalovka, locally dubbed Vagabond Haunt (we resided there for a short while after the NKVD arrested my father). Nakhalovka was a cramped, sullen squatter's slum of hovels tacked together with wood scraps, paper, cloth and discarded boxes. It was Harbin's receptacle for the poorest Russian refugees.

Apart from railroad tracks and some huts, the north bank of the Sungari across from Pristan (near Zatonsk) remained undeveloped. It was called Sunbei, and served as an execution ground during Chang Tso-lin's heyday. After 1932 the Japanese built a morphine factory there.

The privileged position of Pristan and Novy Gorod was enjoyed until 1917 having a status of a foreign concession, which was administered by the CER. Immediately after the Revolution, both Reds and Whites claimed to be the legitimate Russian owners of the CER. However, in 1924 Chang Tso-lin and the Soviets firmly extended their power over the CER at the expense of the Whites, its original owners. Thereafter, Pristan and Novy Gorod lost their autonomy, although they continued to be governed separately from the rest of the city.

Pristan looked just like any provincial town on the Volga. The riverside quays and the paddle steamers could have been transplanted from Saratov, and onion-shaped cupolas of Orthodox churches rose majestically against the Manchurian sky. Tramcars and *droshkies* (Russian four-wheeled open carriages) clattered along cobbled streets. In winter, *izvozchiki* (Chinese cabbies) solicited business in horse-drawn sleds, and man-propelled ice mobiles skimmed across the frozen Sungari, their occupants wrapped in furs and astrakhan hats. Russian children played lapta, a ballgame, on vacant lots and clustered around every *bakaleynaya* (grocer shop), eyeing sausages and candied crab apples called *takhuli*. Housewives with prams, Cossacks, bearded priests and uniformed students strolled down Kitaiskaya, Pristan's main thoroughfare, passing theatres, cabarets, the Hotel Modern (later turned into a movie theatre), Tchurin's Department Store (a cross between Grace Bros and Marks and Spencer) and a Tsarist relic called the Russo-Asiatic Bank. Everywhere advertisements written in Cyrillic letters proclaimed the vitality of bourgeois enterprise that had been all but snuffed out in the Soviet Union. Obviously the same fate awaited Harbin after the entry of the Soviets in 1945.

At the Yalta Conference of February 1945, the Soviet premier Joseph Stalin demanded the restoration of all former Russian rights and privileges in Manchuria as a price for Soviet entry into the Pacific war, an offer readily accepted by his fellow Allied heads of state. In May 1945, Soviet troops began to move from Europe to Asia. On 8 August, the Soviet Union declared war on Japan and invaded Manchuria early on 9 August. By 15 August, the war was over. Nevertheless, the next day, the Soviets captured the Manchukuo emperor P'u-i. Having struck a good bargain for joining the war, the Soviets now plundered Manchuria as a conquered territory, systematically confiscating food, gold bullion, industrial machinery, rolling stock and other stockpiles. So what the Tsarist Russia built and under favourable conditions provided China, the intermediate Chinese warlords, the Japanese conquerors and then the Soviets plundered, stole and misused for their own gain. For former CER employees it was a time of much anguish. But worse still – and to the horror of the population – was the forced expatriation of about 20,000 males from Harbin and its nearby rail-line settlements into Soviet GULAGS. It was a tragedy that many families like my own suffered for decades after.

To the Nationalist (Kuomintang) government, the political damage of the Soviet occupation of Manchuria was even greater than the economic ravages that it had suffered. Under the protection of the Soviet Army, underground Chinese Communist guerrillas united with Communist troops from North China to form the United Democratic Army. Equipped with Japanese arms turned over to them by the Soviets, the Communist force occupied much of Manchuria. The Kuomintang reaction to this was exceedingly slow. It was June 1946 before the Kuomintang occupied Ch'ang-ch'un. By then the countryside was in the hands of the Communists and nearly 500,000 of the elite Kuomintang troops found themselves surrounded by Communists in Ch'ang-ch'un, Shenyang, Chin-chou, and Ying-kou. By the end of 1948 the Kuomintang had suffered military defeat in Manchuria, an event that was the prelude to their loss of the entire Chinese mainland to the Communists in 1949. Since then, Manchuria has been fully integrated into the political structure of China and today is the industrial heartland of the country.

4 REQUIEM

1920-1935

28 THE HILLS OF MANCHURIA

A New Start – what the Vajinskys noticed most of all in Manchuria, apart from the Taiga, were the rolling hills. Manchuria, prior to its subdivision, was bounded on the north and east by Russia along the Amur and the Ussuri Rivers, Korea to the south-east, Mongolia to the west and the remainder joining China to the South. Basically the area was divided into three parts: the eastern mountains, the western plains, and a transitional zone of rolling hills between them. It was these hills that added much splendour to the area and about which a number of romantic songs and poetry was written. Among them an amorous, starry-eyed waltz – On the Hills of Manchuria – often played for the couples at their wedding and/or anniversary.

For the Vajinskys, like for most Russians in Manchuria at that time, this was a transit stop. In a few years the Russian people would realise what they had lost and what evil they had encountered. They would once again rise up and overthrow the menace that had again taken over their land, this time the Bolsheviks, and the refugees would all return to their homeland and rebuild a new Russia. Meanwhile, the Manchurian climate and its geography were very similar to the rest of the Russian Far East. Only the topographic variation of the magnificent hills on the horizon and the nearby Chinese would remind them that they were outside Russia. Anyway, Harbin was an extension of Russia. It was after all built by the Russians and populated by the Russians and neo-Russians; the Chinese nearby were usually friendly. So the refugees could bide their time.

Some even said that if you spelt the current Russian emblem the hammer and cycle – *molot i serp* in reverse it read *Prestolom* – Throne. Thereby Russia would certainly be free one day and under a guidance of a new Tsar. A previous prophecy that foretold that the Romanov dynasty would start and end with Michael theoretically was correct, as the throne had automatically passed on to Nicholas's younger brother Michael after the abdication. But Michael, too, renounced the Crown the following day and the Bolsheviks also murdered him some time later[37]. Others would remind their colleagues that it took 250 years before the Russians freed themselves of the Mongolian/Tartar rule before their newborn freedom was restored. So these were the thoughts that many Russians lived with in exile, grasping at straws, to keep their dream of returning to their homeland alive. Still others like Vasily kept on fighting, unwilling to give up.

Vasily helped his family to safety but then for another year went on fighting against the reds – commanding a gunboat along the Amur River. When he finally returned to Harbin in 1920 he was given command of various steam ships of the Sungari River Fleet. This he diligently discharged for the next quarter of a century. During the Manchukuo period from 1932 he was appointed a Senior Naval Commander. His extra duties included keeping the Sungari River free from Starogirintsi, a one-time Chinese war faction, for which General Nakamuro mentioned him in dispatches.

Boris and Franya settled down in Harbin and watched their girls grow into beautiful young ladies. Franya's daughters helped her to

37 Lenin gave orders to systematically, execute as many Romanovs as possible to avoid any potential challenge to the Communist rule. Grand Duke Michael was murdered by Cheka agents five weeks prior to the Imperial Family.

overcome her profound sadness; the earlier loss of her first three children and her recent discovery that most of her family died back home, some of starvation and some like the four out of her five brothers who served in the White Guard were all killed in battle. To Franya's knowledge, only one or possibly two sisters of the total ten siblings and her parents survived at least until the 1930s, after which all communication ceased.

29 THE CAPTAIN'S DAUGHTERS OR THE BELLES OF ST...

As Vasily was usually at sea, his two daughters attended a private boarding school in a convent, because it was probably too much to expect his new young and inexperienced wife to cope with these two lively girls as well as a newborn son, Valentin. During the school holidays, the girls usually stayed with Aunty Franya and Uncle Boris and their three cousins. Owing to the high spirits of the girls, the Captain more than once would have to beg and bribe the nuns to keep his daughters on at school. It was on one such occasion when Vasily returned from one of his long trips that he noticed a frown on his brother's face and his daughters nowhere to be seen.

"Trouble?" he asked.

"I'll say!" replied Boris. "The girls are all but expelled." Vasiliy's mood immediately changed from calm to that of a hurricane.

"I will skin them alive if you tell me that they have hidden the nuns' habits or been into the Communion wine or missed classes again."

"Well I don't know if they did any of that again." replied Boris. "However, when they arrived home last month for the summer break, I asked them about their yearly reports and they answered, 'Oh, they are sending them out by mail this year.'"

"And what about your books for summer work?" I asked. "You know they often have to catch up with schoolwork during summer for what they missed during the school year."

'We did not have to this time, as we did very well this year,' they both responded.

"Then two days ago, when Franya and I were both cleaning up the house from top to bottom, we found their exercise books with comments and a letter from the Head Nun nailed to the underside of the table. The envelope contained their yearly reports with very low marks for everything but gymnastics. The accompanying letter was addressed to you asking you to show cause why the girls should be allowed to be re-admitted next fall and allowed to graduate."

"After a thorough belting!" Vasily roared. "I think I should visit the Head Nun and once again throw myself at her mercy and offer her a barrel (about 2½ litres) of herrings and a barrel of smoked sturgeon."

"You better add a barrel of caviar as well this time," commented Boris. Finally, in desperation Vasily asked, "Do you think the nuns will take them back?"

"If you go in your naval uniform, put on your best smile, offer your gratuity and remind them that it will be Eugenia's last year if she graduates."

"Yes, yes! I think that should work, thank you, Boris. Is there something else? You still look a bit perturbed."

"Well, it's nothing really."

"Come on spill it little brother."

"Well now in retrospect, it's almost amusing. Last Sunday afternoon, Franya and I were relaxing when all the girls screaming and yelling suddenly startled us. We immediately responded and rushed to their aid. We saw Klava and Musya covered practically from head to toe in what looked like blood. Tina only had a few drops on her. Natalia and Eugenia looked bewildered and were also covered in red, except that Eugenia was also dragging what looked like a white blood-stained sheet and talking nonsense … 'Dyadichka-Uncle, it's not our fault, the devil made us do it!'"

"What are you talking about, Eugenia?" I said. By that stage, I could see that what looked like blood was one of the berry wines that Franya makes. So I again said slowly; "What is going on here?" Eventually Eugenia took the lead with Natalia helping.

"'It's like this dyadichka; we liked it so much in church this morning that we thought we would repeat the Communion process ourselves while playing in the cowshed. We got the sweet wine that *tyetuchka* (aunty) makes out of the *pogreb* (cellar) and your trophy cup that looks like a chalice. We filled the chalice with the berry wine and I put the bed sheet around me to look like a priest. Natalia was the Deacon. Klava was first to take the Communion wine, followed by Musya and then Tina, when suddenly from the adjoining shed came a repeatedly beastly sound. Natalia was so startled that she screamed and knocked the chalice out of my hands, which practically covered all of us in wine. I tell you, *dyadichka,* it was a devil of a sound and it sounded like Beelzebub[38] himself. *Dyadichka,* you can whip me if you like and I won't upset you by counting again.'

"The last time whilst I was giving her a whipping, she continued to count each administered stroke to mock me – Once, *dyadichka*! Twice, *dyadichka*! And so on … until I gave up before I burst my boiler. This time she sounded truly repentant. So I told them all: 'You must never make fun of Communion – it is not a game and because you have, God has already punished you. Now go and clean up the mess before I change my mind and stay out of Franya's *pogreb*'. I then checked the adjoining cowshed and to my delight I found that our Munya (cow's name) gave birth to a lovely new heifer."

---

38 Referred to as the prince of the devils in the Old Testament.

30 FATHER AND DAUGHTERS

Boris's daughters were also energetic and thirsty for knowledge, but unlike their cousins they were less mischievous as they inherited their father's desire for reading mainly classics and mystery novels. However, their thirst for the inexplicable also led them into researching the supernatural. By the time the girls were in their late teens they took up the holding of séances – communication with the spirits – which was recurrently in vogue. The practice of calling on the dead particularly to foretell the future, as with astrology can be intriguing and absorbing to young and old alike particularly for the impressionable – and the sisters certainly were.

The girls enjoyed the secretive and mystical atmosphere created during a séance. They organised their sittings as per researched instructions. These usually took place in darkness or dim light, around a table free of nails, because strong light and metal links are said to hinder communication. The created atmosphere was exhilarating. Their favourite was the use of a self-made ouija[39] board consisting of a rectangular piece of cardboard with letters of the alphabet inscribed along its longer edge in a wide half-moon. On top of the board the girls placed a *bludichko* (saucer). Hence,

39 French and German words for yes – *oui* and *ja*

they called this entertainment *bludichko* rather than ouija board. Each person lightly placed a finger from each hand on the *bludichko*, which then moved about freely because of the resultant pressure. The pointer on the *bludichko* paused at different letters, sometimes spelling out words and even sentences.[40] Like crystal set enthusiasts the girls were thrilled and convinced they had communicated with the other side.

As they became proficient with this form of entertainment, they considered advancing to the next stage. The holding of a real séance – also sitting around a table, in a group of six to eight persons who, by holding hands, formed a circle. One of the group, an experienced medium, would then communicate with the spirits. There was no shortage of professed mediums in Harbin. But their parents' permission was needed particularly if held at home and as this encounter with the occult was at odds with their Christian upbringing.

When Boris heard of his girls' experiments his already elevated blood pressure nearly went through the roof. But since he prided himself on his self-control, he took time out to consider how best to deal with this situation. His daughters were the love of his life and he would have to find a way how best to discourage them from this newest fascination. Boris also knew that he would have to appeal to their minds as well as curb their emotions.

The family was seated in their living room after lunch following the Sunday church service. "So my dears you are seeking entertainment by probing into the occult," commenced Boris. "Entertainment it may be! But what you should ask yourselves is, is this the type of entertainment you really want? Occultism centres on the presumed ability of the practitioner to manipulate natural laws for one's own benefit; such practice can be regarded as evil when it also involves the breaking of moral laws. It's a practice that seeks

40 In the late 19th century, when the Ouija board was already a popular pastime, it was fashionable to ascribe such happenings to discarnate spirits. However, the more recent opinion is skeptical.

knowledge of the future or the unknown by supernatural means. It is a phenomenon that has existed since ancient times and can be practised for both good and evil. When used for evil it is known as black magic. When used for good it is known as white magic. The distinction between white and black is not always clear; hence, there is much grey area. Even the experienced shamans, magicians, gypsies and others can get into trouble. Your great grandmother Marina was said to dabble in fortune telling, to what end we do not know. The skill of understanding mystical agents is often better left alone. One of your favourite authors – Sir Arthur Conan Doyle once said: 'Obsession with the supernatural has been the ruin of many an exceptional intellect.' People have been known to lose their minds or as some say, become possessed. Our own religion advises us to stay away from these practices ... Lead us not into temptation, says the Lord's Prayer. So do not become tempted or lured by some evil force that is far stronger than most of us think! On that note, my dears, I will end my sermon to you and trust that you will reach the right conclusion." After that discussion, the girls lost their interest in this type of pastime.

31 DOG STORIES - MAN PROPOSES AND GOD DISPOSES

Boris loved his dogs and on more than one occasion some of them saved lives of a family member, like Duke, who saved Franya from a villain back in Russia. On this occasion Boris had returned from a hunt while Vasily remained behind stalking his prey with Boka – a favourite stray that Boris befriended. Vasily was so absorbed with his prey that he did not notice the change in the murky swamp that became like quicksand engulfing him slowly and little by little. Vasily knew the dangers associated with this type of entrapment. He attempted to remain as still as possible as with every move the body is sucked more and more into the dark, murky, sinister funnel of no return. He called out to Boka: "Boka, fetch Boris!" Like lightning Boka raced home. On seeing Boris he began to bark and tugged Boris in the direction of the forest. Boris at once realised that something had happened to Vasily. Almost subconciously he grabbed some rope, told Franya to get help from the neighbours and followed Boka back as fast as he could. By the time Boris reached his brother, Vasily was engulfed to his chest using his rifle to provide some support under his extended elbows and armpits.

Boris quickly threw a rope with a prepared sling which Vasily put around his head and armpits while Boris ran the rope around a tree to hold Vasily until further help came. A few shots from the rifle helped the searchers to locate them. Boka was given an extra treat that day and became a hero of Boris's pack.

Two or three years later when Boris and Franya were having their evening meal, Boka came in the household and licked Boris's hand, then proceeded to the back door and into the back yard. Boris stood up, looked at Franya and followed Boka. When Boris reached the back yard he saw Boka lying dead under a tree. In those few minutes before his death Boka had come to bid his last farewell to his loving friend and master. (As a dog owner myself, I never cease to be amazed how strong the bond between a human and an animal can be.)

Franya remembers Boris saying, "All my kinfolk except Vasily are gone, now Boka, I feel it won't be long before I go too."

"Do not talk such nonsense, Boris, you are only 49 and we have everything to live for." The year was 1933. Boris would meet his maker in two years' time – Man proposes and God disposes.

32 I WANT TO BE A STAR

At the age of 16 and still ebullient, Eugenia graduated from the convent and now lived at home with her father, her young stepmother and little brother but continued to be a handful. The Captain was sharing his frustrations with his brother Boris.

"She will be the death of me I tell you, Boris. Do you know what she did this time?"

"*Papachka* (a term of endearment for father)! You will be proud of me," said Eugenia running into the room.

"And why is that dearest?" inquired the Captain apprehensively, fearing the worst from Eugenia's excited and determined voice.

"You know that place on the edge of Old Harbin near the brickworks, well I lately heard the new young communist league – The *Komsomoltsi* – have been holding their secret meetings there. But everyone knows about it anyway".

"Eugenia, you haven't joined them? Have you? Oh! God help me".

"*Papachka*! You are wrong, so please listen to me before you burst your boiler. I crept up on them in broad daylight, snatched their red banner hanging off a broken down brick wall and ran."

"Oh my God!" exclaimed the Captain in shock horror.

"Listen, listen, *papachka*, the red atheists could not catch me, I am too fast for them and I know some of the underground tunnels there which they don't. So I got down into one of them and came out about half a kilometre or more down the track. I then waved the flag to them and yelled out: hey you red bastards cop this. I then spat at their flag, threw it down on the ground and trampled it. To infuriate them further I then bent down, showed them my backside, and ran off through another tunnel. Aren't you proud of me?"

"I tell you, Boris, I was left speechless. The only thing I remember asking her was: what possessed you to do it, *dochenka* (term of endearment for daughter)?

"Moreover, with great pride she said she did it for me and that she is as much of an anti-communist as you and I. She reminded me of the painting you and I were admiring one day in which the Cossacks were writing a letter to the Turkish Sultan and where the letter ended by saying that the Sultan could kiss the Cossacks' arse. She thought that that was most appropriate and that is what she yelled out to the Komsomoltsi. I literally did not know whether to laugh or cry."

By 1923 when she was barely 17, Eugenia had to marry Vladimir Boiko and that same year she gave birth to Yuri (George). By the time, Yuri was three Eugenia had had enough of her husband. One day she tipped a saucepan of soup over his head, picked up Yuri and left Harbin for Shanghai to become a star.

It was not easy. After some time, however, she began to appear on stage, written about in the local paper and noticed by foreigners that mattered. She favoured a style that made her look on stage a cross between Gloria Swanson and Marlene Dietrich with a similar tattooed beauty spot on her face and a *munshtuk* – long cigarette holder like Marlene's. Her highly lavish manner, her impeccable and obviously provocative attire that best suited her lovely model-thin body and her pretentious classic features attracted many men.

But Eugenia knew what she wanted – she wanted to be a star and thereby her liaisons were restricted to those who could help her progress. And progress she did. Eugenia took on a stage name

– Gloria Star. She danced through South East Asia; Hong Kong, Singapore, Malaya, Burma, French Indo China, Java, India and back to Hong Kong. It was there that she met Jack Woolard, a British Public Servant who served in the local fire service. She finally fell in love and stayed with Jack or rather he with her for the rest of their lives.

Yuri was able to go to a private school; first in Hong Kong and later in England. Jack did not mind Eugenia's lavish style and extrovert behaviour. He understood that she was a performer and needed to be loved and desired by others. They went on holidays to the United Kingdom and far out places like Jamaica, a place that they loved and vowed to return to one day.

By the early 1930s Eugenia decided to go back and visit her father Vasily, her Uncle Boris and the rest of the family. She came back and was known as Aunty Gene from Hong Kong, a former black sheep of the family now a big time lady with plenty of money. The poor girl from nobility who became a star and married an Englishman. Her profession was still frowned upon, but everyone still enjoyed seeing her. She really had a good time and when everything was over, on her way home she boarded the Chang Tso-lin Express owned by a famous Chinese War Lord – Chang Hsüeh-liang[41] the son of the late Jan Tso-lin. This express train was an armoured train and of course it was fair game in those days to try to derail it.

Eugenia got herself a sleeping berth but a couple of passengers, an older woman and her daughter, came up and said to her, "Look young lady, can you please move to another bunk as this bed is more suitable for me seeing that I am older then you and I just can't climb up that high". So Eugenia shrugged her shoulders and

---

41 Chang Hsüeh-liang assumed control of Manchuria and part of North China, after the Japanese killed his father. He mainly fought the Japanese. Unlike his father who fought the Communists and the Japanese. Chang Hsüeh-liang after the Sian Incident (1936), compelled the Nationalist leader Chiang Kai-shek to form a wartime alliance with the Chinese Communists against Japan.

moved to the upper bunk. By doing so it saved her life, because a few kilometres down the track the train hit a mine, the train was blown up and the old lady with her daughter were killed. Eugenia only suffered a few fractures and lived to perform on the stage for many years to come.

33 THE ACADEMIC

Vasily Georgievich Melihov was a 1921 graduate of a Harbin Commercial High School and has very fond memories of the educational system during his time there. His son G.V. Melihov, now living in Russia, documents some of these memories in his book *Manchuria the Far and Near – Manzhuria Dalyekaya i Blizkaya* Moscow 1991 pp 242-246. My grandfather A.A. Vassilieff together with some other teachers receives high praise for their conscientious and outstanding teaching ability. The educational system in Harbin also receives high praise. The key features of the educational system at the time included: A highly participative Parents and Citizens Committee; a number of welfare initiatives overseen by the P & C Committee including hot breakfasts and financial assistance for the under-privileged; religious, musical, games and sporting instruction with an annual sporting and games carnival between all Harbin Schools; school uniform and a high broadly based academic syllabus.

Alexander's career unlike his marriage prospered. Although Alexander was a good provider he was far too absorbed in work and part-time studies. Alexandra constantly complained to her parents and sisters. Being young and spirited she began to neglect her son Vladimir, often leaving him with her family in order to go out. Young Vladimir often complained to his father that he missed them both.

So Alexander decided to show greater interest in the upbringing of his son. In one of their *deep and meaningful* exchanges, Alexander finally said to Alexandra: "I have provided you with everything that a husband can give his wife: accommodation, food, clothing and money for Vladimir's education. I know I have not been able to give you enough of myself as I have been trying to secure a future for all of us. You, instead of showing some gratitude, have spent the housekeeping money on vodka and parties. That is not the example our son should have. I am separating from you and will bring up Vladimir myself."

Alexander was true to his word. His older married sister Lidia and at times his two younger brothers helped in Vladimir's upbringing, but in general Alexander tried to make up for lost time and was a good father. He encouraged Vladimir in his educational and sporting activities to the level where Vladimir began to show great potential. Alexander's younger brother Nikolai, who was a teacher in physical culture, for a brief time, instructed Vladimir in gymnastics until Nikolai decided to move to Stalingrad in the USSR. Alexander's youngest brother Sergiey, an employee of the CER – Russo/Japanese translator, helped Vladimir with languages and also introduced him to the Dobrovidov family. Alexander N. Dobrovidov (the son of Nikolai N. Dobrovidov, one of the few prominent Chinese language specialists in Harbin) at one stage coached Vladimir in Chinese and English and was impressed with his ability to pick up the languages quickly.

In 1926 Alexander, by this time a fully qualified Engineer Technologist (Mechanical and Electrical), was offered the posting of a member of the academic staff at the recently established Harbin Polytechnic Institute lecturing in advanced mathematics. The Polytechnic like most other educational institutions was subsidised by the CER. For a while, things went well. Father and son learnt how to bond.

34 I WANT TO GO HOME

As with a haughty smile she says;
"Am I not worth your love like Venus?
Mark what I choose to tell you, then.
I may forget the gulf between us
And make you happiest of men.

Here is my challenge-who will meet it?
For sale, I offer peerless nights.
Who will step forward-I repeat it –
And pay with life for his delights?"

Cleopatra 1835
A. Pushkin[42]

By the age of 17, Vladimir developed into a handsome strong-minded young man. Although he lacked a proper family upbringing, particularly the mother's touch, he was nevertheless well mannered and well spoken with a potential in engineering or athletics. But his secret desire was Russia. His High school col-

42 A Yermolinsky – The poems, prose and plays of A Pushkin – Random House New York 1936

leagues were equally divided into pro-white and pro-red school debates. Unlike his father, he saw a great future for the USSR. The new economic policy with the new five-year plans being implemented in Russia would, Vladimir believed, in no time put Russia back on the map so to speak. Uncle Nick wrote back saying how fast things were moving in the USSR and what an honour it was to live in a city named after its new leader – Stalingrad. So Vladimir began to brood more and more and say "why should everyone else live in their own country except some of us Russians – relics of the old regime".

He told his childhood friend Michael Koliagin that he was going home as soon as he finished High School. I may join you too, Volodya (a diminutive of Vladimir), after I finish my mechanics course. But, tonight there is a party and I will introduce you to the Vajinsky sisters.

That Sunday night Vladimir met the Vajinsky sisters. Alexander Dobrovidov – his former tutor, who recently returned from a brief stay in Australia, accompanied the eldest, Valentina. The middle one Musya and the youngest Klava were with Michael. Vladimir was immediately enchanted with Klava and as the evening progressed the three couples revelled in enjoyment. After the party, Vladimir and Klava sometimes saw one another. However, Vladimir's infatuation with his mother country grew by the day.

At one of the last class meetings, a number of them made a vow that within the next two years they would go back to their homeland. Vladimir in excitement mentioned his own plans to one of his school colleagues, Natasha, and she in turn told him that she and her future fiancé Valentin Pogozhev were also planning to move to Stalingrad in about two years. They both laughed and said wouldn't it be funny if one day we bumped into one another in the street amongst our own people.

Finally, Vladimir told his father of his intentions. Alexander was horrified.

"*Sinok* (son), is that how I taught you to think, are you thinking with your brains or your backside? Oh it's my fault I know, I should have spent more time with you."

"It's nobody's fault, papa, it's the way things are today. You have been so engrossed in your work and study, study, study that you have not noticed the changes occurring back home. Russia is moving forward with its new economic policies, its five-year plans, building factories, hydroelectric schemes and linking rivers with canals. Meanwhile the Samurai are expanding their forces in Korea and eagerly waiting to jump into Manchuria the gateway to China. Papa, I want to go home. Harbin is not ours anymore."

"Oh! My dear *Vovachka* (a term of endearment), what can I say, as your parents we have not been the best to you. But we do want the best for your future. Who knows you may be right. And I am aware of the things you have just said. I am not altogether blind! These are uncertain times. The world is changing. The world depression may make nations do things they otherwise would not. Maybe, we would be safer back home. But this is my home, my Russian Harbin. Go ahead, spread your wings ahead of time if you must. But if you are so intent on going, first get a professional qualification."

"So I can end up a lonely man like you and live in a foreign land with no future?"

Alexander was lost for words. Vladimir realised he was too brusque and offensive and moderated slightly.

"All right, papa, because I do love and respect you, I will finish my ninth class and then do a chauffeur's course and before my 18th birthday I will go to Russia.

35 MANCHUKUO - THE NEW LANDLORD - OBEY OR DIE

I have outlasted all desire,
My dreams and I have grown apart;
My grief alone is left entire,
The gleanings of an empty heart.
The storms of ruthless dispensation
Have struck my flowery garland numb-
I live in lonely desolation
And wonder when my end will come

Untitled 1821
A. Pushkin[43]

The Japanese takeover of Manchuria on 9 March 1932 made it an independent state – Manchukuo – with Chang-chun as its capital. Once again, life in Harbin changed; although the Japanese did not officially terrorise the Russians for fear of a total exodus by them (more than half left anyway), because the Russians who built Harbin were still running it and their en masse exodus would have

43 A Yermolinsky – The poems, prose and plays of A Pushkin – Random House New York 1936

collapsed the city infrastructure. Furthermore, a large number of Harbin citizens held Soviet passports and the Japanese were not quite ready to confront the Soviet Union. But that frustrated the local Japanese Administration and their military – a frustration that from time to time they took out on the Russians for the least excuse.

And so it was with Alexander. He was not a subservient person. He was hard working and strong willed and a man with little to lose. No wife and the only love of his life – his son in the USSR safe out of the clutches of these new upstarts with a deluded vision of a master race in Asia. The bowing and scraping was not his style.

That attitude must have been noticed very quickly. Within a few months of the Japanese takeover of Harbin in June, 1932 Alexander was called out to the Japanese Gendarme (Gestapo-like) Headquarters for questioning. His brother and sister were terrified for fear of being next. After all most of the family had Soviet citizenship and some of them lived in the USSR. For obvious reasons no information of that time is available other than that he was tortured. All that is known is that within a week of his release he died at home.[44, 45]

Any obstacles to the invading Japanese Imperial rule, no matter how subtle, had to be quickly eliminated and an example set. Otherwise disobedience would spread – a *Dictum Sapient* that was often given savage expression by the conquerors.

Ironically and unknown to Vladimir, soon after his father's death a cruel fate was also dealt to young Vladimir.

---

44 Alexander's burial is listed in the monument-album p 218 (V Pamyat ob Usopshih v Zemlye Manjurskoy i Harbintskoy) Melbourne Australia.

45 The CER was a contentious issue to the Japanese militarists and they attempted all forms of intimidation; blackmail of CER employees, spreading agents among them and attempting to recruit them. Disagreeable individuals were dealt with harshly.

36 BACK IN THE USSR

Vladimir's arrival in the USSR is best outlined from his records in the KGB file (the former NKVD) accessed in 1999 after the fall of the USSR: Vladimir Alexandravich Vassilieff (Registered Case No. 44249 Moscow Administration FSB – previously KGB files). (Translation of the language was somewhat challenging owing to the use of Soviet jargon, sometimes a poor standard of words and phrases, by the records agent, and/or possible improvisation of evidence.)

> Vladimir Alexandravich Vassilieff first arrived in the USSR in January 1931 from Harbin China where he had lived since his birth with his relatives.
>
> He was arrested in April 1933 for his involvement, together with D.E. Haritonov, a former chekist (forerunner to the NKVD) agent of the Ryazan operational sector, in performing a robbery under the guise of carrying out a search of Mr. Lobanov's premises in Malokozihinskomu Street in Moscow.
>
> The acquired evidence of the crime was from a confession provided by the accused Haritonov and Azarov Alexander. (Translator's note: Azarov is apparently another accomplice

out of a total of six probably unknown to Vassilieff at that time.)

Prior to the arrest Vassilieff V.A. worked as a chauffeur at the auto depot of the *Narkomindela USSR.*

From the court documents: *Under the pretext of a search (warrant) for the OGPU* (another forerunner to the KGB) *the accused executed a robbery of the Lobanov flat(s) confiscated manufactured items and subjected the victim to temporary detainment* (July 1933 Moscow).

Out of the charges laid the established resolution and the chosen measures taken (form No 28) from 10.07.33, Vassilieff V.A. is accused under article 59.3 of the Criminal Code RSFSR, is to be held under guard, until completion of the investigation.

Signed: Authorised OO OGPU MVO

Bekorevich

INVESTIGATION 7/1933

As part of the investigation from the words of Vassilieff V.A. the investigator fills out a form with an ink pen, where he points out:

Address prior to the arrest –

Moscow, Malaya Polyanka lane. House No 10. Flat 11.

Relatives Remaining in Harbin (abbreviations made by the agent filling out the form):

Mother – Vassilieff Alexandra Vladimirovna, age 39, Seamstress.

Uncle – Vassilieff Sergey Alexandravich, age 36, Interpreter Japanese language in the Administration of the China Eastern Railway.

Aunt – Podkamenskaya Pod Alexandravna, age 38, Pensioner.

Aunt – Vishnevskaya Lidia Alexandravna, age 42, Home

duties. Her husband: Vishnevsky Nikolay (patronymic illegible) age 38, Teacher of a manual trade.

Aunt – Krivova Anna Trofimovna, age 44, Home duties.

Aunt – Shuvalova Mar. Vladimirovna, age 39, Home duties.

Aunt – Shuvalova Anna Vladimirovna, age 32, Home duties.

Relatives Living In Russia:

Auntie – Kazanskaya Elena Alexandravna, age 32, works in a factory *Geodeziya*

Moscow, Malaya Polyanka lane. House No. 10.

Uncle – Vassilieff Nikolay Alexandravich, age 32, Teacher Physical Education in Stalingrad.

From the interrogation protocol: Vassilieff V.A. Came to USSR legally, at first he lived with his uncle Vassilieff N.A. in Stalingrad where he worked for a business enterprise. In September 1931 he moved to Moscow.

From all the evidence obtained through interrogation of Haritonov Dmitry Efremovitch, date of birth 1910, it became clear that he is a group organizer of flat searches.

Altogether, the accused had performed eight flat raids. Haritonov D.E. – a military serviceman, in hiding from the Ryazansky operational sector of the PP OGPU MO, is accused of a crime under Section 193 p.7 of the criminal code. During a search of Haritonov's premises by the investigative agents a number of blank forms were found that gave him authority for searches of premises – *62 examples of a small format and 84 examples of a medium format,* this is shown in the charge document, dated 14.07.33. The charge is signed by:

Authorised L. Bekorevich,

Agreed Officer in Charge 2 OTD OO OGPU MVO Fainberg
Assistant Officer in Charge OGPU MVO Ilyn

Excerpt from the protocol of the Troika meeting of the PP OGPU MO DATED 13.07.33:

Resolution: *Vassilieff V.A. to be incarcerated in a GULAG for a term of three years, the term commencing from 10.07.33.*

From work notes OPER OD PP OGPU MO from 17.07.33: In the room flat of Vassilieff V.A. M/Polyanka lane, House No. 10, flat 11 during his arrest his aunt Kazanskaya Elena Alexandravna was also residing in that flat with a 10-year-old child and without a signed authorization. *The aunt has her own house in Ryazan and a flat in Moscow. It is requested that she be urgently offered to urgently leave the premises for her previous place of residence at Pyatnitsky St, House No. 3, Flat 13. Vassilieff V.A. belongings to be left in the room, marked to be kept until further notice*

Signed: Asst O.C. OO OGPU MVD =Ilyn=

Excerpt from the protocol 16.09.33:
Resolution: Haritonov Dmitry Efremovitch – to be shot, belongings to be confiscated.

So at the age of almost twenty, Vladimir blindly fell into a web of deceit which was played out by a former chekist with criminal expertise (a trait often common to the chekists of that and later times) preying on his victims and unknown young accomplices. This sentence would haunt the young naïve Vladimir from Harbin for most of his life.

37 THE ESCAPE

It was early winter in 1934 when Vladimir, with two other escapees, crossed the Russia/Manchuria border where the Amur River freezes and one can literally island hop from Soviet Russia into Manchuria. On the day of the escape, Vladimir convinced his two GULAG inmates that while they were delivering supplies to the camp with the aid of a packhorse, escape to the Chinese border and freedom was less than a day away. Thus with much hardship, hunger and danger of being shot if caught, they made it. However, Manchuria was not the same as he had left it three years before. It was now a puppet state of Manchukuo under the control of the Empire of Japan. Nevertheless, he was free and he would seek out the Soviet Consul and prove his innocence. After several days' exhausting walk, hitching a ride when they could on horse-driven snow sled, they made it to a CER station. There, as stowaways, they sneaked rides how ever they could to Harbin and parted company.

Vladimir made it to his uncle Serge's house, told him of his ordeal leading to his escape and asked for more information about the premature death of his father. Uncle Serge, a younger brother of his late father, also worked for the CER as a Russian/Japanese interpreter. Serge tried to console his nephew and gently told him the little that he knew.

"As you may have heard by now, Volodya, shortly after you left for the USSR, in 1931 the Japanese began the take over of Manchuria. They desperately need the control of the CER, which is still in a peculiar position. The Russians, correction, our Soviet friends, own it! They lease it from the Chinese but the Japanese control it. Most of the staff are white Russians like your father and I. But, as you know, before you left, if we wanted to remain employed by the CER we had to take out Chinese or Soviet citizenship. Very few took Chinese citizenship, some left for Shanghai or Tientsin. They were the smart ones. Most, like your father and I, took Soviet citizenship. We thought it would be better for you also and our brother Nikolai, with whom you stayed in Stalingrad for a while.

"But, alas it only brought us misery. The Soviets still sentenced you and the Japanese resent us. They can treat the Chinese as they like but they have to show restraint with us, as they do not want to antagonize the Soviets just yet. But every now and then the Japanese Gendarmes flex their muscles and overstep their boundaries.

"So it was with your father. He, still with the CER, continued to lecture advanced mathematics at the Institute and was much admired by the staff and students. One day he told me he had had a disagreement with a Japanese official and that the Gendarmes wanted to see him. He thought it either might have been to demand more respect for the Japanese or to accuse him of spying as some relatives such as Nikolai and yourself were living in the USSR. It was in June 1932 – less than a year before the NKVD arrested you – that he was taken in by the Gendarmes and held for several days. I could not get in touch with him. They warned me not to make waves or they would take me in for questioning as well. Your father died at home less than a week after he was released. I believe the bastards tortured him and possibly infected him with something. When we buried him, we kept the casket closed during the service as he was badly beaten. We buried him at the Uspensky Cemetery and marked the grave with a monument. I will show you how to find it.

"There are also rumours that outside Harbin the Japanese are experimenting with some biological germ-warfare. Your father mentioned this to me shortly before they arrested him. Who knows what he stumbled on? Yes, he was only 39; I loved him dearly just as I know you did. Apart from his state of mind that is all I can tell you.

"Oh! And another thing; he frequently appeared depressed of late. He was lonely you know, what with our parents gone, his long separation from your mother, the family split between Manchuria and the USSR and you languishing in the homeland and then the bloody Japs – he had nothing to live for. Sometimes he buried himself in his work. Sometimes your father and I, and (our older sister) Lidia and her husband Nikolay would get together and talk, just as we had done in the old days. This would help us unwind and summon up the courage to go on for a while but not for long.

"You know, Volodya, you need a new beginning and you won't get it here. Go to Shanghai maybe, make some money and then go to America. That is where I am going. I will not stay here much longer. For now, Russia and Manchuria are finished. Get yourself a nice girl and get married. Here, take some money. It will get you started, and don't forget to visit your mother."

Vladimir thanked his uncle and embraced him. "Thank you for everything, Uncle. I will take your advice, but first I must do something."

So Vladimir visited his mother. "Thank God you are alive and well," she said. "I don't want to speak ill of the dead but your fool of a father should have stopped you from going back. He boasted that he could look after you better than I. Well did he? He couldn't even protect himself against the Japanese."

"Mama! Let it go, I don't want to argue with you as soon as I return."

"Yes you're right, Volodya. Look at you! You're skin and bones! Come and have something to eat. And tonight we will have some friends over to celebrate your return; we will have some *zakuski*, *pelmeni* and *vodochka*. Now go wash up and change. I think I still have some of your old clothes in the back room."

After the homecoming celebration and a full stomach, Vladimir felt better than he had since his arrest almost a year ago now. The nightmare briefly reappeared in his mind, the set up by Haritonov – *the rotten scoundrel*, the arrest, the humiliation and then a Siberian GULAG. What a mess, with that record he could never return home. He had to clear his name.

The first thing Vladimir did that morning was to visit the Soviet Consul. Shaved, groomed and dressed neatly he sought audience with a Consulate official. He attempted to explain his story of the false accusation leading to imprisonment and escape. The official took Vladimir by the arm, led him to the door and threw him out saying; "You young fool, be grateful that you are still alive, get out of here and don't ever come back." His pride hurt and, bitterly disappointed, he realized he could do nothing.

"Find yourself a nice girl." He thought of what his uncle said, which made him reminisce. I wonder how Klava is? So he decided to seek out his childhood friend Michael Koliagin. His own parents separated and his upbringing alternating between his parents and other relatives and Michael not knowing his, since he was brought up from childhood by adopted parents. They made a good pair. He found Michael working on a car in a small garage.

"So I see you are mechanic now."

"Volodyka[46]! When did you get back? God, what has happened to you? You look like death warmed up. What did they do to you back home? I am sorry about your father." And so the two friends caught up with each other's lives. "What miserable luck, Volodya. Never mind, maybe we could get you a job here in the garage. You are partly a mechanic. You have done your chauffeur–basic mechanic papers. I'll talk to the boss for you."

"That's great. Thanks, Michael. By the way, how are the Vajinsky sisters?"

---

46 Rough term of endearment for Vladimir.

"Well, the oldest Tina she is now married to Alexander Dobrovidov, the fellow that used to tutor you in Chinese."

"Oh yes he's not a bad guy. I think our fathers might have known one another, through some teaching connection and the CER. Anyway, what about the other two, God they look alike."

"Musya is my girl. I plan to marry her one-day, so hands off. Klava, the one you fancy, has a boyfriend, Igor Petrov. She sees him sometimes – don't think they are serious. I'm going over next Sunday for dinner. Come with me. I'll warn Musya I'm bringing you along. Her parents are very hospitable, real Russian nobility; the father is not well, poor circulation I hear."

"Thanks again, Michael. You don't have to worry about Musya. I'll only steal a kiss from her when you're not looking. Yes it's Klava that I fancy but I don't have much time for this nobility business. They got rid of it all back home and everyone is equal."

With the snow melting and Easter approaching, that Sunday afternoon Michael and Vladimir drove up in a car borrowed from Michael's garage. They entered the modest Vajinsky cottage and were greeted like old friends with typical warm Russian hospitality. The house was warm and cosy, decorated with the small, white flowers called *podsnezhniki* – snowdrops. An Icon of the blessed Virgin with the Saviour and a glowing *lampada* – icon lamp, hung in a corner. A white tablecloth covered the table and on it were a variety of non-meat *zakuski* (owing to the Great Lent) and other delicacies that Vladimir had not seen in a long while. Sturgeon caviar, herring and other variety of marinated fish, *pirogi* (pies) with cabbage, carrot and mushroom filling, several varieties of marinated vegetable dishes and of course salted gherkins, vodka and a number of home made liqueurs. The hostess, Efrasinia Stepanovna Vajinsky, was a master cook and her daughters good students.

The host, Boris Nikitich Vajinsky, greeted the two young men warmly, introducing the newcomer Vladimir to his wife, his three daughters and Valentina's husband Alexander Nikolayevich Dobrovidov, Sasha as most friends called him. "But, of course I believe you two gentlemen have met before, Alexander Nikolayevich used to tutor you in Chinese," said the host, looking at Vladimir.

"Yes," Alexander Nikolayevich intervened, "he was a good student."

"Ah, a student is only as good as his teacher," responded Vladimir.

"Part of the credit must go to Alexander Nikolayevich's father," replied the host. "Nikolay Nikolayevich is still considered one of the prominent Chinese language specialists in all Harbin and if we live here in the Orient we should all try to speak the native language."

"Which native language do you recommend?" said Vladimir with slight sarcasm. "Chinese or Japanese?"

"Either, one, or both," said Boris Nikitich, "and you are right of course, young man. Klava speaks basic Japanese and works as a cashier at the well-known Aspitian's delicatessen and pastry store, which the Japanese frequently visit. Oh forgive me, young man, may I call you Volodya?"

"But of course," replied Vladimir, sounding perplexed.

"Here we are discussing languages and the Japanese. I have heard of your sad loss. Please accept our deepest sympathy on the untimely death of your father."

"Thank you, you are most kind, Sir."

"Do not be judgmental of all the Japanese, the Gendarmes like the NKVD tend to attract the worst kind. My boss is a Samurai and he has treated my family with the utmost respect and now that my health is suffering he has displayed extra kindness to me."

"Forgive me, Boris Nikitich, if I don't share your views, the Samurai and you are of noble birth and maybe there is some affinity there. But, my father who was an engineer and an academic highly respected at the CER and the Polytechnic did not receive the appropriate respect. On the contrary he died from disrespect, abuse and torture and for that I will never forgive the Japanese and if any one of them ever gets in my way I will show them some of my respect!"

At that moment to break the tension, the hostess beckoned all to the table.

The rest of the afternoon passed – more light-heartedly. The plentiful and delicious meal washed down with home-made wine and liquors and vodka made every one very chirpy and as often at Russian dinners everyone spoke at once. Even Vladimir lightened up, telling jokes and stories. So when Sasha asked him what he did in Moscow before his arrest, with a straight face and without the blink of an eyelid he answered, "I drove Stalin around on several occasions, I was a chauffeur at the Ministry of Transport and that was part of my job." At that point, the table became very quiet until Michael burst out laughing.

"He tells everyone that. The closest he got to Stalin was when the NKVD gave him a *putevka* – a free trip to a GULAG resort in Siberia; see how they fattened him up." And so the conversation became lively again, but the host glanced at Vladimir in an uncertain way as though trying to weigh him up.

Prior to going home, Klava and Volodya made plans to meet in town. As the weeks followed, the two met more often. Although, not often enough. Vladimir's job at the garage and Klava's long hours at the store gave little time for any get together. Sometimes they would snatch a brief moment to be together or Vladimir would go to the store where Klava worked to buy something as an excuse to talk to her. On rare occasions, they would go to the movies on a Sunday afternoon.

Late one Sunday evening after they parted company, Boris Nikitich sat down with his daughter for a chat. "So Klavunka," as he would address her in an affectionate way, "how do you find Volodya?"

"I love him papa," was her brief reply.

"But what about Igor; your steady boyfriend?"

"Igor is a good man and I like him, but I don't love him."

"Dear one, I don't want to run your life, you are getting to a stage where you will have to make these decisions for yourself. But, I do not think that Volodya is the right man for you. He may be handsome, funny, and a go-getter but he is also impulsive, unstable, comes from a broken home, he is without means and romanticizes Russia the way it is not. Precious, I ask you to reconsider your feelings for him or at least do not rush into anything for which you may be sorry later. If in a year or two you still have feelings for one another I will not stand in your way and you will have my and your mother's blessing."

Next time the two saw one another, Klava mentioned her father's apprehension about their developing relationship and suggested that maybe they should not see each other quite so often.

"We hardly see each other now," Vladimir protested, adding, "He probably does not like me, because I am poor and he thinks I am a Sovietsky. Well I will make something of myself; maybe I will become an engineer like my father, a businessman or a top athlete to prove to him that I can look after you because I love you. You wait and see, nothing is going to keep us apart."

But fate stepped in. A couple of weeks later, coming home from work tired and angry at the world again, Vladimir spotted two Gendarmes beating up a drunken Russian. Visions of Gendarmes torturing his father flashed in front of him and Vladimir reacted impulsively. Without any hesitation, he ran to the rescue of the victim and making use of his school-time boxing lessons within a brief minute he knocked out cold the two Gendarmes. The victim thanked him profusely.

"May God bless you, young man, for helping me, but now they will be after you. You must leave town now or they will kill you."

Thus having recently escaped from the Soviet NKVD GULAG he now had to flee once more, this time from the Gendarmes and Japanese-occupied Manchuria. After having said a quick good bye to his mother, then Michael, who drove him to Harbin Station and promised to pass on to Klava the message that Vladimir would send for her when he was re established in Shanghai. Meanwhile Uncle Serge helped to arrange a quick passage on the SCER to Tientsin from where Vladimir would make his way by boat to Shanghai.

38 THE END OF A VAJINSKY

And Lensky, left eye closing, aimed-
But just then Eugene's pistol flamed...
And the poet, without a sound,
Let fall his pistol on the ground.
Eugene Onegin
A. Pushkin [47]
(Almost prophetic to Pushkin's death)

Boris's health was worsening rapidly; his blood pressure was high, his nerves were strained, his body was puffed owing to the onset of oedema[48]. Boris was advised to take sick leave. His superior and long acquaintance Tanaka-San,[49] a Japanese senior manager of

---

47 A Yermolinsky – The poems, prose and place of A Pushkin – Random House New York 1936

48 An abnormal accumulation of watery fluid in the intercellular spaces of connective tissue. Oedema is most frequently a symptom of disease rather than a disease in itself, and it may have a number of causes, most of which can be traced back to gross variations in the physiological mechanisms that normally maintain a constant water balance in the cells, tissues, and blood. Among the causes may be diseases of the kidneys, heart, veins, or lymphatic system. 1994-2001 Encyclopædia Britannica, Inc.

49 The exact name is not certain.

the Samurai[50] class visited him on a regular basis. "Borya-San you must not worry, your job is safe, and when you are better you will return. I look forward to seeing you back soon." This, Tanaka said even though he was pressured by the military Gendarme to fill this and other management positions with their own officials.

"You must remove the sick old man from this important position; and not let our efficiency be hampered by your personal feelings towards this decrepit, worthless being to our cause."

"*Choti mati kudasai* (Just one moment) – you overstep your boundaries, Colonel. I am the one responsible for the productive output of this factory. Vajinsky-San has given many faithful years to our enterprise and my honour does not allow me to treat my faithful employees like dogs. If you continue to interfere in my business, I will personally see General Nakamura to restrain you. As you know, the General knows the Vajinskys. He personally awarded Boris-San's brother Captain Vajinsky with a bravery award in his service to the Manchukuo."

"Forgive me, Tanaka-San, I only meant what was best for our cause. I did not want to dishonour you in any way."

"I understand your zealousness, Colonel; perhaps we each better run our own businesses as we are meant to do. I bid you farewell. If I can be of any service to you please do not hesitate to call on me again. Sayonara."

Early in the morning on St. Georges Day – 6 May 1935 (23 April – Julian calendar) – Boris Nikitich Vajinsky died.[51] Like my paternal grandfather – Alexander – he was buried at the New Uspensky Cemetery (now demolished). I recall visiting his grave with my mother and sister prior to departing Harbin for Australia. For my mother who loved her father very much, this farewell was particularly poignant.

---

50 Member of the Japanese warrior class. The term Samurai was originally used to denote the aristocratic warriors (bushi), but it came to apply to all the members of the warrior class that rose to power in the 12th century and dominated the Japanese government until the Meiji Restoration in 1868. 1994-2001 Encyclopædia Britannica, Inc.

51 Boris' burial is listed in the monument-album p 268 (V Pamyat ob Usopshih v Zemlye Manjurskoy I Harbintskoy) Melbourne Australia 2000.

39 BERLIN

Although during the early twenties to the mid thirties close to 200,000 émigrés from Russia settled in Berlin, few tangible remains can be found there today. The phenomenon of Russian Berlin, the cultural and intellectual centre of the emigration declined almost as swiftly as it flowered. Mainly because of World War II and its immediate after effects. Prague, Belgrade, Constantinople, and Paris appear to have kept longer lasting pictures of the past than Russian pre-war Berlin, with its once-dynamic life, which only remains a memory. The past of the Russian Berlin appears to have fallen into oblivion. And yet today since *Perestroika* Berlin once again has attracted tens of thousands of Russian immigrants.

Berlin's character of myth and symbol as a city of the imagination, reached its peak, not during the existence of imperial splendour but during the time that followed, the period of the troubled Weimar Republic in the 1920s, the *Goldene Zwanziger Jahre* – the Golden Twenties, when Berlin developed an extraordinary reputation for cultural brilliance and intellectual ferment. Fritz Lang chose the city of Berlin in which to direct his famous movie *Metropolis,* and Walter Ruttmann the film *Berlin: die Symphonie einer Grossstadt* – Berlin: Symphony of a Metropolis. The theatres, clubs, cabarets, and other amusement enterprises that made Berlin notorious in the 1920s continued into the postwar period.

After many years, Berlin once again is a cultural centre. In 1988, it was classed as the cultural capital of Europe. The city convinced the sceptics that art and cultural life were just as attractive and significant as the Kurfurstendamm (Ku'damm) or the Brandenburg Gate. The city organised stunning spectacles: theatre, dance, literature, film, music, exhibitions, international symposia, and many sculptures along the popular Ku'damm. The four major museum complexes – Museum Island, the Tiergarten, Kulturforum, the Dahlem Museums and those at Charlotenburg Palace were reorganised and made more *user friendly.* A year later Berlin was once again a unified city.

By the time in 1996 when my wife and I visited her birthplace, we were astounded with the beauty, order and elegance of the city. I recalled my late mother-in-law's frequent descriptions of how beautiful and efficient the city used to be. Being young and inexperienced, I did not take as much notice as perhaps I should have.

Now in the new millennium, Berlin once again is the capital of reunited Germany, attracting visitors from all over the world including thousands of Russians from Russia and abroad.

40 PARIS OR BERLIN

Elena eventually made her way to Paris. It was one of the favourite Russian émigré centres. After a while, she got a job as a housekeeper with Kira and Emil Herrmann. The husband was a successful and probably the world's foremost violin dealer. Their daughter Tatiana later married Coast Guardsman Serge Sikorsky, the inventor's son. By 1919 Dasha went to a pensionate – a Russian language Church school on Rue Daru. The school was on the grounds of a beautiful Russian Orthodox Cathedral, which was built by the Russian Nobility who frequently went abroad during the previous century.

Dasha made a number of friends at school with whom she kept in touch for many years to come. Amongst them were handsome young Count Nikolai Sheremetyev and Marina (later Alekseeva) daughter of her mother's friend. An interesting convergence of paths particularly between Dasha and Marina would unexpectedly and repeatedly occur, during their next two generations of family.

In the 1920s, the big attraction for the Russian expatriate in Germany was Berlin, with its promise of employment, an elegant lifestyle and the cultural support of a large Russian Community. Unfortunately, by the time Dasha finished her schooling and moved there with her mother Elena it was 1929 and the time of the Big

Crash – followed by the Great Depression. That all began with the catastrophic collapse of the stock market prices on the New York Stock Exchange in October 1929.

In Europe, the Great Depression intensified extremist forces and lowered the values of liberal democracy. In Germany, economic anguish directly contributed to Adolf Hitler's rise from the infamous beer-halls of Munich to power in Berlin in1933. The Nazis' public-works projects and their rapid expansion of munitions production ended the Depression in Germany by 1936.

Elena and Dasha found it difficult at first but ultimately each found work. Better still, Dasha found the love of her life – Ivan Wownenko. They met at a Russian/Ukrainian community gathering and were quickly attracted to one another. Over a cup of coffee and a cigarette they each told each other their past.

Ivan was the eldest of two sons and three daughters to Arhip and Ecapitalina Wownenko. He was born in Ivanovka near Dniepr opetrovsk in the Ukraine in 1902. He fled the Ukraine during the Russian Civil War.

He came to Prague Czechoslavakia in about 1920 and completed his degree in Mining Engineering. By the late 1920s, he came to Berlin for improved opprtunity. Although he could not progress from a draughtsman to an engineer owing to the depression it was still a reasonably well-paid job.

By 9 October 1932, Ivan and Dasha married with Elena's blessing.

5 WAR AND PEACE

1935-1950

41 SHANGHAI

To many the fascination of life in Shanghai in the 100 years before the 1949 Liberation lies in its strange remoteness from the world of China today. It was almost like a different parallel universe. Shanghai was a cross between the Paris of the East and the Whore of Asia or the Yellow Babylon.

You could say that it started with the defeat of China by Great Britain in 1842, which led to the signing of the Treaty of Nanking and the opening of Shanghai to unrestricted foreign business. The British, French, and Americans took possession of designated areas in the city within which they were granted special rights and privileges, calling them concessions. The Japanese received a concession in 1895 under the terms of the Treaty of Shimonoseki. The granting of concessions led to the establishment of major European banks and multipurpose commercial houses.

Shanghai's potential as a leading centre of foreign trade was further enhanced when its rival port Canton in the southeastern coastal province of Kwantung, was cut off from its hinterland during 1850 to 1864 by the Taiping Rebellion. As a result of this and future potential threats to the expansion of their commercial operations in China, the British obtained rights of navigation on the Yangtze in 1857. Owing to the natural outlet for the vast hinterland of the Lower Yangtze, Shanghai rapidly grew to become China's number one leading port. By 1860, it accounted for about 25 per cent of the total shipping tonnage entering and departing the country.

The city's abundant and cheap labour supply, with local raw materials, and inexpensive power induced the flow of foreign capital particularly after the Sino-Japanese War of 1894-95, thus establishing light industries within the foreign concessions. The foreign zones were under extra territorial administration, maintained their own courts, police systems, public utilities and armed forces.

By contrast, local Chinese investment in Shanghai's industry was minimal until after 1960 with the minor exception of World War I when foreign capital was diverted from China. In that hiatus, Chinese investors were able to gain a tenuous foothold in the scramble for industrial development but, this initial involvement was short-lived, as the post World War I resurgence of Western and Japanese economic imperialism – followed closely by the Depression of the 1930s – overwhelmed many of the newly established Chinese industries. Competition became difficult, as cheaper foreign goods were dumped on the Shanghai market, and labour was attracted to relatively higher paying jobs in foreign-owned factories. During the Sino-Japanese War of 1937-45, the Japanese occupied Shanghai and the city's industrial plants suffered extensive war damage. After the war the International Sector of Shanghai continued to live, on borrowed time. From 1949, Shanghai's development was temporarily slowed because of the emphasis on internal regional development, especially during the period up to 1960 when close cooperation was maintained with the Soviet Union. With the cooling of relations after 1960, Shanghai resumed its key position as China's leading scientific and technological research centre, with the nation's most highly skilled labour force. Modern Shanghai is fast becoming the *Wall Street* of China, particularly since its rapid development of the former Pudong wharf area across the Huangpu River.

42 THE REGIMENT

How the Regiment was formed – The Shanghai Volunteer Corps was established for the defence of foreigners in 1853 in response to the then Chinese riots threatening the lives of Europeans living in Shanghai.

At the outset, it numbered only 300 people. However, by the time the Russian immigrants began to arrive in Shanghai after the Russian Revolution in 1917 the Corps numbered in excess of 1,500 people. It comprised two English Companies of Infantry, Scottish, Japanese, Portuguese, and other units. There was, also, a Squadron of Cavalry, a machine gun Detachment, about 30 armoured personal carriers, an engineering Company and a band unit.

It is interesting to review how the Russian Regiment was established within the Corps as documented independently by two one-time residents of Shanghai. A former serving officer of the Regiment – V.D. Jiganov previously a White Army Captain (a hero of his own time), later a teacher, and an author of a large number of Russian Historical Reviews published in Shanghai and Sydney. The other, V.P. Petrov, a Russian journalist at the Shanghai Zarya and later an author in the US of several publications including *Shanghai on the Huangpu* (in Russian).

In 1922, the remains of the White Russian Army in Primoriye

in the Russian Far East under superior pressure of the Red Army retreated into China. Part of the Army crossed over by land to Manchuria. The balance of about 9,000 military and civilian personnel sailed to the Korean port of Genzan (now Wonsan) in 15 ships and other small unworthy boats. That same year only 3,000 of the refugees set sail for Shanghai in 12 of the better ships.

The standoffish British in Shanghai reluctantly accepted the refugees – half-worrying that these refugees would become a noose around their neck. Still, they were given permanent residence. At that time, the Shanghai International Settlement did not require entry visas.

From the 6,000 refugees remaining in Korea about 4,500 dispersed mainly to Harbin and some to Mukden both in Manchuria, with a small part dispersing to other parts of China. Left over was a small Far Eastern Cossack Group of 1,500 Cossacks under the command of one of the most meritorious warriors of the Russian Imperial Army – Lt. General F. Glebov. This group was determined to get to Shanghai. By September 1923, this group of three ships finally arrived in Shanghai. It rather dropped anchor at the Port entrance with the Imperial Russian colours at the ship masts and guns trained on the city. At this demonstration, the authorities immediately issued an ultimatum to leave.

However, the General responded with a decisive refusal. He also declared that the ships had nowhere to go and that he would not commit his command to any further suffering. They already suffered enough during the last two wars (World War I and the Russian Civil War). Hearing this, the Shanghai Diplomatic Corps and the Municipal Authorities decided not to oppose the last remains of the Imperial Russian Army and the ships were left alone.

Shortly afterwards, all of the Glebov's command was allowed ashore and thereupon received permanent residency, accommodation and employment. However, the staunchest patriots did not leave the ships until 1927 and when they visited the city they did so in the uniform of the Imperial Russian Army.

By the turn of 1926/27 China was on the brink of a civil war. Along the border of the mighty Yangtze River stood troops of the Northern Coalition Alliance headed by Marshal Chang Tso-lin. Within the close proximity of Shanghai were the forces under the command of General Sun Chuan-fun (a protégé of Chang Tso-lin). From the south and the west advancing onto Shanghai was the Cantonese Red Army under the command of General Chiang Kai-shek (pro communist at that time). Chiang Kai-shek had already taken Hankow and forced the British to withdraw from their concession. Sun Chuan's armoured trains entered the Shanghai suburb of Chapei to meet up with Chiang Kai-shek for a showdown with their southern counterparts.

Shanghai was at a flashpoint – a situation that filled its citizens and the Civic Authorities with dread. Realising that the 30,000 British troops despatched to deal with the crisis were still stretched between Suez and Singapore and that the 1,500 strong Volunteer Corps was quite unequal to meet the oncoming challenge, the City Council in desperation turned to the Russian refugees it reluctantly accepted back in 1923.

General Glebov agreed to help immediately, but with the condition that the Russian Unit be officially known as a Russian Detachment under the command of Russian officers including the Commanding Officer and that the adopted policies and procedures were that of the Russian Imperial Army. The reputation of the Cossacks was enough to stave off the approaching Chinese forces until the British reinforcements arrived.

The Shanghai Volunteer Corps from its establishment was a volunteer force (similar to the Australian Citizens Military Force/the current Reserve). Its members were unpaid. They came on parade once a week and their uniforms, small arms and ammunition they stored at home.

The new Russian Detachment was a professional unit, founded upon a regular army basis. The soldiers were paid, and they lived in barracks. They were also uniformed and were fed and subjected to the routine of regular professional training. This with the strict discipline maintained by General Glebov made the Detachment the pride and glory of the Shanghai Volunteer Corps.

In 1932, after the conclusion of Chinese/Japanese military actions, the Shanghai Authorities recognised the Russian Detachment's commendable contribution and renamed it the Russian Regiment. On parade in front of the city and an audience of several thousand, a visiting Senior British Staff Officer handed its Colours to the Regiment. The same Colours that the authorities initially refused recognition back in 1923. At the centre of the new silken white, blue and red tri-coloured banner was a crest in the form of the letter Y consisting of the 16 flags representing all the nationalities of the international settlement of Shanghai.

Shanghai Russian Regiment Colours

43 THE REGIMENTAL SPORTING CHAMPION

The Regiment also became a transit workplace for those newly arrived Russians in Shanghai who needed a place to stay until they got on their feet. In return they had to meet the selection criteria of being young, fit, amenable to discipline, not afraid of a little danger and above all a credit to the Regiment.

Almost within days of his arival in Shanghai young Vladimir joined the Regiment, at which time his enrolment form was endorsed with the remark that he had a keen interest in sport. Hence, after his basic training he was immediately sent to the Regimental Sports Section. As 1935 was the year of inter-organisational mini-Olympics within Shanghai and other colonial cities in China, Vladimir was quickly assessed a good all rounder, with a flair for boxing and promptly entered into a boxing tournament. Although a novice, he scored his first victory in the light middleweight division with a technical knock-out against Charles Ding from Hong Kong.

From then on Vladimir began his rapid rise. Although he continued to participate in other sports, namely volley ball, long jump and pole-vault, winning a number of trophies and medals, it was boxing in which he excelled the most.

Vladimir's schooldays sporting activities became very useful. He was extremely fast on his feet and had excellent reflexes. He used the recognized orthodox stance – left hand and the left foot forward. He scored many knockouts by delivering a rapid sequence of blows. Though style remains a matter of individual choice, his swift lateral movement and combination punching have, to a large degree, won him the regimental light middleweight title.

Vladimir, in his spare time, read and watched newsreels on the up and coming American Heavyweight Champion of the World – Joe Louis – who, already in 1934, was a Golden Gloves titleholder. Vladimir modelled some of his stances and movements on Joe Louis.

In his three years with the Regiment, Vladimir did not lose a single fight and retired as the undefeated light middleweight amateur boxing Champion of Shanghai. At the end of his time with the colours he was given the honour of leading the regimental sporting parade witnessed by all of Shanghai dignitaries.

While still in the Regiment, Vladimir wrote to his beloved Klava calling on her to join him in Shanghai. Klava was full of uncertainty. On the one hand she loved him dearly. On the other hand she could not leave her mother so soon after her father's death. To add to her dilemma, her mother and Musya were against the marriage. Musya now married herself to Vladimir's best friend Misha Kolliagen. Nursing her newly-born baby daughter Lyudmilla (Milla), reminded her younger sister of Vladimir's, impulsiveness and instability that had already landed him in hot water – the Soviet GULAG from which he escaped not so long ago.

Vladimir also realised that although he was widely acclaimed his wages were very small and would not be enough to support a wife. He discussed his quandary with his boxer friends who best understood him. His closest companion Anatol Kalkey – a Spencer Tracy lookalike and another Mardensky (full of heart and pudgy-looking when I met him years later) – gave him closest council.

"If you want your loved one to marry you, you have two choices.

Become a professional boxer earn some big money and in a few years if she is still free and you are rich and scarred she may join you. On the other hand, you are well known in Shanghai, you have a good personality and people like you, you have the ability to sell yourself so why don't you start your own business."

It was having his own business that appealed to Vladimir. It was a thought that had been coming to him for a while, but having his colleagues voice it, made him feel more confident. Seeing opportunity in the widespread demand for hot water in Shanghai, Vladimir after some extensive inquiries enrolled in an American school of engineering correspondence course on installing and marketing hot water systems. He also realised that he needed some initial capital to start off the business. So he decided to make use of the benefits of an honourable discharge, which ended his military/sporting career but not before his volley ball team was awarded a silver medal in 1937 in a close match against the series winners. It was a medal that my sister and I would often play with even later in Australia reminding us of our father, until one day it disappeared.

44 VASSILIEFF AND VAJINSKY UNITE

After his discharge, Vladimir worked at a service-station. His driver's certificate was helpful as it qualified him to carry out minor repairs, deliver vehicles and attract customers. He was now grateful that his father had insisted that he complete something after high-school prior to his trip to the USSR. The thoughts of his homeland made him shudder. He was too ashamed of the events that led up to his arrest. The guilt, associated with those memories of the past, was something he could not share with anyone. One day he must clear his name. Until that day the past would continue to haunt him.

Finally Klava came to him. She left Harbin in June 1937 and was farewelled by her mother, Musya and Misha and her closest friends.

On the way to Shanghai, Klava stayed in Tiensin for a few months with her older sister Tina, her husband Sasha and their daughter Marina, who was three by then. The Dobrovidoffs accompanied Klava to Shanghai as they too were attracted by Shanghai's lure. Although Tiensin had a more cosmopolitan life than Harbin, Shanghai was like a magnet to all foreigners and Chinese alike. It was the largest city in China. Apart from its romantic glitter the

Bund on the Wampoo like Wall Street in New York attracted more capital than any other city in China.

On 27 February 1938, a long-awaited wedding of my parents-to-be took place. They lived in a small place on the Wayside – International Concession where most Russians who were not well off lived. Vladimir and Klava wrote to the Koliagins inviting them to join the rest of the clan in Shanghai saying that Misha could join Vladimir in his new hot water system business venture when it got established. In the meantime Misha could join the Regiment. Life in Harbin was becoming more difficult and more and more Russians were leaving for Tientsin, Shanghai or going overseas like Serge Vassilieff who eventually made it to San Francisco, USA. As visas were hard to get in Harbin, Misha went ahead of Musya. Vladimir helped him get established.

45 THE OTHER REGIMENT

Unfortunately, with so many Russians coming to Shanghai and joining the Russian/British Regiment, the numbers were full with a long queue to get in. Vladimir's contact in the Regiment said:

"If your brother-in-law hurries they are still taking them in over on the French Concession into the Russian French/Detachment". This was a new Unit which was recently reduced from a Regiment to a Company-sized Detachment of the French Municipal Police.

Thus, Vladimir helped Misha in joining the French auxiliary unit, with the understanding that as soon as Vladimir got his business established Misha would join him. Misha did not particularly like army life – its regimentation – however, he stayed in the unit for about one year. He hated the sergeants ordering him about and the corporals even more. The officers in his opinion were relics of the past. He missed his wife and daughter and he waited for the day when Vladimir would set up the business venture.

46 THE BUSINESSMAN

The day finally came. Vladimir sold and installed his first hot water unit. Initially his Chinese friend from the service station helped him with the installations and the use of a light second-hand pick-up truck which Vladimir eventually bought from him on good terms. Finally orders started to come in and Misha was able to get his discharge.

A partnership arrangement was struck and Misha joined Vladimir in the hot water system business. The arrangement was convenient as it allowed Vladimir to concentrate on the marketing and customer service side of it and to occasionally assist Misha on the installation and repair aspects.

Misha's joining was very timely, as the demand for hot water installation was growing and Vladimir's reputation had preceded him. Most people had heard of him as a successful sportsman and more recently as a businessman who provided a good deal with a quick and reliable service. Thus with Vladimir's reputation, his marketing ability, and his general business acumen and Misha's technical background the business just boomed.

In addition to the general shortage of hot water units, which had at first caught Vladimir's attention and fired his imagination the business was helped along by the growing of Shanghai's European population in the 1930s. Owing to migration from Manchukuo, Peking and Tientsin the Russian population in the city surged to about 40,000, almost doubling by 1939. At the same time the Jewish community also increased significantly, some like Russians came from North China but the main immigration stream was from Europe, seeking sanctuary from the Nazi persecution. The Jews were Vladimir's and Misha's best customers as they had more money than the Russian refugees and paid well for a job well done.

Adding a finishing touch to the success of the joint venture in Shanghai in 1939 was the achievement of Musya in Harbin, who at about this time, with commendable perseverance acquired for herself, her daughter and her mother the last visa for Shanghai, which saw the extended family, reunited. The Vajinskys rejoiced at being together again and the joy of the Koliagins who had been separated for over a very difficult year was complete.

To help them get established, the Vassilieffs assisted with getting a flat near them on the Wayside. Vladimir even agreed to take in his mother-in-law Franya so that the reunited couple might have the privacy they longed for.

47 MIRROR, MIRROR ON THE WALL

When the three Vajinsky sisters, their families and their widowed mother Franya were together in Shanghai, they stayed in close touch, helping one another wherever they could. They followed the family tradition – based on the advice their parents had given them – "We are family and we stick together!" This principle was demonstrated to them repeatedly by the Vajinsky brothers – Vasily and Boris – who always said, "In these difficult times if we do not help one another who else will?"

Now, however, the Vajinsky clan was partly separated. Since the death of their father and the changing circumstances in Harbin, the sisters and their widowed mother progressively moved to Shanghai, establishing their new lives and expanding their new families.

Vasiliy's family was more fragmented. Eugenia, her son George (Yuri) and her new husband Jack lived in Hong Kong. Natalia with her husband Ivan and their two sons Yuri and Nicholas remained in Harbin. Vasily with his second wife, Tasya (Natalia) and their son Valentin lived in Zatonsk – across the Sungari River in Harbin.

By 1944, life in Shanghai for the Vassilieffs improved significantly. On 15 June 1939 their first child was born. They christened her Valerie (Lera). Early in 1942, Klava said to Vladimir: "I had a dream last night that we will have a son and in it an Indian Guru told me that he will be a loving son and a leader amongst his own kind."

Vladimir was at first dismayed and answered Klava: "You and Musya are getting as bad as Valentina. All you women talk about are dreams, spirit beings, palmistry and fortune cookies! Between the three of you, four daughters to date have been produced and the likelihood of your dream coming true is zilch. You know we are not ready for a second child. Let's abort it and have one in about two years time. I know by then we will be better off financially."

Klava put her foot down: "I have already had two abortions and I will not have any more. We are having this child and that is my last word on it."

On 9 September 1942 son Alexander (Shurick/Sasha or Alex) was born. Vladimir checked his toes and proudly pronounced, "He is a Vassilieff!" On occasion Vassilieff males have slight syndactylity – webbing between two toes – a trait barely visible unless checked for.

Vladimir later admitted to Klava, "Thankfully I respected your wish".

Vladimir's partnership arrangement with Misha Koliagin worked very well. Their hot water system business continued to flourish.

Franya lived with the Vassilieffs since her arrival in Shanghai. Although she was not overly fond of her youngest son-in-law: his pro Soviet views, flirtations with the opposite sex, his insufferable humour and his coarse practical jokes, such as tickling his mother-in-law, disgusted her. Still he was a good businessman and provider, respected by the Shanghai community and loved Klava. In her view, her oldest son-in-law Sasha was more of a gentleman and a staunch anti-communist (Boris always said that), who showed no inclination to womanise and did not put up with Valentina's dramatised nonsense. It was not his fault that as an accountant he could not get a well-paid job, initially because of the depression and now the war.

Her second son-in-law Misha, although approved of by Boris,

was at times also disappointing as he was noticeably influenced by Vladimir's pro-Soviet attitude and coarse behaviour. Together they sang pro-Soviet songs, cheered pro-Soviet victories and acted like a pair of comedians whenever the family got together. Initially after Boris died in Harbin, she lived with Misha and Musya and was aware of Michael's outbursts and hot temper, but he made Musya happy and was also a good provider and a loyal husband. Their second child Vera was born in September 1941, making her five years younger than her older sister Milla.

Now that the Vassilieffs had moved to an elegant apartment in the French Concession on Avenue Haig Franya had her own room and every week her other two daughters with their families gathered there. The Dobrovidoffs also lived close by on the main road of Avenue Jofre. Marina would often come around to visit her aunt, grandmother and her younger cousins. As always the extended family would sit at a table covered with a fine white tablecloth, eat tasty food in abundance that Franya in the main would prepare, followed by some moderate drinking and plenty of singing, in particular by Vladimir, Misha and Klava. They all had excellent voices.

The Vajinskys usually celebrated occasions such as Name Days, Birthdays, Easter, Christmas and New Year together often at the Vassilieff's. It was New Years Eve 1945 and all the children had gone to bed, Franya and the three couples sat down to enjoy their candle-lit supper. Just before midnight, one of the candles went out and the mother and her three daughters – all a touch superstitious – looked at one another. Valentina was first to speak.

"I don't like this; it's an omen something unpleasant is going to happen."

"Don't be superstitious Valentina. I am going to make passionate love to you," said Vladimir jokingly.

"Sasha, tell Vladimir to stop teasing me," responded Valentina.

"Volodya, stop teasing Valentina, you know how impressionable she is, she won't be able to sleep for the rest of the night now that you promised her passionate love," interrupted Misha.

"Oh, come on you hot water-guys leave my poor Valentina alone, I alone can satisfy all her desires," Sasha broke in on the conversation.

"Children!" said Franya loudly, "I think it is something serious. I have had this unpleasant feeling that something has happened to Vasily. I have been feeling it most of the day."

Musya and Klava agreed. "We too think that uncle Vasya may have joined our father."

Vladimir did not like the way the conversation was going and reminded everyone that it was one minute to midnight. After wishing each other a Happy New 1945, they all hugged and kissed. Vladimir said: "I have a positive feeling for the year but with a few reservations. The war is coming to an end. Our armies are pushing the Nazi invaders back to Berlin. Two years ago, we beat them at Stalingrad. A year ago, we beat them at Kursk with our tanks. Six months ago, the allies opened up a second front in Normandy. Now Hitler is being squeezed from both sides. It is likely that the war will be over in three to six months. However, I do not believe that the Japanese will give up so easily. Shanghai could end up another Stalingrad. We may have to leave this place."

"Volodya could be right. If only we could see the future in a mirror, as the fortune tellers do with candles and mirrors,"[52] said Valentina.

"No, I do not want to. I have never been as happy as I am now and I would rather not know what awaits us in the future," said Klava.

"Volodya, bring Klava a cardigan. Look how cold she is. Her arms are covered in goose-bumps," said Franya.

"Klava will never want for anything, not while I am with her," said Vladimir covering Klava with a cardigan and placing his arms around her.

On that note, everyone parted with an uneasy feeling.

---

52 An old Russian belief of telling the future by couples with candles standing in front of a mirror.

48 THE BREAK UP

Shortly after the New Year celebration, Franya received a letter from Vasiliy's wife. It confirmed their earlier fears. It read:

"My beloved Vasily had passed away from heart failure at 8.20 a.m. on 31 December 1944 – just one day short of his Name day[53]. We buried him on 2 January 1945. The Service was held at Zatonsk Church across the Sungari River, performed by Rev. N. Starikov and attended by a large farewell of friends and colleagues including S.I. Dolov Director General of the Bureau and B.S. Baranov who gave the eulogy. A large number of representatives from the River Transport Mantetsu and the Management Team of the Russian Organisation of the Sungari Water Transport were also there. He recently returned on the SS *Van-Ta Shan*, the North Manchurian River Steamer. This was his last command. Harbin lost one of its oldest associates from our community. May he rest in peace."

By early March 1945, the Dobrovidoffs left Shanghai for Shimen, an unknown small town some distance south of Tientsin. Sasha had responded to a Japanese advertisement offering well-paid jobs and accommodation. Work was hard to come by and their financial situation was modest.

53 In the Orthodox Faith, the Names day is even more important than one's birthday.

Although Vladimir's business was still doing well the Dobrovidoffs' move made him wonder how he might be affected by the Japanese occupation in the event of a confrontation with Russia – which was not beyond the realms of probability in view of their historically strained relations and Japan's ongoing war with Russia's allies. Like most Russians in Shanghai, he was encouraged by the allied victories over Nazi Germany and the imminent collapse of the Third Reich. Although he shared the general anxiety over what the Japanese might do in the event of Russia entering the conflict – as their wartime atrocities in China were well known.

As he saw it, if Russia entered the war the Red Army would come in via Mongolia or Manchuria and that it would be better for him to be closer to the liberating forces in some small and insignificant place rather than in a big city. Besides, Stalin had also appeared to have changed. He had restored many pre-revolutionary customs, encouraged churches to reopen and had told Russians at home and abroad that all past sins were forgiven. The rhetoric sounded very convincing particularly to him, at a time of such uncertainty as well as the stigma that he still carried which could now be finally removed owing to the undeserved sentence that he received in his youth. No doubt, the Dobrovidoffs had been right in moving to a small and insignificant place.

Vladimir did not have to try very hard to convince Misha, who shared his beliefs at that time. So they sold the business and Vladimir set about persuading Klava with brochures similar to those that the Dobrovidoffs had acted upon saying: "Look, darling, promise of a better future – jobs and accommodation in Kaifeng[54], not too far from Shimen. We may even visit the Dobrovidoffs at times and we will have your mother with us. It's not a well-known place. The Japanese are bringing in Russians and other Europeans to live and work there

54 Kaifeng, city is in northern Honan sheng (province), China. Until 1955, it was the provincial capital (now transferred to Cheng-chou). Kaifeng is situated in the southern section of the North China Plain, to the south of the Huang Ho (Yellow River), in an area where a number of streams flow southeastward into the Huai River.

but they would not fight for it like Shanghai once our Army comes. It's also closer to Tientsin and Harbin. We will be safer and better off in the coming days. Just once do something for me please". Finally, Vladimir wore Klava down. Reluctantly she agreed to go.

Misha was less successful in convincing Musya. In fact, he was very unsuccessful. After many days of deep and meaningfuls she finally said to him: "If you want to go so badly then go, but the children and I are staying here". She qualified it further. "Have you forgotten so soon I was left on my own once before with our three-year-old Milla and mother, while I was waiting for that confounded visa to join you, Vassilieffs and the Dobrovidoffs in Shanghai. Things were getting worse by the day in Harbin. I could not wait to get out of there. Why would I want to go back there now or some other God-forsaken place in the middle of nowhere. We came together here for a purpose and when the time comes we will be saved. I feel this. I could not stop the Dobrovidoffs and I will not be able to stop the Vassilieffs, even though like me Klava and mother do not want to go and I don't know if I can stop you, but the children and I will not go".

Finally, Misha caved in. He was not going to leave his family again – a year apart showed him how much he loved them.

When the Vassilieffs arrived in Kaifeng, they were horrified just as the Dobrovidoffs had been about two months earlier in Shimen. Both places were the pits, attracting in the main the worst kind of people – alcoholics, criminals and generally those down on their luck.

The sustained tension during the months that followed resulted in an irreconcilable break-up of the Dobrovidoffs family. Whatever were the earlier differences between Sasha and Tina the unbearable conditions in Shimen made their situation worse. Therefore, when a lonely heart – a recent divorcee – Dimitry Yanchevsky (Jim) arrived on the scene the stage was set for a love affair. Upon which Sasha issued a stern warning to Valentina: "If you choose Yanchevsky over me than I shall keep our daughter Marina."

On 2 September, the surrender of Japan was signed in Tokyo harbour on the battleship *Missouri.* The war was over. Sasha and Marina, Tina and Dimitry made their way to Tientsin as did the Vassilieffs.

On Tientsin station, they all met and recounted their experiences, accompanied by many tears and hopes of a better future. However, there was a difference in their destinations. Jim convinced Tina that under no circumstances should they go to Harbin, which the Red Army under Marshall Malinovsky, a World War II hero, now occupied – since 18 August 1945. Jim's marriage had broken up because his first wife with their son left him to go to Harbin and then onto the USSR. So he was determined to return to Shanghai. Now free from the Japanese, Sasha decided to follow them in order that Marina could be close to her mother. He did not want her to suffer any more than she already had. Her whole world was collapsing around her. During the past six months her immediate and extended family, her home and her surroundings had all changed to her detriment.

Vladimir, however, did not want to deviate from his original plan. The thought of being so close to his homeland made him even more determined than ever that his family should proceed as planned to Harbin and then all the way home. He had had enough of the foreign existence. The last four miserable months in particular showed him that the Japanese could not be trusted. He wanted to be back, amongst his own, now that all was forgiven. The motherland on the verge of ruin welcomed ex-patriots to help rebuild mother Russia. The Soviet ministry of propaganda echoed comrade Stalin's words and thousands of patriotic Russians were answering the call to go home. Ships and trains now and for the next few years would bring back Russians from China and Europe with their savings and treasured possessions to help restore and rebuild the home they had longed for.

Franya also had a wish. She said to Klava: "You must follow your husband where his heart takes you. Your late father and I escaped from those atheists back in 1919. I do not believe their slogans. I do not want to go back. May God bless you all, particularly the little ones. Please let me go back to Shanghai with the others". Mother and daughter embraced and wept openly. Vladimir on hearing the conversation between mother and daughter approached his future brother-in-law and asked: "Dimitry, please take Franya back to Shanghai with you?" Receiving his assurances, the families parted, the trains carrying them in different directions. The following night as the train sped towards Harbin, the Vassilieffs celebrated their son's third birthday as dark clouds gathered over the horizon.

49 BACK TO THE LION'S DEN

From the moment the Vassilieffs stepped off the train at Harbin Station, everything looked different. Klava briefly remembered that bright, colourful day in June 1937 when she was farewelled with flowers at this same station. She was then on her way to a new sunny future. Harbin was in blossom and happy memories remained in her head. Compared to those memories, this September day was bleak and grey. A chill was already present in the atmosphere. Red flags and Soviet soldiers were everywhere and lengthy trains loaded with railway stock were moving north. In the midst of all this, she noticed a large Icon of St. Nicholas the Protector hanging on the station wall. The kind eyes were looking down on her.

The Vassilieffs settled in a pleasant apartment in Novygorod and Vladimir very quickly found a job. Although the city was different, it was still the old Harbin, of Klava's childhood. In a couple of months, she rekindled some of her old friendships and began to correspond with her mother and sisters. Although everywhere, things looked normal and perhaps her worries were unfounded but from time to time, there were whispers going around town that the NKVD were arresting individuals and sending them back home. The usual reason was that they had collaborated with the Japs.

Somehow, Vladimir lost his sense of urgency to return home to the USSR, but still spoke of it as his ultimate wish. One December afternoon Klava answered a knock on the door. When she opened it, a neatly dressed man addressed her: "I am an official from the Soviet Consul. May I see comrade Vassilieff?"

Klava felt a chill come over her, her heartbeat started to race. "He is at work right now and won't be back for two to three hours," she replied.

"Oh that's all right. I will wait if you do not mind."

Klava could not remember what she and the official spoke about during the next two to three hours. The only thing she recalled later was that when she and Vladimir embraced and parted, she slipped two pairs of woollen socks into his coat pocket as he had at times complained about his feet being cold since they had arrived in Harbin. Touched by the emotion of the moment the official reassuringly said: "There is no need of that. Do not worry. They only want to speak to him for about five minutes."

50 THE HELL-HOLE OF HARBIN

Will the hour of my freedom come?
'Tis time,' tis time! To it I call;
I roam above the sea; I wait for the right weather,
I beckon to the sails of ships.
Under the cope of storms, with waves disputing,
On the free crossway of the sea
When shall I start on my free course?
Eugene Onegin
A. Pushkin[55]

In the Soviet Harbin *a woman with two children had no needs* – for the next three days Klava stood at the window looking and waiting for her husband but he did not return. Her shocked mind could not grasp the immensity of the situation. As time went by, information trickled along the grapevine and was shared by many women who were in similar circumstances.

The NKVD arrested Vladimir and forcibly expatriated him to the USSR to serve in a Government labour camp – GULAG. He was

55 A Yermolinsky – The poems, prose and plays of A. Pushkin – Random House New York 1936

after all a former escapee. Stalin and the long arm of the NKVD never forgave or forgot, irrespective of the wartime rhetoric. Klava found some solace with some women who had had similar experiences like Lena Suvorova and Irina Ivashkova (future Resaeva). Both told her the same stories. Each in turn comforted one another and provided a shoulder to cry on. Work was unavailable by Soviet decree to wives whose husbands were politically accused and forcibly repatriated. Some women for the sake of their children hastily remarried. Others quickly mastered gainful skills to sustain themselves as an alternative to prostitution, for which they had no inclination. Klava began hairdressing and did manicures while she prayed and waited. She eventually built up a small clientele largely consisting of considerate Soviet officers' wives as they at least had money and appreciated her predicament better than most.

51 THE SLAVE CARAVANS

In his *GULAG Archipelago* Solzhenitsyn wrote about the slave caravans – the Soviet system of labour distribution. This system extended to Eastern Europe and beyond and applied to anyone who sided with the Germans against the Soviet Government. Namely; the Cossacks, Vlasov's Liberation Army comprising of captured Red Army officers and soldiers, and many others who may have fled the USSR or were forcibly taken captive by the then invading German Armies. In the Far East, the caravans extended to Soviet-occupied Manchuria and included Russians who moved there before or after the revolutionary period.

The rumour mills in Harbin in the postwar years produced a figure of about 10-20,000 victims, mainly men who were taken away from their families in cattle wagons (standing room only) by the NKVD and incarcerated in various GULAGS throughout the USSR. This so-called cheap labour was to help the USSR rebuild itself after its devastation by the Nazis. However, in its implementation the scheme made it difficult to work out who was worse, Stalin or Hitler.

Vladimir Vassilieff, my father, was one of these people. A further review of his KGB file reads:

I was arrested and sent to Alma-Ata Kazakhstan where I was incarcerated together with the Japanese in a Prisoner of War Camp (POW). For a long time they could not find an appropriate article under which to sentence me, then they dressed me into a Japanese uniform and declared me a POW accusing me of fighting against the motherland. From my overall state and the condition I was in, I contracted typhoid after which I was kept in solitary and questioned and requested to confess that I was a spy. From a healthy and a strong former athlete of 180 cm tall, I was reduced to a skeleton of 46 kg. For lack of evidence my case was sent to Moscow where I was convicted by a special meeting and was finally sentenced to 10 years under article 58.4

18 THE CAUCASUS 1914-1917

Commander V N Vajinsky

28 THE HILLS OF MANCHURIA

L-R: Klava, Tina and Musya

33 THE ACADEMIC

34 I WANT TO GO HOME

Did Vladimir's love for Russia repay him in kind or like Cleopatra? He paid with life for his delights.

35 MANCHUKUO - THE NEW LANDLORD - OBEY OR DIE

Alexander II

Alexandra Snr

37 THE ESCAPE

Boris with his youngest daughter – Klava & Chinese peddler in the background

38 THE END OF A VAJINKSKY

Boris Vajinsky

41 SHANGHAI

The Bund – Shanghai in the 1930's

42 THE REGIMENT

Shanghai Russian Regiment

43 THE REGIMENTAL SPORTING CHAMPION

Vladimir's love of athletics

Vladimir leading the Regimental sports parade

44 VASSILIEFF AND VAJINKSKY UNITE

Farewell to Klava Harbin

Wedding Reception at the Kavkaz Restaurant Shanghai

45 THE OTHER REGIMENT

Russian Volunteer Detachment of the French Concession prior to its reformation into an auxiliary Unit

The Officers of the Russian Company Auxiliary Agents of the French Municipal Police

47 MIRROR, MIRROR ON THE WALL

Klava and Vladimir with children Shanghai 1943

52 EARLY MEMORIES OF LITTLE ALEX

Little Alex – Harbin 1946

Day Nursery Centre – Yasli Harbin for the underprivileged and semi and/or orphaned children. The mosaic over the building entrance displays Little Red Riding Hood Photo by B Statsenko 2002

Russian Orthodox Cathedral of St Nicholas in the former Harbin central square – a circular perimeter built entirely out of wood and assembled without a single nail. Destroyed by the Red Guards during Mao's Cultural Revolution.

58 RECONCILIATION

L to R: Gregory with his two granddaughters; Olga & Alexandra & daughter Dasha Oberammergau – 1947

59 GOODBYE HARBIN

The two Demagogues – Iosif Vasirionovich Dzhugashvili Stalin & Mao Zedong – 1950

62 GOODBYE GERMANY

From top to bottom L-R Babushka Elena, friend with dog, Dasha with little Alex & friend at Munich DP Camp. Little Eugene Alexandroff & Alexandra in the snow 1948. Ivan, Alexandra, Dasha and Elena aboard the SS Castelbianco.

67 KLAVA'S ILLNESS

Klava at Gladesville Mental Hospital 1954

68 SCOUNTING FOR BOYS - THE RUSSIAN SCOUTING DIASPORA

Founder of the Russian Scout movement and Chief Sct for life Col. O.I. Pantuhov – 1882-1973

Former Commander in Chief of Anti-Bolshevik Forces General Wrangel among Russian refugee Scouts in Constantinople early 1920's

69 UP SOAR THE FALCONS LIKE THE EAGLES

Scm M.M. Plehanoff Shanghai circa 1935

Russian Group Novgorod ORUR with several participating NORS scoutmasters at the Archbishops residence in Croydon 1974

ORUR NSW Sc Leaders 1974 L-R Top down: Gr Scm M Korovnikow, A/Gr Scm & Tr Scm A Vassilieff, Snr sc H Ritdake, A/Gsm G Kent, A/Gsm I Kent, Reg Comis Scm L Apolonoff, Ins O Kazansky & visitor from Vic Sn Scm R Joukoff Sydney circa 1973

Annual camp – Kentlyn 1982 – my son Vlad just became a Rover, seen here holding the Group flag

Nick and I of the Kookaburra patrol White Bear Camp Lilyvale 1958

A Blast from the past when old friends meet-R-L: Snr Sc NORS N Gileff & ORUR Res Scm A Vassilieff Sydney 2001

Father and children – Vlad and Helen off to a scout meeting Carlingford 1974

L-R former Sn Scm – ORUR R. Joukoff, Scm I. Holahoff-Nat Sec, Scm in Res M.Alexis, Scm N. Donner-Nat Comis Scm L. Apolonoff-Reg Comis, Scm A. Vassilieff-A/Grp & Tr Scm 1974

Above R – ORUR Leaders incl' Rovers & Snr sc's National Conference at Hillsvile Vic 1960 L-R from top row down Ins O Berns(V), Gr Scm Amburger(SA), Ins N Rogovaya (V), Snr sc M Protopopoff(V), Snr sc V Tan (V),A-Gr Scm N Donner (SA), M Alexis Gr Scm (NSW), Nat Com Scm R Joukoff (V), Rov S Joukoff (V), Snr sc D Trofimov (NSW), TrScm A Donner (SA), Snr sc A Ilyn (V), Tr Scm A Grechko(V), Ins V.Sergy(NSW), Ins L Gerasimova (V), Ins K Joukoff (V), Rov H Bernikoff (V), Rov W Wayne (NSW) & Rov A Vassilieff (NSW)

ORUR Scout Leaders in Australia – Noojee Vic National Camp 1975/76

72 TALES FROM THE SCOUTING PAST

ORUR Scout Leaders west coast USA circa 1973

74 THE APPRENTICESHIP

My apprenticeship at STC 1959-1964

75 CITIZENS MILITARY FORCE

Reserve Forces Day – George St, Sydney1998

76 I´M IN THE ARMY NOW

L/Cpl A. Vassilieff & Cfm J Trofimov Singleton Army Barracks 1962

RAEME 7th Fd Regiment Light Aid Detachment Workshop Annual Training Camp at Singleton Army Barracks 1963

77 VIETNAM

S/Sgt W. Wayne & Sgt J. Binham Phu My Village after TET offensive 1968

Above and below left – Memories of the Wedding Day and the Honeymoon

Vassilieff's at 63 Ferry Rd, Glebe off to a Russian Party – 1969

Lena and Vova at 32 Robin St, Carlingford off to Roselea Primary School – 1974

83 THE KNIGHT RETURNS

L-R top row: Klava, Vova, Lou, Musya, Eugenia, Jack, Daria, Alex L-R front row: Marina, Misha,Valerie & Shura At our place in Carlingford during my father's visit Sept, 1975

Klava and Vova Bondi Beach 1975

Misha and Vova Carlingford 1975

84 HOW TO BEND WITH THE WIND

Our first overseas family holiday – a Pacific Cruise – Pirate Night on the MV Taras Shevchenko May-76

The Russian Orthodox Parish School of St John of Chronstadt at Strathfield St Peter and Paul Cathedral consisting of two former parish schools – Croydon and Strathfield which amalgamated on the initiative of both schools and the of both schools and the Blessing of the then Archbishop Theodosius 1977

86 THE GRADUATION

Conferring of Degrees & Diplomas NSWIT 12/5/1982

87 THE CLUB

Former Club Presidents Y.A. Davidenkov & I.M. Nesteroff

L-R G. Shatrov Long Standing Board Member A. Vassilieff – President and two former Presidents I.M. Nesteroff & A.P. Kisliakoff

L-R ?, P. Shahmatoff, A. Vassilieff, W. Wayne, V. Baitch & D.Zhdanovitch

Nights to remember with visiting dignitaries such as – Sydney Lord Mayor – D. Sutherland, former ALP Federal Minister A. Grasby, Lib State Parliamentary Secretary P. Zammit and future Lib Federal Minister Philip Ruddock at the Russian Club 1984 to 1986

90 THE RETURN

Alex & Alexandra in front of the Temple of Heaven – Beijing 1988

The balcony of our former appartment which we left in 1945 Ave Jofre Shanghai Revisited in 1988

Shanghai Water Executive and I visit the former French (Jesfield) Park 1988

Former Russian Orthodox Cathedral, Shanghai

93 RUSSIAN ETHNIC COMMUNITY COUNCIL

Addressing the gathering at the NSW Parliament House 1995

Reception for M. Zadornov – visiting Delegate of the Russian Duma at the Russian Club 1997

B. Nemtsev the then Governor Nizhny Novgorod-Russia and A. Vassilieff President RECC Sydney 1995

Mrs Tania Hartung, Vice-President, RECC, Mr Alex Vassilieff, President, RECC,
Mr Pyotr Bourdykin, Consul-General of the Russian Federation;
Mr Alexander Losyukov, Ambassador of the Russian Federation,
Cr Frank Sartor, Lord Mayor of Sydney and Cr Peter Woods, Mayor of Concord
and President of the Local Government Association of New South Wales. 17.1.97

The PM John Howard joins the RECC Representatives with their new President N Maximov for a photo at Burwood RSL Multicultural Night – 1997

95 WHEN A GIRL MARRIES

Rear: L – R G Nash, M Koliagin, A Vassilieff, Musya Koliagin, M Nash, I Smith, V Vassilieff, M Smith and A Vassilieff Middle: L – R A Dobrovidoff, G & H Cook the Wedding Couple, Fr: K Moss and V Vassilieff

98 THE OLYMPICS

Welcomed to SOCOG by the CEO – Sandy Hollway 1999

Rear L-R Prue & George Kozlovsky (Nash's kin) Alex Vassilieff, Mila Smith, Gary and Marina Nash. Fr L-R Alexandra Vassilieff & Ian Smith. Some of the current descendents carrying the Torch circa 1997

52 EARLY MEMORIES OF LITTLE ALEX

My mother saw the first winter through by pawning and selling all our valuables. Apart from the little jewellery that she had, our father's suits and coats, all his sporting trophies and medals (except the volley-ball silver medal – perhaps it was not worth much or maybe she wanted some small momento of his to remain). She sold anything she could.

It was spring and the money had run out. We could not afford the flat in Novygorod any more. They say when you are on your way down you do not stop until you hit the bottom of the pit. Well our next stop was Nahalovka (Vagabond Haunt) or the sullen slum of Harbin. It was many times worse than the Redfern or Erskineville slums of Sydney. From flashes of memory it may only have been a few weeks or months that we lived there. I do, however, vaguely remember the dirt floor, small windows, unguttered dirt roads and sitting in some cowshed eating a *zhmih* – cow feed made up into a grain oil cake for storage. To encourage us to eat it, our mother repeatedly told us how healthy it was for us, which was probably true.

My sequences may not be as accurate as the events that took place. But, many of these events were firmly etched into my mind. Two events I remember prior to Nahalovka. The first when I swallowed a small lead nugget and my mother and sister held me by my feet and shook me until I coughed it up. The next was when some older boys in the street playing with a water-pipe wacked me on the forehead and I ran home covered in blood. I carry a reminder of that event as a small dent in the forehead which is still visible today. One can only wonder how my poor mother coped with these and other forgotten events.

By the time I turned four, my mother had to put my seven-year-old sister into a convent and my paternal grandmother Alexandra, who lived in Stary Gorod, agreed to look after me. I certainly was not a quiet little mouse and was probably full of mischief just as my own children were later and now my grandchildren. It was probably autumn and I must have done something wrong at the time for which I was severely beaten by my grandmother. My screams attracted the local Chinese children, who hopped up on the other side of the fence to see what animal was being slaughtered. My grandmother momentarily interrupted my punishment to shoo the spectators away with a wave of the stick and a burst of meaningful Chinese. When my correction was over she took me inside the house and showed me the other side of the stick which had protruding nails. She then warned me that should she ever have cause to beat me again it would be with the other side of the stick. Obviously I was terrified.

That night I was made to sleep in the dining room and told to face the wall on which hung a rug (a common method of decoration in the East and among the Russians). I was also told to sleep and not to blubber while grandma entertained her guests.

For some reason I remember that they were Red Army Officers. A lieutenant who heard my sobbing picked me up and sat me on his knee. He gave me some watermelon and I quickly forgot my misery and looked at his revolver. Seeing my interest he took it out of its holster and let me play with it. Grandmother made some protest, but he assured her it was safe. After that I soon fell asleep.

The next day or shortly after the event my mother visited us.

When grandma was out of the room and we were stoking the stove with wood I begged my mother to take me home.

"Don't you like it here with babushka?" she asked.

"No!" I said "And I will do anything to help you, but please don't leave me here." On further questioning I told my mother about the beating and the threat of nails next time. All I recall then, was that my mother was furious and said something to the effect: "I came to you for help in a moment of need and this is how you treat and terrify your own flesh and blood. You are worse than Volodya told me. I am taking my son home and I never want to see you again."

After that incident, I think I was sent to an orphanage for a short while which I do not remember, and soon after I was accepted by a day-care centre.

In the course of my research I came across a picture which immediately jogged my memory. It was the picture of a day-care nursery in a bi-monthly paper entitled *In the Hills of Manchuria No. 100 Nov-Dec 2002* produced by the Harbin Association in Novosibirsk Russia with distribution around the world and locally represented by G. Kositsin in Sydney. The article and picture brought back many memories. The nursery, or *Yasli* as it was known then, was already in operation by 1941, and still stands today. It catered for 40-60 children at a time from early morning to late in the evening for working mothers who had no other alternative for minding of their children as they had to work to support their families, particularly so after the war as the children were semi-orphaned with fathers in a GULAG, incapacitated or dead. At the *Yasli* the children were fed throughout the day and were looked after by volunteer nannies.

I still remember a day: as I looked out of the window during a fierce thunder storm a large tree came crashing down.

"It's a typhoon," shouted one of the nannies. "Make sure none of the children get out." I learned a new word that day. The next day I saw the large fallen tree in the garden and obviously felt the urge to climb on it and for some reason it is that memory of the outside of the nursery and that fallen tree that I have filed away in my mind which the picture *In the Hills of Manchuria* brought back so vividly when I saw it.

Somewhere about that time, or possibly when I was in an orphanage, my mother brought both of us home. Lera had pneumonia and we were both covered with fleas (not uncommon in China then). Mum washed and scrubbed us both, then standing us on a stool she smeared us with methylated spirits. The next few nights my sister would wake up crying and my mother would give her a spoon of sugar to suck and she would settle down. We were all skin and bones then and possibly my sister was suffering with malnutrition as well as pneumonia.

Another unpleasant memory that I recall was when my sister and I were given *chumisavaya kasha* – a cheap Chinese grain porridge to eat. As I finished my plate, I noticed my sister emptied her unfinished plate to a stray cat that we had acquired. I dobbed my sister in to our mother who was sitting in the kitchen. Mum burst into tears saying: "I gave my portion to you to eat and you throw it away to a cat. How could you?" This distressing incident must have affected me subconsciously as I have never dobbed on anyone ever again as I felt I had upset both my mother and sister by doing so.

By the time I was six I was taken every morning by a neighbour, Ashot Mihailovitch, to a kindergarten nearby where he worked. It is the first time I remember that before class started all the children and the adults sang prayers which I did not know. It was then I recall sometimes going to church. It was the beautiful St. Nicholas's timber Cathedral, or Sabor as we referred to it. It was there that the picture of me was taken which appears at the beginning of this chapter. I also recall that I was about eight when mum took Lera and me to my first Easter midnight mass.

Hope sometimes is all we have when almost everything else is lost.

In the year or two that followed Vladimir's captivity, mum went to a fortune teller. Some of what she told her was obvious. That mum was a woman in dire straits left with two children to bring up by herself, but that she would overcome her trials and tribulations. She would eventually go overseas to a far away land and raise her children there. Through the efforts of her son she would see her knight in shining armour once again and would live her remaining days like *cheese rolling in butter* – luxury. Whether that was guesswork or some form of sixth sense, it gave my mother some badly needed hope.

It was about late 1940s when the local authorities insisted that the Icon of St. Nicholas, the Patron Saint of Harbin that hung in the foyer of the Harbin Railway Station, be removed. The Icon was highly revered by Russians and Chinese alike. People felt safe when boarding a train. Many believed that St. Nicholas the protector looked after them on their journey. During the late days of the war, Harbin Station was to be bombed three times by the Japanese and the Soviets in turn. Yet each time there was a low fog preventing the bombers from making their run. The blessing was attributed to St. Nicholas. So there was great reluctance to remove the Icon. Finally the impasse was solved and a church procession followed by a great number of parishioners accompanied the Icon's transfer from the Station to the Sabor, where it was hung in a prominent place.

The night before this event my mother attended Saturday night vespers, which from time to time she liked to go to. On this occasion, after the service she began her slow walk home. She felt the cold through her worn out winter boots, the soles of which needed urgent repair, but she had no money to get them done. The light drizzle of snow obscured her vision and the street lights gave the atmosphere a fuzzy mellow glow but through it all, unexpectedly, a kind voice enquiringly and serenely called out to her from behind: "You look very worried, my dear, as though all the world's problems are on your shoulders?"

Mum looked around and saw the silhouette of an elderly man

with just a faint view of the Sabor behind him. Before she had a chance to respond he asked: "Would you allow me to walk alongside you for a spell, I live nearby and would appreciate your company". As mum let him catch up with her she saw his deep grey kind eyes emanating from almost a wrinkle-free face covered with a silvery beard. She somehow felt safe with him beside her. They conversed briefly and slowly strolled along the boulevard. The main thing I remember when mum retold that story over the years was that she felt very hopeful and her despondency began to disappear as they moved on. "God will protect you and your children, of that you can be sure, you have nothing to fear, just be brave for a while longer, my dear. Now if you will forgive my intrusion I must get back to my new dwelling". As mum looked around to see where it was the old man was going, he disappeared, yet the fainter view of the Sabor was still just visible.

Whenever my mother attended sevice in the Sabor she would try to stand close to the Icon of St.Nicholas as he reminded her so much of the old man on that snowy night.

53 WAR SONGS

1 September 1949 I started school – School No. 2 in Novotorgovaya Street, Novy Gorod. About that time, I recall mum playing records on the crank-up gramophone that were so popular during the war and postwar years. These songs helped to inspire and lift morale among the Russian people during the dreaded days of the Nazi German invasion of Russia. They gave hope for the future enveloping normal life feelings and beautiful melancholy Russian melodies. Here are a few verses of some of these songs that I still remember, with my mediocre translation.

MAIDEN'S FAREWELL (Na Pozitsii Dyevushka)

A young maiden farewelled her departing front line fighter
They bid their goodbyes in the dark of the night on the steps of her porch
And until he reached the fog line glancing back
He could still see from her front window the shining light

A new welcoming, frontline family met the young recruit
All around were comrades all around were friends
But his familiar street he could not forget
Where is my darling sweetheart? Where is my darling light?

THREE LANCERS (*Triy Tankista*)

On the borderlands, the clouds were dark and stormy
And the atmosphere was stern and quiet
That's the night when the Samurais decided
To cross the border near the riverside

But the Intel, was quite exact and timely
And a strike force was sent out
To repel the advancing forces
And send them back from where they came

Three tanker-lancers, three happy friendly fighters
A crew of a deadly fighting men-machine

KATHY'O (*Katusha*)

As the apple and the pear trees blossomed
And the fog departed over the riverbanks
Young Katusha came out
On the high steep and abrupt river bank

She came out and sang songs of her loved one
Of the one, who left her behind
About the stepped blue-grey eagle
About the one she loved so dearly and whose letters she cherished so much

Eh! You song, you maiden's song go flying
To the far and distant land
And to the soldier I love so dearly
Send Katusha warmest and her best

DARK IS THE NIGHT (*Temnaya Notch*)

Dark is the night
Only the shells that keep flying through the steppes
Only the wind that is blowing through the lines
And the stars that are twinkling

Dark is the night O! My darling I know you are not asleep
And by the cradle, you sit wiping away your tears darling waiting for me
Oh! How I love the depth and the love of your eyes
How I would love to come near them again

Oh! How I love and believe in you
My dearest friend and soul mate
And the hope that we will meet again
And your love and faith is the only thing that keeps me alive

These songs infuse a feeling of the patriotism, determination and reflect the anguish of the Russian fighters and the loved ones they left behind defending their homeland. Even in the postwar years both young and old would often listen to these songs. I remember them well.

54 RAINBOW

Babushka Alexandra was probably sorry the way her actions cut her off from her only grandchildren. To make it up, she one day took me out of school and took me to the Churin store, bought me some sweets and a toy and something for my sister. In the afternoon she brought me home. After some discussion with my mother I think they made up, but we never got close.

Our mother would sometimes take us visiting, which we loved. We met our Auntie Natasha (Vasily's younger daughter) with her two teenage sons Nicholas and Yuri and an adopted son Victor of similar age. The boys were all about 10 years my senior but they entertained Valerie and me. Nicholas was an engine driver in the former CER. Later he would become a famous train engineer driving the renowned Red Arrow train between Vladivostock and Moscow. The Soviet paper would refer to him as the 'Man with the Golden Hands' – he could fix anything. Natasha was eventually reunited with her husband Ivan after his release from the GULAG in the mid 1950s and the family settled in Krasnoyarsk.

We also visited Natasha's stepmother Tasya, Vasiliy's widow in Zatonsk. It was fun going across the Sungari in a rowboat. To take us across, the Chinese rower would charge the equivalent of a few pennies. There my mother and Tasya would share in their misfortunes. Tasya confessed that she had been very miserable when Vasily died, but after the arrival of the Red Army and the NKVD had taken away her only son Valentin she was devastated. It was only months later when she began to recover that she actually thanked God that Vasily had died in his sleep eight months earlier. Had he still lived, God knows what they would have done to him. "Klava!" she said, "as hard as things are, count your blessings you still have your two children. I have no one". Whatever happened to Tasya I do not know. In doing my family research, I heard that she finally had a mental breakdown. Whether she ever recovered is unknown to me.

She probably never again saw her son Valentin Vajinsky, who was released from the GULAG about the same time as my father. Valentin, like his father Captain Vajinsky, after the release served in the commercial navy but, unlike his father, as an accountant. He married and had two children who settled in the Russian Far East – Nahodka. The time in the GULAG probably weakened his system as he died in his forties.

One day our mother met her former fiancé – Igor Petrov – who immediately reproached her.

"How could you not tell me earlier of the situation you are in? I had to find out from other people. I could have helped".

"How?" asked Klava. "You have a wife and a daughter and I would never ever consider putting my situation between you and your happiness."

"For one thing I can help you financially. You did not have to starve all those years! For another I can try and put you in touch with some people that can give you a decent job. Here is some money. Buy yourself and your children some food and clothing".

"But ..." Klava began.

"No buts," said Igor, "I have a very well-paid job in the forestry. I can afford to help my old friend without sacrificing my family's needs. If you feel indebted, pay me back when you are better off and you know me well enough to know that I would never demand anything from you. At the moment I have to go into the Taiga again, but after I am back in a couple of months I will help you again. Now go and see these people." He gave a name and address. "I will talk to them before I leave. You can do some real estate work for them. If you help them sell a house there will be a nice commission for you."

"I have never sold anything. How could I do it?"

"When I first met you, you worked at the Aspitian's French Patisserie; you were one of his best sales girls. You also told me you had to sell all your husband's possessions to survive. If you could do that, you can sell a house, who could resist your womanly charm.

Consequently, mum sold her one and only house. Real estate was not a booming business in Harbin under Communist Government. But, one could do some business on the side. Mum's commission and help from Igor on two or three occasions allowed us to live a little better. About that time, we moved from the tree-lined Bolshoi Prospect to one of its side streets, No. 5 Telinskaya. Years later, I found out that at that time a teenager who lived at No. 3 was the last Russian to later graduate from the Harbin Institute of Technology in Civil Engineering before the Institute was turned over to the Chinese. It was Valerie Gounko, a former Engineer with the Federal Department of Public Works in Sydney and like many others contributed many years to the Russian community in Sydney.

Igor Petrov was a very good and decent man. Not only did he help us in a difficult situation but also every time he would come out of the Sabor he would give alms to all the beggars outside the churchyard. I sometimes wondered how different our life might have been if my mother had married Igor instead of my father. Again, years later his daughter and I joked about what if? We could have been a brother and sister. But then, I would not have turned out to be me.

Igor and his wife turned out to be incompatible. They separated in Sydney but never divorced. He became increasingly pious and turned more and more to the Church. I remember when I once visited him in a small flat at Redfern how he made his visiting daughter and me stand and pray for a long time before and after a meal. He eventually became a deacon in the Archbishop's Chapel in Croydon and later moved to the Jordanville Russian Orthodox Monastery in New York, USA, where he became a monk. He died in 1983 about the same time as my father.

55 THE KOREAN CONFLICT

In September 1950, the Korean conflict was in its third month. It resulted from the North Koreans with tacit Soviet support moving southward, across the 38th parallel. By mid December, General MacArthur's forces were approaching the Yalu River, the border separating Manchuria from North Korea – the closest point being about 450 kilometres from Harbin. However, by the New Year the tide had turned with the entry of 180,000 Chinese volunteers. The United Nation forces were repelled to the 38th parallel. As a counter measure, MacArthur requested the blockade of China's coastline and the bombing of its Manchurian bases. This Truman refused, avoiding the prospect of the Soviet Union entering into the war and thereby leading to a global conflict.

In retrospect, enigmatically years later I would favour MacArthur's request to blockade and bomb China. Had that happened, I may not have lived to form any view or write this book, because Harbin would have been bombed as one of the bases that supported the pa-lu-din – the Chinese 8th Army. Perhaps Truman was wiser than MacArthur after all. To me this enigma is even greater when another dimension is added and one considers the former stories of the Harbinites that Harbin was spared three times from the proposed bombings during the late days of World War II by the

Japanese and the Soviets in turn. This blessing was attributed to Harbin's Patron – St. Nicholas. Did the blessing of St. Nicholas protect Harbin from the well-intentioned but misguided General MacArthur as well?

I still remember the time during the first term of that year when all students helped to cut strips of paper and with the help of rice glue reinforce every windowpane in each classroom. At the same time, trenches were dug in many of the streets. There was one such trench dug outside our front gate of No. 5 Telinskaya. This was my introduction to that War.

By the following spring, after the snow had melted the trench on the other side of our gate appeared full and its surface was covered with weeds and spring flowers, but I was told many a time to keep well away from such trenches. On one June Sunday afternoon dressed in my Sunday best: shorts, shirt, socks and shoes my mother let my sister and me to go to a local soccer match. A few minutes later my sister brought me back filthy, covered in mud and God knows what else from the neck down. The next thing that I remember was being totally stripped, washed in the bath and simultaneously belted with a strap, to which I was yelling "*bolshe ni budu mamachka*" (I won't do it again mummy), that is, stand on the trench surface to see if it was solidified.

This was to be my last summer in Harbin. Our situation further improved when we heard from our relatives who made their way from Shanghai to Sydney via the Philippines.

56 FROM BERLIN TO MUNICH

After the 1936 Berlin Olympics, life was really picking up in Berlin. Wownenko's transport business was growing. Ivan handled most of the transportation issues and usually drove one of the vans or trucks himself. Dasha handled the administration and coordination of their business. Elena looked after the apartment and did most of the cooking and cleaning. Later, as business improved a housekeeper assisted Elena. From the one modest van their vehicle fleet would eventually grow to a dozen vans and trucks. The Wownenkos were now able to afford some outings and community participation. Ivan played a leading role in the local Ukrainian community and Dasha was a Chief Sister in the Church Sisterhood.

They would attend prominent functions and performances of Anna Pavlova, Theodor Shaliapin and other performers whenever they appeared in Berlin. One day the Wownenkos were overjoyed at a performance at the Berlin Concert Hall, where they once again heard their favourite performers – The Don Cossack Choir with their renowned choir master Sergey Jaroff. The performance as always was outstanding and deeply stirring. The flowing Russian and Cossack melodies touched everyone's hearts and brought back memories of their homeland – *The Legend of the 12 Robbers,*

Evening Bells and the ones that the Germans liked in particular – *Cossaken Patrool* and *Stenka Rasin.*

During the interval, they saw many of their former countrymen now living in Germany dressed in their Cossack national costumes. Dasha recalls an interesting incident as they approached a table where two Colonels sat, a German and a Russian Cossack – Shkuro. As Shkuro was vaguely familiar to them, the Wownenkos nodded their heads in recognition.

"Come and join us," responded the highly spirited Shkuro, who was well known in the Russian community. Shkuro introduced the Wownenkos to his German colleague. As they all sat down, the German Colonel dropped a five pfennigs coin which rolled under the table, whereupon he got on his knees to pick it up. Shkuro, a comedian at heart, not losing an opportunity to humour and show off, promptly took out five marks from his wallet, lit it from a table candle and joined his colleague under the table so he could better see where the coin was.

"Dunke schön," replied the German, and then burst into laughter saying, "Mein Got diese Russiche Cossakens sind verrückt."

Similarly Shkuro said, "A mein liebe Colonel, what is life if you cannot live it to the fullest and not laugh at ourselves when we can. Tonight I am overjoyed. It's like being back home. If only Stalin and his bunch of thugs were not there I would go back to my homeland tomorrow."

"And if Deutsches Reich was at war tomorrow with Russland, would you join our Fuhrer's call to fight the Russiche?

"Ah! mein *Oberst*, it's not the Fuhrer I would be fighting for. I would be an ally of Deutschesland fighting against Stalin and his cohorts but not the Russian people".

"My dear friend," said the German, "I understand what you say, mein frau ist Russiche as you know, but you must be more careful to whom you say it. If the SS or the SD or indeed the Russich NKVD overhear what you just said the only thing you will be doing is facing the firing squad."

On that note, the first intermission bell rang and everyone excused themselves and returned to their seats for the second half of the performance. But Dasha felt a pang of foreboding after that conversation because the reality of a war was becoming more and more probable.

The Devastation of Berlin like the rest of Germany did not take long. But when you live through horror, the timeline appears to stretch. In the course of the war the Wownenkos suffered in direct proportion to the destruction of Berlin. At first they lost their daughter Lyudmilla. She died of pneumonia at the age of four, as antibiotics were not yet available commercially. Ivan felt her loss acutely and carried her photograph in his wallet until the day he died. Shortly after Lyudmilla's death, they lost their son Vladimir just before he was a year old – also from pneumonia. The Wownenkos were desolate. They were surrounded by death and destruction. But then, unexpectedly, Dasha found out that she was pregnant again.

On 3 January 1944, their daughter Alexandra – Shura – was born, a brief respite of love and joy in the middle of a living hell. Shura was born in an air raid shelter as the hospital had been destroyed the night before. By now Berlin had become a symbolic objective of the allies and in the stark contrast of winter snow was a conspicuous target. Berlin was pounded every night and living conditions deteriorated accordingly. Babushka Elena was always in close proximity to Alexandra. When the parents were working she would protect her granddaughter with her life if the need arose. Food was rationed and Dasha would have to travel miles for basic necessities. Heating was difficult as fuel was scarce and Dasha and Babushka carried the warm milk bottles in their bras so that the contents would be warm enough for their baby to drink. The loss of their elder children caused the Wownenkos to be over protective of Alexandra. She was warmly cradled in a pram and never left alone. Babushka Elena was always there to take care of her whenever her parents left the place. It was at this time that Elena, fearing the worst, fortuitously stored the family's silverware in the pram under the baby's mattress.

Late one evening in the springtime, responding to an air raid alarm which had now become a regular feature, the Wownenkos went down to the local bunker. Dasha and Elena carried the baby's milk as they usually did and Ivan came along with a kettle of hot water and some cups for tea. As they settled in for the night, they heard a series of loud explosions nearby. When they emerged from the shelter they discovered that their apartment and the nearby garage with their vehicle fleet had gone. They were left with what they stood in and the silverware in the pram. The silverware in the pram would be remembered for a long time as it has by the grace of God been saved to be passed on to Alexandra's children.

Likewise, most of their street was destroyed, tram-tracks were uplifted and twisted, remains of buses and cars were in pieces and smouldering, building rubble was everywhere, but the worst that imprinted on people's memories was the burnt flesh and body parts lying around. The family had nothing left in Berlin and it was no longer safe to remain there. Consequently they moved to the outer suburb of Gross-glienike. Several months later they were aware that the tentacles of the regime they had once fled were fast approaching. So they moved to Bad Kissingen for about three years and eventually to a Displaced Persons camp in Munich. Had they remained in Berlin, they would certainly have been caught up in its future occupation and perhaps even repatriated to the USSR.

57 THE AFTERMATH

After the war, the Wownenkos were classed as *staatenlos* – Stateless. Along with many others they were placed in a DP camp where they resided in barracks for a few years and were able to get work with the American occupying forces.

In 1947, Ivan's 19-year-old nephew responded to a call to return home to the USSR, from which he had escaped during the war. He returned and shortly after he was executed by a firing squad for his earlier escape. He was one of thousands who was either executed or sentenced to a GULAG. About that time, the Wownenkos read in the papers about the Soviet trials of 1946 and 1947 of Russians who were classed as enemies of the state and were forcibly repatriated to Soviet authorities by the allies. It was a shameful sequel to the agreement reached between Roosevelt, Churchill and Stalin at Yalta at the end of the war. Although some of the repatriated people might have deserved the hangman's noose, the majority did not. Among those that were executed were Senior Cossack Officers, non Soviet residents and staunch anti-communists under the leadership of P.N. Krasnov, the former Imperial Russian army officer and a commander of anti-Bolshevik forces during the Russian Civil War. During World War II, Krasnov helped organize anti-Soviet Cossack units for the Germans and urged the creation of a Cossack state under German protection. Other generals included Krasnov's son and General Shkuro. The grandson Krasnov was sentenced to a Soviet GULAG from which he was later released in Kruschev's time and allowed to leave for South America where he wrote his novel *From the Double-Headed Eagle to the Red Banner.* In the book Krasnov relived the Russian tragedy of Communism.

The Soviets during their executions differentiated between non-Soviet citizens and Soviet citizens. The non-Soviet citizens were hung or shot as enemies of the State. General Vlasov and his senior staff who were former Red Army officers but could not stomach it under Stalin any longer and turned, were classed as traitors against the State and hung with the addition of a meat hook. (Author's comment: It's a pity someone did not hang Stalin by a meat hook for murdering millions of innocent Russians including most of his senior general staff just prior to World War II, leaving Russia poorly prepared against the coming Nazi invasion. The execution of senior Red Army officers in 1938 by Stalin's decree was reason enough for the future Vlasov rebellion against the communist state.)

58 RECONCILIATION

In the autumn of 1947, Dasha heard her father was unwell. She thought that it was time to settle their differences and visit him and her half-related family. She travelled with her daughter Alexandra from Munich to Oberammergau. After an overnight stay there, she returned by bus via Innsbrook, Austria. These three places are very close to one another. So Dasha took the opportunity to do some sight seeing and shopping. While in Innsbrook, on the advice from her father, a shoemaker in his later days, she visited the Salamander Shoe store in Innsbrook and bought herself, her mother and Alexandra, Salamander shoes. A brand which still today is in high demand for its superior quality. Almost fifty years later in a sense of deja-vu, Alexandra would relive this experience while shopping and sight seeing in Innsbrook during a stop-over on the way through from Oberammergau.

In March the following year, Dasha received a telegram that her father had passed away on the thirteenth of that month. She later visited his grave in Oberammergau which is in the cemetery at the foot of a mountain guarded by the Kofel[56]. Standing there she felt glad that she answered his call and that they all had the chance of

56 The tallest peak – 1343 m in Oberammergau surrounded by the Austrian Alps

seeing one another, and meeting her new half relations who were not Russian but German. A people and country that she too had learned to love. She further reflected upon the twists and turns life makes – from the steppes of the River Don to the mountainous countryside of Oberammergau and prayed that he might lie there in peace overlooking the peaceful surroundings that had become his more recent home. But, for herself she felt that her new home would lie elsewhere – somewhere overseas.

In 1950 at the age of six little Alex started school. Very soon she spoke three languages; Russian and Ukrainian at home and German at school. But the *staatenlos* had to be settled. Some of her Russian friends like the Alexandroff family had already departed. They left for a far away land called Australia.

When the Wownenkos' turn came, they had three choices of destination: the USA, Argentina and Australia. Almost everyone always ticked USA as their first preference as the Wownenkos did as not much was known about Australia then.

However, when their approval for America came they had to reject it. The approval was for the Wownenkos but not for Babushka Kolesnikoff. So once again they had to wait for a place that would take them all together. Ultimately the approval came for the whole family to set sail from Bremerhaven for Australia early in the new year.

6 EXODUS II

1950-1965

59 GOODBYE HARBIN

No tear shall fall on the lonely grave and
No one will ever repair the Cross or bother to say goodbye
Only the local old Chinaman will whisper to a passer-by:
Quiet, a Russian sleeps here don't linger and just go by
After the Russian Civil War Cadet D. Tarto
Tai Ku – China

That autumn of 1950 during the Korean conflict, after a long three month summer break I started second class. I was now a cut above the new starters and considered myself an established schooly so much so that when I saw an older boy picking on my older sister and her girlfriend I came to their aid and pushed the boy aside. He fell and we ran away whilst the boy waved his fist at us. Only later did I notice that by coming to the girls' aid I cut my leg against a metal spur protruding from a wartime abandoned jeep in which I was playing at the time of the incident. The little scar on the inside of my right lower leg reminds me of the chivalry I exhibited then.

About that time, I started a modest stamp and coin collection. One of the stamps, which I still have, displays above the 1950 handshake between two dictators – Stalin and Mao Zedong. It may be referred to as the handshake between the two demagogues which was doomed to failure[57]. The agreement might have survived had Stalin not died in 1953 and had he not been denounced by Khrushchev in 1956. As it stood, apart from economic aid and technology transfer from the USSR to the People's Republic of China more than half of the Russian population living in China was encouraged by the Soviet/Sino policy to either return voluntarily or be repatriated to the USSR.

We were one of the lucky ones and owe it to our relatives, particularly the Koliagins, who helped us to emigrate from China to Australia in 1951. This is how it happened.

57 "In 1945, Stalin wanted to prevent China from making a revolution, saying that we should not have a civil war and should cooperate with Chiang Kai-shek, otherwise the Chinese nation would perish. But we did not do what he said. The revolution was victorious. After the victory of the revolution he (Stalin) next suspected China of being a Yugoslavia, and that I would become a second Tito...". Mao's declaration in the 1960s.

60 THE INTERNATIONAL RELIEF ORGANISATION

By 1949 The International Relief Organisation (IRO), a temporary specialized agency of the United Nations, assisted the Russian refugees in Shanghai with resettlement. The IRO, during its existence from 1946 to its termination in January 1952, assisted refugees and displaced persons in many countries of Europe and Asia who could not return to their countries of origin or were unwilling to go back for political reasons.

The IRO, in liaison with the Russian Emigrants' Association in Shanghai headed by G.K. Bologoff, after a great deal of organising finally acquired a refugee holding camp on the island of Tubabao in the Philippines. Tubabao is just off the southern tip of Samar, some 600 kilometres southeast of Manila and just north of the equator. So between early January and late May 1949 almost 6,000 Russian refugees were evacuated from Shanghai to Tubabao. The Tubabao camp continued to function until its destruction by a typhoon in December 1951. However, most refugees lived on the island about six to twelve months. One of the people who helped the refugees to eventually find sanctuary was their bishop. Bishop John[58] made successful representation to the UN in New York and

58 Bishop John of Shanghai later became Archbishop of San Francisco and

the American Government in Washington for the resettlement of the refugees, mainly to the USA, Australia, South America and France.

I remember my Uncle Misha telling me how impressed the American and other dignitaries who came to inspect the refugees were. He said it was late afternoon when the dignitaries arrived expecting to find dispirited refugees. Instead they found a clean, well laid out camp with a brass band to greet them. The orchestra played several national anthems of the dignitaries' home countries, including the Star-Spangled Banner, God Save the King and the former Russian Imperial National Anthem – God Save the Tsar. Later on, under a large tropical moon and the camp lit up with kerosene and hurricane lamps as well as fakels – island torch flames, the orchestra entertained the visitors with pleasant music.

Shortly after the visitors left, departures for final destinations commenced. The USA took about half the refugees, next Australia, followed by South America. France took mainly the sick and frail in memory of the debt she owed Russia during World War I – where thousands of Russians died to help their French comrades in arms in their hour of need.

My relatives: the Koliagins, Dobrovidovs, Yanchevskys and Babushka Franya all went through Tubabao on the way to Sydney Australia.

---

the West Coast of USA. In 1988 he was canonized for extraordinary spiritual work during his life and for his devotion to his flock and humanity in general.

61 KLAVA AND THE CHILDREN RESCUED

On arrival in Australia Jim Yanchevsky went to work on the sugar cane plantations in Townsville for the first year or so to help him and Tina get started. Sasha, with his daughter and parents, lived in a cabin in Forestville and later he began to slowly build a house for himself and Marina. The Koliagins and Babushka lived in the migrant camp at Scheyville near Windsor for a few years and worked there. They borrowed and bought a 36 acre farm in Oakville. As soon as they all settled down, Musya began taking steps to get Klava out of Harbin.

She approached all their relatives and friends for contributions including Sergei Vassilieff in San Francisco. Sergei at this stage was supporting his wife, son and daughter and in his reply he said he was not in a good financial situation; nevertheless he still contributed a small amount.

Musya was disappointed, even with their own contribution she and Michael could not raise enough money. Later she said; "I prayed for help to come from somewhere". Klava also prayed in Harbin. Their prayers were answered. A co-worker of Musya approached her one day and said: "We hear that you and Michael are trying to raise funds to bring out your sister and her two children from Communist China and that you are still short. Here is an envelope which hopefully will meet your requirements, all the workers in the camp have contributed."

Musya burst into tears and hugged and thanked her colleague. Later in the day when Musya, Michael and Babushka sat down and counted up all their savings and contributions against the proposed expenditure of fares, accommodation and associated expenses to bring the Vassilieffs to Sydney, there was just enough to get the ball rolling.

On 1 September 1951, I enrolled in third class of Harbin School No. 3. But the following week I was saying goodbye to my friends and schoolmates. Two of the schoolmates that I would later meet in Sydney were Adrian Lapardin and Aliosha Tetushkin. We also bade farewell to Auntie Natasha, her two sons Nicholas and Yuri and newly-born grandson, Vasiliy's widow Tasya and my sister's godmother Tamara Petrov and her parents. It was quite a wrench for my mother, who knew she would never see any of them again, but I was too young to understand why there were so many tears. Finally we visited dedushka Boris's grave where more tears were shed.

On the evening of 8 September, we left No. 5 Telinskaya by rickshaw for Harbin Station. Our entire belongings fitted into two suitcases. As a last request, the rickshaw driver allowed me to peddle the rickshaw while he ran along the Bolshoi Prospect. The next day on our three slow days train journey to Tientsin I turned nine years of age. Just as I had almost six years earlier to the day when I turned three on the way from Tientsin to Harbin.

I can imagine the thoughts that were going through my mother's head; her earlier trip from this station to Tientsin on the way to get married, then back to Harbin to avoid the Japanese and into the arms of NKVD and now back to Tientsin and on to Hong Kong and then to Sydney. A land *downunder* and unknown to us. Did she at that moment remember then her fortune teller's prediction? If not then she certainly did later.

Two months in Tientsin made me realise that my old world was disappearing. Instead of rickshaws they had pedicabs – a bike with a side carriage rather than at the rear as in rickshaws. It was warmer here, still no snow when we left in November. Even the Russians were different here. Some of them used English or American words like okay, hello, goodbye, see you. At least we went to the Soviet Club and saw a new free movie – the Kuban Cossaks.

By late November we boarded the *SS Hoopai*, about a 1,000 ton ship. Our cabin just had enough room to roll out a mattress between two beds on the floor for me at night. As a nine-year-old, I loved it. When we boarded the ship I was overwhelmed with the adventure ahead and immediately thanked my mother.

"It's not me you should be thanking but your Auntie and Uncle. Don't forget to do that when you meet them in Sydney." We sailed along the muddy Wang Ho – Yellow River – for about a day until we came out into the Yellow Sea, then the East China Sea and through the Straits of Formosa near the Island of Amoy. We were warned that the Taiwanese bandits might take pot shots at us. Fortunately we were spared that experience.

To pass the time away I played chess, a game which I picked up from seven years of age. Even the Captain found me an interesting challenge. From time to time he would lose. Either he was not a good chessplayer or he lost to encourage me.

On the seventh day, we found ourselves in Victoria Harbour between Kowloon and Hong Kong Island. I was overwhelmed with the view of the Harbour and later on again viewing the Harbour from the Peak. I recalled that memory when many years later I saw Hong Kong again. We stayed on the island at the Victoria Hotel on Victoria Road – which must have been demolished a few years later to make room for progress. Hong Kong is a dynamic place, always changing. In 1951 it had a population of about one million compared to today's of just under six million.

Finally, on 1 December, we departed from Kai Tak airport bound for Sydney on a Qantas flight – DC 4 propeller engine aircraft (leased from BOAC). That same day in the afternoon we stopped overnight in Sarawak, Borneo, where we northerners found the heat unbearable. At that time there would have been one to two feet of snow in Harbin. The following morning we left for Darwin, where we landed at 6 p.m. There we were taken by bus to a hotel for a shower and dinner and at 10 p.m. we left for Sydney.

62 GOODBYE GERMANY

In January 1951 the Wownenko family waved goodbye to their homeland of many years. To young Alexandra it was the only homeland that she knew. They travelled by train from Munich in the south to Bremerhaven in the north. From there they sailed in the *SS Castelbianco* to Australia. In those days, the voyage took 40 days via the Suez Canal to Aden, Fremantle and finally Melbourne where they disembarked.

Years later, Alexandra wrote in her memoirs of the trip:

Amongst the passengers on board were Dasha's classmates from Paris – Count Nikolai Sheremetyev and Marina now Alexeiva with their families. Count Sheremetyev was also an inspector on the ship and specially took my family on a tour of the ship and allowed me for a while to steer the ship.

My family lived in old army barracks in Munich where as displaced people we were settled after the war. We had chickens, turkeys and pigs and grew our own vegetables. The home-grown produce was then bartered for milk, fruit and other needs. A big change for city folk from Berlin. This rural environment was heaven to a five-year-old child. I recall the meadows strewn with red poppies, fields of wheat, fruit orchards and my favourite, lilac trees. Bombed-out buildings also surrounded us and craters made by bombs were put to good use in winter for tobogganing.

One day we left all of this behind and set off by train to Bremenhaven to board a ship that would take us to our new home in Australia. The journey was long and tiring. In a cramped carriage amongst luggage I tried to sleep in my mother's arms. I woke to exclamations of – There it is! Our ship the Castelbianco. Opening my eyes I saw the sparkling blue sea, which I had never seen before and for me an enormous ship.

From a Distance, as in Bette Midler's song, all looks great but life on board was a challenge. Forty days and nights we sailed through cold rough seas as well as hot sunny days watching flying fish. Most people suffered from sea sickness and I recall two burials at sea.

The converted cargo ship had two holds – one for men and one for women. There were rows and rows of beds all curtained off with little sick bags attached to each bed. Mama, Babushka and I were together and papa on his own in the men's quarters. The Bay of Biscay was very rough and most of the passengers were ill with sea sickness or other ailments. However, my mother coped and even helped other people whilst I fetched water for drinking, washing and medication. Mama even managed to eat in the dining room where crockery, tables, chairs and piano slid fom side to side.

Our first stop was at Mont-St-Michel in the English Channel – between Brittany and Normandy, which was a fascinating excursion and a welcome break from the ship. Now I know that the place is almost circular measuring about 3,000 feet (900 metres) in circumference and consists of a granite outcrop rising sharply to a height of about 256 feet (78 metres) out of Mont-St-Michel Bay. Amongst the number of monastic ruins was the surviving Chapel of St. Michael which apparently dates back to the 15thcentury. Most of the time Mont-St-Michel is surrounded by vast sandbanks and becomes an island only when the tides are very high. At twilight we hurried back to the ship across the sandbars before the tide came in.

As our journey continued, we sailed through one of the world's most heavily used shipping lanes – the Suez Canal, which extends 101 miles (163 kilometres) between Port Said in the north and Suez in the south. The canal is a gateway between the Mediterranean and south of Suez which flows into the Red Sea. The canal separates the African continent from Asia, and it provides the shortest maritime route between Europe and the lands in the region of the Indian and western Pacific oceans.

Our next stop was Aden (then a British crown colony – now Yemen) where we splurged on a souvenir – a leather ottoman which we had as a reminder of our visit for many years. Then on to the stifling heat of the Indian Ocean and the Equator. Below deck was unbearable so many tried to sleep on deck but the mosquitos and other insects were worse.

King Neptune ruled the celebrations at the crossing of equator and everyone received a certificate. After the remaining long stretch across the Indian Ocean at last land was sighted at Fremantle. We made our way across the Great Australian Bight disembarking in Melbourne.

63 THE NEW AUSTRALIANS

The Wownenkos had to start all over again. From Melbourne they made their way by train to Bonegilla – a migrant camp at Albury near the Hume Reservoir. However, Babushka Elena by having a different surname had to proceed to a different camp at Cowra, about 90 kilometres southwest of Bathurst. There they were housed until they could acquire appropriate employment.

After about a month, in early April, the Wownenkos were allocated live-in employment in a house at Bellevue Hill. Ivan was employed as groundsman and Dasha as cook and housekeeper. Meanwhile Babushka Elena also received live-in employment as cook and housekeeper with a lovely Jewish family, the Bandos in Bondi. After about a month in that position, Ivan could not face feeding prime red meat and cutting out the fat to over 20 little dogs that the landlady bred. As they had just left a war-torn country and near starvation, he could not tolerate this indulgence. Consequently they left the Bellevue Hill house and found a room to rent at 32 Wigram Road, Glebe, where they both found jobs.

Dasha found herself a lifetime job at the Royal Prince Alfred Hospital in the catering department, where later on she achieved a supervisor's position in Glouchester house diet kitchen. Ivan found himself a job as a storeman at a local independent petrol company

– Purr Pull Oil. After two more years, in March 1954 and for the next 10 years, he received employment as a storeman-driver with the State Rail.

Finally by mid 1954 the whole family was reunited and all moved to 106 Derwent Street, Glebe.

64 THE VAJINSKY FAMILY REUNITES

Our plane landed at Kingsford Smith Airport at 8.00 a.m. on 3 December 1951. As I rushed ahead of everyone I saw leaning over a barrier, a man and a woman who so much resembled my mother. The man addressed me and asked: *"Malchik, ti znaesh semyu Vassilievih?"* Boy, do you know a family Vassilieff?

I nodded and immediately rushed back to my mother and sister saying: "Mama, mama! the Koliagins are here and Aunty Musya looks so much like you". After arrival formalities, we all hugged and kissed and the sisters cried. I was used to the crying by then. Misha Koliagin led us all to the car and we drove to the Scheyville Migrant camp, where the Koliagins lived. I very soon noticed and voiced the observation that there were no Chinese anywhere in sight, asking why that was so? My uncle explained that this was a European country. It all seemed very strange to me as I had only known China and Hong Kong and the Europeans there were only a minority. Here, suddenly almost every one was white. The language barrier had not yet had its full impact on me.

By about midday with the temperature soaring, something that we would eventually have to get used to, we arrived at Scheyville. Again more embraces with Babushka and, later, my cousins Milla and Vera when they came home from school. The camp I thought was terrific. There were many barracks, people, places to play and even a picture show. We spent two days there and I was disappointed when we left for the Koliagins' farm in Oakville, where we would live together with Babushka.

The Koliagins were to visit us on the weekends (another new concept[59] and an English word that I learned). They had only recently bought the 36 acre property and were heavily in debt. When we arrived at the farm the first thing I noticed was how desolate it was. I could see only two other farms, each in the opposite direction and the haze of the Blue Mountains in the distance. I also found out progressively that water was scarce and you drank it from the water tanks outside and that the Australian dunny only surpassed the worst Chinese toilets on the outskirts of Harbin. There were frequent electricity black-outs and we had to use kerosene lamps as a standby. Oakville in those days resembled the outback.

The house, had it remained to the present day, would have probably been heritage listed. It was, from my recollection, constructed of mud and some other additive mix. A leaky corrugated iron roof with hessian bag ceilings and lime-washed inside and out. I was alarmed in December/January 1952 to see the Blue Mountains ablaze. The year was recorded as the worst bush fire up to that time and for many years to come. Uncle Misha, who was one of the volunteer fire fighters, assured me that if the fire spread to Oakville unexpectedly we could always save ourselves in the small dam that he had on the property. Not knowing any better, I was reassured.

The property had a few fruit trees, some chickens and a cow that Babushka milked. We helped with farm work, particularly during the school holidays. Some vegetables were planted that required regular watering with a watering can (just as it is now in the 21st century during the drought) and a few eggs were gathered every day. Mr Hanckell next door allowed us to gather a bucket of oranges and mandarins for two shillings whenever we wanted. My mother soon

59 In China, we had no concept of weekends. Everyone went to school and/or work six days a week.

found a job as a process worker at a Rosella factory in Windsor. She would walk about three kilometres every morning to Scheyville where she caught a bus to Windsor, and then do the reverse in the evening. She had a powerful soprano voice and would sing on the way home, walking through the bush track. Valerie and I could hear her about a kilometre away; then we would run to meet her.

After Australia Day we started school in Oakville about one and a half kilometres from home, to which we walked each day. I was not used to having all classes in the one room with the same teacher, who taught all classes and I was embarassed when I was placed in second class as I could not speak English. When the teacher noticed that I was more interested in doing fourth class arithmetic than second class, he allowed me to continue with the fourth class maths at least. I learnt very little English that year. The only English that I was exposed to was in school as we all spoke Russian on the farm. The teacher as I recollect spoke Australian *Ocker.* During a dictation I would copy word for word what he dictated, thinking that English like Russian was phonetic, e.g. Da kau jumpd ova da mun. Obviously my teacher was not impressed.

Soon after our arrival we met more of our relatives. First the Yanchevskys – Aunt Tina and her second husband Jim, whom she married in Shanghai after her divorce from Sasha. The sisters remembered the sad farewells at Tientsin railway station over six years ago. On Christmas Day all the relatives got together. I could not understand why Christmas came 13[60] days earlier in Australia but was happy to experience two Christmases each year from then on. On that day I met my eldest cousin Marina and her father uncle Sasha. As I was already a coin collector I was thrilled that Marina gave me a Christmas present of 10 shillings in five silver florin coins whereas my sister received a 10 shilling note. I already had in my little metal box Chinese, Hong Kong, Russian and other coins.

---

60 As noted earlier many Christian Orthodox celebrate their Holy days by the Julian calendar, which is 13 days later, unlike most of the West who use the Gregorian calendar.

When uncle Jim found out that I also saved stamps he gave me his old stamp album, which I still have today.

The things my cousins, my sister and I remember most about these gatherings are the nights when we would all sit by the fireplace – at times with only the light of the kerosene lamp – listening to stories from the past as told by the adults. The youngsters would listen with great interest – tales of Old Shanghai, Tientsin, Harbin, my father's and Uncle Misha's hot water installation business, the War, the parting of the Family, my father's forced expatriation and mum's fortune-teller, to mention a few.

When Tina and Jim first came to visit us on the farm, Tina immediately remarked how skinny and scrawny I looked and that I would never match my father's strength or agility. It was like waving a red rag in front of a bull. I immediately challenged her to a wrestle. She unhesitatingly responded that she would put me down with her little finger. That was all the encouragement I needed and immediately assumed the wrestling position that I learned back in China – a cross between Mongolian and Greco-Roman wrestling. As my aunt put her hands on my shoulders I tripped her and forced her on her back with my right leg, jumped on top of her, grabbing and squeezing both her wrists in a surrender – hands up position. Tina at once began to squeal and yell for help from her husband who did not react, thinking she was putting on a perfomance for my benefit. When I asked her if she surrendered she agreed without any hesitation and complained to her husband for not coming to her rescue. Jim replied that he thought she was only joking. Tina, by then furious, exclaimed "He is just like his father, a prankster with hurtful hands, look at my wrists they will swell up by tomorrow". I could not have had greater praise, than to be compared with my father. My scrawniness was forgotten. These memories come back to me when I feel my muscles and bones ache after wrestling with my little grandsons.

Very soon my mother learned how to use the railway system and get about. I recall one Sunday afternoon when mum took my sister and me by train from Vineyard (about five kilometres from the farm) to Quakers Hill to visit my mother's cousin – my oldest aunt – Eugenia who, after her extensive travels as an exotic dancer, settled in Australia moving over the years between Sydney, Brisbane and the Gold Coast. Again we embraced, laughed and cried. Eugenia introduced us to her guests. Although after breaking her leg she now had a limp like her sister Natalia in Harbin, she still performed on the stage at the Russian Club in Sydney. It was an enjoyable afternoon where there was much talking, drinking and singing. I played under the house and became friendly with a girl my age whom I would meet again in the future when I joined the Scout movement. As it turned out, she would not be the love of my life but a passing fancy who was destined to lead a colourful Bohemian life.

It was Eugenia who suggested a place in Marayong which we could rent. Mum decided that we should move as we had lived in Oakville about 12 months. In the lead up to our move I began to notice occasions of friction in the house, particularly between Uncle Misha and my mother, with Aunt Musya intervening to calm things down. At that stage I did not know what was happening, other than my uncle making certain demands that should be met on the farm and my mother replying: "If you wanted cheap farm labour seven days a week then you should have left us in Harbin and hired yourself someone else! I am not a labourer. I give you what I can from my weekly wages! The children and I help as much as we can with chores around the farm! But I also need some rest."

When I asked my mother "Are we moving because of the arguments?" she replied: "Yes. The Koliagins are in debt, the farm requires high repayments. Misha wants me to work on the farm and give up my factory work. If I work on the farm it would help him more with his repayments as my weekly contributions from my wages are too small. But I am not a farmer and lately I have been getting more and more tired. I know it was a considerable cost to them to bring us here and maybe one day I will be able to repay them for their kindness, but for now I cannot take this situation anymore."

So we moved to Marayong and I think Uncle Misha helped to move us. It was a small two-room fibro garage that a Ukrainian market gardener and his wife rented out to us. I went to fourth class at Quakers Hill Primary for the next six months, and Valerie to first year High School in Windsor.

Half way through the year we moved to Homebush. Valerie and I changed our schools accordingly and Mum got a job much closer. We rented a room in a private house from a Russian gentleman who was rather keen on our mother. I even slept in his room while mum and Valerie shared the one we had rented. Mum mentioned to both of us that he wanted to marry her, to which we both replied, "Great, when?" However, she said that she still had hopes of reuniting with our father one day and would prefer to wait for him. By the end of that year there was a dreadful row between my mother and the gentleman-landlord with my sister yelling, "leave my mother alone." I was rather disappointed that things took such a bad turn as he seemed to be a nice man.

Soon after that incident we moved to 232 King Street, Newtown – a three-storey boarding house owned by Mr Doolye, a Greek bootmaker who had his workshop on the ground floor. Our room was on the third floor and across from us lived a Russian Priest – Rev. Nikolay Golubev/Grey, his wife and their 20 year-old-son Nikolay (Nick). We became very friendly and Nick sometimes took Valerie and me out. He bought me a present once – a double-barrelled cap-firing pirate musket. I was over the moon and constantly taunted my sister, who would then respond physically and Nick would laugh. While mum and Valerie painted and cleaned our room, the Reverend and I scrubbed the stairway in turn and cleaned the communal kitchen. He explained to me the importance of doing good to others and the need for the righteous way of life. Although not a movie-goer he took me to see *Quo Vadis* – "Lord, where are you going?" a time about Nero's Rome and Peter's crucifixion. He also showed me how to defend myself, as I was frequently bullied at school having a foreign name and speaking with a strong accent.

I was in the fifth class now at Newtown Primary and almost every day on the way home I would be bullied and called a "Commo", which I found very hurtful. Although I could take care of myself in a one on one situation, it was difficult to fight off four or five boys at a time. With some coaching by the Reverend, plus some of my own innovations in self defence, the next time I was taunted on the way home I grabbed the ring leader in a headlock and told him to tell the others to leave me alone or I would break his neck. It worked. But, after I let the culprit go he promised that the next day they would surround me and belt me up.

Upon hearing this, my mother and I fronted up at the Principal's office the next day. I was asked to point out all the offenders in the classroom and the Principal led the bunch out into the corridor where their punishment was clearly audible as each received a cut of the cane. From then on I had a peaceful existence.

65 THE CURSED INHERITANCE OF THE NKVD

La lueur de Lumière –
The gleam of light
The illness of
Depression surrounds me,
But like through a telescope
A glittering of light stands out...
As at the same time hope fills the room...
Unknown poet

Klava's family was to fall apart once more. I began to enjoy settling in at Newtown Primary, when one afternoon after school as I arrived home Babushka unexpectedly was there to greet me. Babuska's knowledge of English was limited to a few animal farm words, basic niceties and *sharap you bloody cow.* She could get around by public transport, with the help of a note, showing our address in English. Sometimes with the help of such a note she would arrive at Newtown Station, whereupon she was helped by street folk to find us. She also became known by the local Newtown Police Station who more than once helped her – first with a cup of tea and then delivering her to our place. Babushka, as well as my mother and later myself, found places on the assumption of an old Russian proverb – *Yazik do Kieva do vedyet* – the tongue will get you to Kiev, or put another way – ask and you shall receive. Babushka would occasionally come down for the weekend and we all would go to the chuch together at Robinson Road, Centennial Park, where Father Nikolay was one of the two priests. He usually conducted the choir. On this occasion, Babushka sat me down and explained that my mother was ill and had to be hospitalised. It was something that she called a nervous breakdown, which I could not understand. She assured me that everything was going to be alright and as soon as she was better we could go and visit her. Meanwhile we could stay with our aunts. Valerie with the Koliagins and me with the Yanchevskys.

"Why can't I go with my sister and stay with Aunt Musya too?" I cried out. Aunt Musya reminded me very much of my mother and I felt very comfortable with her. Babushka explained to me that space was limited and that it was easier to accommodate all three girls together, now that all of the Koliagin family and Babushka lived on the farm and that as a boy I would be better off with the Yanchevskys. Besides, it would not be long before my mother would be better and we could all reunite.

And so the next day my sister and I were separated once more. On Monday I started at a new school in Liverpool. My Aunt made me tasty sandwiches, cheese and dates as I remember, which appealed to me, as I have never tried that combination before. They were also cut up into triangles – the Australian way. Again that was new to me as I usually ate Vienna bread with cheese or salami or jam the *wog way.* My stay at Liverpool Primary was short.

Two weeks after we moved to Campbelltown, the Yanchevskys were made a good offer from a Russian couple who lived in Canberra and had a chicken and duck farm in Campbelltown. The deal was: free board and all the eggs, chicken and duck we could eat in exchange for managing the farm and gathering and selling eggs.

The terms did not literally apply to me but I had to pull my weight before and after school and on weekends. My Aunt was very good at making things clear to me. She taught me how to cook porridge and have a good wholesome breakfast. Check the chicken pens and change any dirty water for the 200-300 chooks and a small number of ducks and later geese as well, and get rid of any dead chickens. Then I would get dressed, say goodbye to my Aunt, walk to a bus stop from where the bus would take me to Campbelltown Primary. By the time I left for school my Aunt would engage herself in a make-up ritual of cosmetics, cream and facial massage that she religiously followed every day for about two hours or so because she was concerned with keeping her youthfulness as she was eight years older then her husband. During her morning ablutions she would listen to the morning radio serials of the time such as *When a Girl Marries, Blue Hills* and others.

Uncle Jim was one of the hardest working people I knew. He would travel to Sydenham Railway workshops every day where he was on shift-work and regular overtime. He did this at first by bicycle to Campbelltown Station, then by rail the rest of the way changing trains at Liverpool from a steamer to electric, and once again at Redfern for the Southern Line. Later he upgraded to a motor-bike and eventually a car. On weekends he would do all the heavy farm work such as cutting lucerne with a saw, moving 60-pound bags of wheat and mash in order to refill the weekly chicken feed hoppers and any other jobs that needed to be done. My task was repetitive. Every afternoon after school I had to hand-feed the chickens with wheat grain, make sure their water was clean and pick up any remaining eggs that were laid following the collection by my Aunt during her earlier rounds. After dinner we would all clean the eggs and pack them in the wooden egg containers of 12 dozen per box, which would take about two or three days and which would be picked up the next day – about three times a week.

After about three months on the farm my Uncle took me to visit my mother at Gladesville Mental Hospital. To me mum looked alright other than being a little subdued and it was a joyful visit. However, I was told that she would have to remain longer. But, that I could visit her more regularly from now on. Having done the trip once with my Uncle I was to memorise the transport procedure and the intricacies of changing trains at Liverpool and Town Hall – where I would catch a bus from York Street to Victoria Road, Gladesville, and repeat the procedure in reverse, walking the last four kilometres home from the station.

In those days I guess I was on auto-pilot. I was not mistreated, but I do not recall receiving any love. It was a rather lonely existence. Primarily because my Uncle always worked so hard that I doubt that he had any energy left for bonding with me. My Aunt, unlike her two younger sisters, appeared to be more concerned with herself and probably did not know how to love a young boy as I was about the same age as her daughter Marina was when she separated from Sasha back in 1945, who kept and raised their daughter on his own. However, I was taught self reliance by the Yanchevskys from the early age of eleven and I always ate well. It was a mutually convenient relationship. I was looked after but I worked for my keep. That helped develop my character at a young age and taught me independence. It also, helped me understand my relatives better and be very aware in the future of the consequence of neglect of a child's need for love and attention.

The following year, my mother was released from hospital and my sister was able to join her. It was decided that for the time being I was to remain with the Yanchevskys to allow mum to settle in her home routine. I had no say in the matter. By the end of the year I completed primary school and found a summer job on a dairy farm close by, to which I would ride on my Uncle's bike at four o'clock each morning, finish the morning milking shift by eight and repeat the milking in the afternoon between two and six o'clock, six days per week. This earned me about one pound (two dollars) per day. At that time the basic wage would have been about eleven pounds per week. It was about two weeks after I started this job, that on a

Sunday whilst helping my Uncle move some wheat and mash bags, I did something wrong. My Uncle exploded and with some colourful adjectives told me what he thought of me. He then said "Bugger off you useless ...", or words to that effect, "... and as punishment when you get home from work tomorrow afternoon you will distribute all the lucerne that I cut this afternoon to the chooks before you sit down to eat."

I brooded all the following day. When I returned home I carried out my punishment chore. It was dusk and I made up my mind that I had had enough of the Yanchevskys. After I completed my task I walked off the farm and hid in the bush. My plan was simple. After dark I would get into the house, pick up my earnings, walk to the station and make my way to my mother and sister.

During the next hour or two my plan and patience were tested as I constantly heard my name being called. I finally gave in. I realised they must be worried. I would return to the house and say goodbye to them the next day. When I showed up my Aunt was in an uncontrollable rage. My Uncle was silent. After much interrogation and reproach I told them I planned to leave.

"After everything we have done for you! Uncle Jim was even thinking of adopting you." The thought of adoption horrified me.

"Please do not make such a sacrifice," I thought, but decided to keep quiet and just ignore the accusations of my ingratitude. I was then told that they certainly would not keep me a day longer than they had to. This was the best news to me so far.

They went on to say, "Anyway Koliagins are on their way here. We did not know who else to call. You could have been abducted or been bitten by a snake. We will discuss with them the best way to deal with you. Now sit down, have your dinner and we do not want to see you when they come."

There was a big pow-wow in the next room when the Koliagins arrived. My cousin Vera sat with me and listened to my side of the events and what I wanted to do.

Eventually the decision was that I would finish work in the next two weeks and then return to my mother. The Koliagins must have helped in smoothing things out, as the situation was more or less calm after they left. When the two weeks were up we said goodbye to one another. I thanked them for looking after me, and with a knapsack, a little suitcase and a lift to the station I went with great joy to meet my mother and sister again.

66 RETURN HOME

It was a joyful reunion – Klava and children together again. We were still living in our old flat at 232 King Street, Newtown. The Golubevs moved to Enmore to their new house. Nick married his beloved Margarita, who had recently arrived from Shanghai. Mum was back in the workforce. Valerie, having finished her Intermediate Certificate, was now working as a secretary and studying for her secretarial certificate at night. I enrolled in first year High School at Ashfield Tech., which was considered better by my mother than the high school at Newtown. Besides, we still had bad memories of Newtown Primary.

The following year, however, my school free travel pass was revoked as another perfectly good high school was available locally. By now I was used to changing schools and it came as no shock to me when I heard the local students referring to the school boldly as Newtown Penitentiary. The change was a mixed blessing. I progressively performed better at school and even became a prefect in third year. In retrospect, I wondered about my slight improvement. Whether it was because the standard may have been lower at Newtown or my English was slowly improving and hence I understood the lessons better, or perhaps the teachers may have been more resilient to cope in a school such as this. I believe the last two points were more likely, as the school "inmates" were rough and tough. The nickname "penitentiary" for the school was a badge of honour for those who looked up to individuals that ended up in reform schools, or better still in gaol. The rough and tough modelled themselves on the 'in' colour, Presley-purple, from the then favourite movie *Jailhouse Rock*. This trend made me fantasise that communal living as in being in a boys' home or even a gaol would be an interesting experience.

This was literally a school of hard knocks where I regularly had to defend myself fighting in and after school. Fortunately I won more often than I lost, and learnt to lose gracefully and use the last defence tactic – where a boxer covers his face and upper torso with his two forearms and clenched fists. That way one walked away only with a loss of pride but unscathed. By now I understood enough and decided that fighting was part of growing up and my mother did not need to know about it. One day I would become a champion boxer like my father, and then even the toughest would not be able to beat me.

On Saturday afternoons I would usually go to Newtown Hoyts for a movie matinee – a movie and two serials. Only Enmore Hoyts two kilometres away was better. It showed one movie and three serials. Seldom having any money taught me to be enterprising. During the movie interval I would swap comics with other kids and at the end of the movie pick up empty drink bottles and cash them in for threepence each at the local milkbar. My criminal tendencies extended to me, with other boys, sneaking in through the back exit door of the theatre to view a late afternoon movie, unfortunately from the front stalls only, and if the usher did not chase us away I would pick up more empties after the end of the movie and my cash reserves would grow.

One afternoon before the start of a movie I was introduced by a mutual friend, Larissa, to Alexandra – my future wife. At the age of fourteen or fifteen I do not recall the meeting, but I do recall the movie – *Smiley*. I was probably in the middle of the more important pursuit of swapping comics. Also, at about that time and oblivious to me, often on the way to school, observant Alexandra, also on the way to her school at Marrickville, would travel in a tram along City Road and King Street, Newtown. She would spot me in a red Cookie jacket (remember – "Cookie, Cookie, lend me your comb" from 77 Sunset Strip who wore that kind of jacket) and play a mental game who would reach the Newtown Station first – the tram or me on foot.

About half way through second year, my mother's acquaintance, Irina Ivashkova (Resaeva), back from Harbin, came to visit us. Her first husband, like our father, was also repatriated to the USSR. Irina Resaeva now remarried, was a Scoutmistress from way back in Harbin, but had suspended her Scouting activities during the Soviet occupation. Now in Australia, together with other Russian Scoutmasters, she was actively involved in developing the Russian Scout Movement in Sydney.

She was aware of mum's situation and encouraged her to allow me to join the Scout movement, impressing upon her that it would be good for my development, particularly as I was growing up fatherless. My sister was already part of the St. Vladimir's Russian Church youth movement and had friends of her own age.

So early in June 1956, I began attending Scout meetings every Sunday afternoon at the Russian Club in George Street in the City. In retrospect, it is interesting to note that most of my memories up to that point are in black and white. From the time I joined the Scout Movement and our family was together again it is as though I had walked into a coloured world.

Knowing that mum felt indebted to Koliagins for their efforts in rescuing us from Harbin, I attempted in a small way to repay some of that debt. Between the ages of fourteen to seventeen on about a monthly basis I would come for a weekend to their farm and help my Uncle Misha, more often than not for no pay and usually by gathering and delivery of animal manure for the mushroom farmers.

We would start in the morning and go out in his old beat-up three-ton Chevy truck to a cattle or chicken farm, where we would spend half a day gathering up with scrapers and rakes cow or chicken manure and then picking it up with a shovel and tossing it into the truck. If there was enough daylight left, we delivered it the same day or the next morning, shovelling it out to the mushroom farmer who in turn would mix it with wheat-straw in several layers and cover it with rice-straw, watering it in between layers. The watering, which helped to heat the process, would be repeated on a weekly basis for up to six weeks until the manure and straw turned into compost ready for transfer to an appropriate dark and cool spot all set for mushroom planting. The different straw we supplied the farmer was picked up by us from Mulgrave Station goods train yard.

The work was hard and uninspiring and during heatwave conditions almost unbearable. To pass the time, Misha would often tell me of the times when he and my father ran their hot water system business in Shanghai or their days in the Regiment and how he hated it. Sometimes we sang, but during heatwaves by the sweat of our brows we worked in silence and waited for the day to end.

When we returned to the farm, we took a much welcomed cleansing shower. Aunt Musya would always have a delicious plentiful meal and somehow the completed day's work did not seem as bad.

67 KLAVA'S ILLNESS

When you look long into an abyss
The abyss looks into you...
F. Nietzsche

When Klava fell ill, everyone was at a loss to explain exactly what type of illness was affecting her. The most common term used between relatives was nervous breakdown or that she was mentally sick. It does not take a rocket scientist to work out that if a person is subjected to prolonged stress and has no one to turn to, in particular one's parents, spouse or other close kin and at times even one's children, the stress is further amplified and that a person may become subject to depression. Intense anxiety about self-preservation tests the limits of mental endurance. Initially it shows up in temporary bouts of depression which are overcome, but in many instances should the experience of anxiety be prolonged even the smallest trial is enough to set off a state in which the person becomes clinically depressed. In Klava's case this was unfortunately so.

The communist Government policies carried out by the dreadful hatchet team of NKVD operatives was felt fully in Harbin during the Soviet occupation. Klava experienced some of the worst treatment a human being could undergo. Enforced separation from her husband, being away from her mother and sisters, difficulty in gaining employment, the need to periodically give up her children, unable to share her inner thoughts with most people for fear of Soviet retribution and experiencing much of this in the freezing cold of the Manchurian winters, where the thermometer frequently fell to minus thirty five degrees centitigrade, left Klava distraught. Most other women either had families to turn to, found a male companion to take care of them, or turned to prostitution. None of these options appealed to her. For Klava they were not the answer to her troubles.

This experience haunted her even when we came to Australia. The cursed inheritance of the NKVD stayed with her for most of her life. She was torn between the obligation to repay her debt to her relatives and providing food and shelter for herself and her children. Whilst living with the hope of the return of her beloved husband, she feared the far reaching hand of the NKVD. Klava needed to stay in control but tragically it finally all became too much for her.

Her first year in hospital included treatment for major bouts of depression[61] with anti-depressant drugs, electroconvulsive therapy and some cognitive psychotherapy. She had terrible memories of the electric shocks – which were later discarded as psychiatric therapy. After her release, she had to continue taking anti-depressant drugs for the rest of her life with significant side effects – drowsiness, loss of concentration, a tremulous leg are

61 The peak for women in succumbing to depression is between the ages of 35 and 45. There is a serious risk of suicide with the illness; of those who have a severe depressive disorder, about one-sixth eventually kill themselves. The loss of one's parents or other childhood traumas or deprivations can increase a person's vulnerability to depression later in life, and stressful life events, especially where some type of loss is involved, are in general potent precipitating causes of the illness. It seems that both psychosocial and biochemical mechanisms are important in causing depression. Encyclopædia Britannica, Inc.

some of the ones I remember. No wonder that at times she would stop taking them, resulting in the return of her condition, often manifesting itself in a state of paranoia. In what was left of her life, she would be readmitted to hospital six more times for this dreadful affliction.

The post traumatic experience of my mother is like a shadow that can be attributed to her earlier sufferings and is well articulated in a different setting by Stalin's daughter – Svetlana Alilueva – "He is gone but his shadow still lingers over us."

68 SCOUTING FOR BOYS - THE RUSSIAN SCOUTING DIASPORA

...And this appointment from above
which gives us happiness and honour
for which our Scouting generation
Shall give the history our report
From Leader's Song

During the Civil War, over one million Russians escaped from the country. Amongst these émigrés were a number of Scouts who laid the foundations of numerous troops in Europe, Latin America, and the Far East. So began the *Russian Scouting Movement in Exile.*

It is a strange fact indeed, and a very sad one, that for about the first 80 years of its existence, the Russian Scouting Movement spent only its first 10 years in Russia! It was founded in April 1909 in Pavlovsk near St. Petersburg. The next year, Lord Baden-Powell – the first world Scout – visited Russia and his visit gave the Russian Movement an impetus, which by 1917 numbered over fifty thousand members all over the country.

After the communists seized power in October 1917, they organized their own groups, the Pioneers, to indoctrinate Russian youth politically. All other independent activities were banned, but despite that, Scouting was carried on underground until 1923, when mass executions and arrests of Scouts put an end to Scouting in the Soviet Union.

Meanwhile the activities of the Russian Scouts abroad were developing outside the USSR. Under the most difficult conditions, where boys and girls were trained in the fundamentals of Scouting and did participate in the Scouting life of the non communist world. Russian Scouts participated officially in the World Jamborees 1920, 1924, 1929, 1933 and 1937.

Russian Scouting was successfully carried on for 20 years in spite of the tremendous material handicaps of life in exile. However, World War II dealt a heavy blow to the Russian Scouting Movement. The Nazi occupation of Europe forced the Scouting Movement underground. Many of its leaders perished in Gestapo concentration camps and prisons. Yet the essentials of Scouting were preserved and even in some respects extended. The Scouting ideals were propagated secretly, in disguised form – to prevent reprisals by the Nazis. Even in parts of Russia, which were temporarily out of Soviet control, Scouting was enthusiastically accepted by Russian youth.

After the war, Scouting rapidly spread throughout the Displaced Persons camps in Germany, Austria and France, where the Russian Scouts soon exceeded 2,000. Some of these boys and girls escaped from the USSR with their parents, some never saw Russia. By the early 1950s most of them migrated to different countries, spreading the Russian Scout Movement all over the non-communist world.

A natural question that arose during those times was what was the reason for the existence of the Russian Scout Movement in exile? Could not the Russian boys and girls join the Scouting associations of the countries of their asylum? The simple answer was that most Russian Scout leaders of the time wanted to preserve the Scouting ideals, which had developed in pre revolutionary Russia, for the day when Russia would be free again, thereby re-igniting the Scouting flame all over Russia once again.

In the late 1950s, the Russian Scouting Association ORUR, also known as the Pathfinders, issued four commemoration stamps.

The first stamp commemorates the founding of the first Scout troop in Pavlovsk near St. Petersburg in April 1909.

The second stamp commemorates the suppression of organized scouting in Russia after 1923, when more than a thousand Scout leaders were executed or sent to concentration camps, particularly the Solovetski concentration camp, a former monastery in the White Sea.

The third stamp commemorates those who had died and those who had survived the communist and Nazi persecutions. They wear this badge of honour for loyalty. The deceased are still remembered on Remembrance Day.

The fourth stamp symbolizes the world brotherhood of Scouting which, to be real, had to include the youth of the enslaved nations (as frequently it did not).

69 UP SOAR THE FALCONS LIKE THE EAGLES

Unlike those in Europe and the Middle East, the Russian Scouts in China and Manchuria were not harassed by the Chinese, or later by the Japanese, only by the communist forces after 1945. Hence, in Manchuria, Russian Scouting ceased to exist with the entry of the Soviet forces in August 1945 and in the rest of China – mainly Tien-tsin and Shanghai – by 1949. However, thousands of Russian Scouts had passed through Europe and China between 1920 and 1949. When several thousand Russian refugees left Shanghai in 1948/49 and lived in transit on the small island of Tubabao in the Philippines, the Scouts came to the rescue. They helped in the erecting of a tent city, hygienic methods of drinking water distribution, garbage disposal and toilet blocks and with a number of other practical daily needs. At night, there were regular Scout campfire yarns and sing-alongs. Many parents and friends joined in. The Scouts helped in keeping up the morale and hopes of a better tomorrow in the middle of a Pacific island jungle full of insects, reptiles and unbearable heat in the middle of nowhere. The island was a transit camp for about three years, on the average just under a year per family. From there the Russian refugees made their way to North and South America, Australia and a few sick oldies to France – as France never forgot how the Russian soldiers gave their lives for France during World War I.

When old scouts meet Rev M. Protopopoff (Vic) & Reserve Scm A. Vassilieff (NSW) annual scout camp Kentlyn circa 1980

70 THE LOVE OF MY YOUTH - PRELUDE TO A POSTSCRIPT

As the dawn breaks in the east, 'tis time
To depart our native camp fire...
Our Scouts' beloved parting campfire song

As I vividly recall, it was over five decades ago that I joined the Scouts in June 1956. As mentioned earlier, the meetings were then held in George Street, Sydney, near Central Railway. I was able to get to the weekly meetings on Sunday afternoons by tram from Newtown. My first Scout Commissioner was M.M. Plehanoff. He started his Scouting career in 1917, back in the Russian Far East in Nikolsk Usuriysk. Plehanoff was a civil war refugee. After a few years in Manchuria, by 1927, he arrived in Shanghai where eventually he became a Group Scoutmaster. He came to Sydney via the Philippines in 1949. In 1959, he migrated to Los Angeles, USA. Shortly after, at the young age of his early sixties he, to my knowledge, married for the first time. His active Scouting career then ended. He lived to the ripe old age of about 80 plus. He foretold one thing before he left for the USA, that a life long colleague of mine, Nikita Gileff, whom I met at my first meeting would one day reach the top of the Scout tree.

Unlike myself, Nick remains in the Scouts to the present day and holds the position of Senior Scout for the Russian Scouts – NORS.

As the Russian Scouting organisation went into exile after its exodus from Russia it became geographically split in two parts of the world, in essence Europe and China, prior to its further exodus to the *new world.*

As in Europe, and later the Americas and Australia, the Russian Scout Movement in exile evolved into two separate parallel organisations after World War II. The National Organisation of Russian Scouts (NORS) from 1919 and the Organisation of Russian Scout Youth (ORUR) mainly postwar later incorporated as *Pathfinders.*

In Australia, both branches commenced their work at about the same time after 1949. NORS on a centralised basis mainly in Sydney and ORUR decentralised throughout southeastern states with its headquarters initially in Melbourne and later until 2006 in Adelaide.

In 1959, the Sydney NORS Group split up. Some of us left and joined ORUR. Thereby extending the ORUR Movement to Sydney with its local headquarters in Croydon, in the grounds of the Archbishop's residence. In the early 1980s, ORUR moved its group to Strathfield after NORS had moved its location. At varying times both NORS and ORUR experienced peaks and troughs in its numbers. Today NORS continues its active existence with a good active cadre of Scoutmasters in Sydney.

By the mid 1990s, ORUR, owing to the declining numbers of the Sydney group, left its Strathfield premises. Scm. G. Skorniakoff and later Scm. G. Kent represented the Sydney lone Scout/Scoutmaster group in Sydney. Late in 2006, Scm. G. Kent was elected as the new National Commissioner for ORUR.

The Sydney ORUR Group experienced two periods of intense activity in the course of its existence. The first was from 1959 to

1964 and the second from 1969 to 1976. During those periods, the group had a good cadre of Scoutmasters: achievement levels were high and membership was in the vicinity of seventy people comprising four subsidiary units. These were a Rover Crew, a Boy Scout Troop, a Girl Guide Troop and a Mixed Brownie and Wolf Cub Pack. The group also had a small lone – Scout representation during the seventies in Wollongong and Canberra.

The annual camps were usually held at Kentlyn /Campbelltown near Georges River on the Russian Orthodox Monastery grounds. Regular mini jamborees of ORUR in Australia were held at either Campbelltown or Noojee in Victoria.

What is most significant about the Sydney group is that all its Group Scoutmasters beginning with Scm. M.A. Alekseeva, L.S. Apollonov (the longest serving and who was also Assistant Commissioner of ORUR in Australia) and M.D. Korovnikow made significant contributions to the Russian Scout Movement in general. Apart from contributing to the bringing up of good citizens, their major objectives were always to reunite the movement of ORUR and NORS and have Scouting reborn in the new Russia. These dreams, especially the reunification, were shared by most of ORUR, but particularly the Sydney group, which had many of its friends and colleagues in the Sydney NORS movement.

ORUR and NORS are today united in Russia and are part of the World Scout Movement, but abroad both subsidiaries are semi-autonomous and continue to work independently but in harmony with each other.

Although the re-emergence of Scouting in Russia occurred mainly with the efforts of ORUR from the USA, both NORS and ORUR worldwide made significant contributions, with a number of NORS and ORUR Scoutmasters making frequent visits to attend Scout camps and meetings in Russia.

During my 25 active years in Scouting, I had many friends and a number of mentors, R. Joukoff from Melbourne and N. Donner from Adelaide amongst them. But, my first and dearest mentor and friend as mentioned once before was a returned (British) army ex-serviceman – World War II and ten-year Malaya veteran – Scm. Peter Sokoloff. He was a Russian Cossack by birth. The boys and girls of my time loved him. The life that he had as a soldier and the wounds he had suffered in the course of his (time with the Colours) Service denied him and his devoted wife the joy of having children. However, this cross in no way deterred him from having a house full of teenage Scouts who shared many happy hours – and some sad ones – with him. On a personal note, it is a matter of pride to me that he took the place of my father on my wedding day. The following year, when he was 59, he died of lung cancer as a result of chain smoking and was sadly missed by Russian Scouts and Scoutmasters all over Australia. His dying words were "I am so disappointed that I will not live to see free Russia".

These are my brief recollections of the Russian Scout Movement, particularly that of the ORUR in Sydney in which I participated at different times as either a Troop Scm., Rover Scm. and/or Assistant Group Scm. I still keep in touch with many of my colleagues as a Scoutmaster in reserve. Both of the NORS and ORUR Sydney branches for a long time were members of the Russian Ethnic Community Council in NSW. The ORUR Branch in Victoria is still a member of the Russian Ethnic Community Council of Victoria. Many of the members of both the ORUR and the NORS have played active roles in setting up, developing and participating in other community organizations in Australia and overseas. Looking back now they were the best days of my youth and practically all the boys and girls that I associated with, made good and worthy citizens wherever they settled.

71 A DAY IN A SCOUT CAMP

0600		Reveille
0605	0625	Physical exercises
0630	0730	Wash up, tents and camp clean up
0735	0800	Raising the flag and orders of the day
0805	0835	Breakfast
0840	0915	Camp and tent inspection
0920	1120	Scout studies and exercises
1125	1230	Swimming
1245	1330	Lunch
1340	1410	Quiet time
1410	1510	Free time
1510	1645	Sport and games
1650	1750	Swimming
1800	1845	Dinner
1900	1920	Lowering the flag
1920	2010	Patrol leaders' council
2010	2120	Camp fire
2125	2140	Milk and preparation for sleep
2145		Signal to tents
2200		Last post

72 TALES FROM THE SCOUTING PAST

This tale is an excerpt from The Russian Scout News No. 3 Yale Sta. Connecticut, USA, July, 1958 – as was relayed by a former Scout – later a bishop of' the Russian Orthodox Church abroad.

In the Manchurian taiga there is something mysterious in this name designating the vast territory covered by the Manchurian forest. Flora and fauna are most curious. Coniferous and tropical trees grow together. Bobcats, bears, foxes and wolves are found alongside the Siberian tiger. Camping in the taiga was a real adventure where a night watch had to be kept to protect the campers from animal and man.

We came to Manchuria during the Revolution. My Scout troop was transferred in its total numbers and we went on with our activities almost without transition. We were planning a summer camp and needed money badly to buy equipment. One of us suggested a rather unusual means of reaching our goal. Thousands of years ago, giant beetles used to live on our planet, and geologists are still finding their fossils in Jurassic strata. These very same beetles could be found in Manchuria, alive – any collector would have paid "cash on the barrel" to obtain a single live specimen. We therefore planned special raids into the taiga to try to catch those huge insects.

On one-of these errands, we were suddenly overtaken by a storm and were forced to seek refuge in a huge cave on the rocky side of the hill. On the floor at the very entrance of our shelter, we discovered a mark on the ground. It was the imprint of a foot, which doubtless belonged to a huge feline. With the help of a torch we examined it and were rather dismayed to find it even bigger than that of a tiger. There was nothing reassuring in this discovery and some of us panicked. Why? If there are still prehistoric beetles roaming around, could there not be some sort of a Sabre-toothed tiger? We all gathered at the farthest end of the cave, watching the entrance and fidgeting the triggers of our rifles in a rather nervous way. Suddenly, a pair of phosphorous green eyes appeared at the entrance and stared at us. We all fired at the same time. No one could think of sleeping after that, we were all waiting for the next pair of eyes. After all, in all the hunting stories we have ever read, the mate appears to take revenge on the killers of her male ... Nothing happened. At the first break of dawn, we cautiously peeped outside. On the rocky slope, a dead bobcat was lying, its body torn to pieces. A closer examination of the foot mark showed that it had been imprinted in the stone thousands of years ago."

73 ORUR SENIOR SCOUTMASTERS

B.B. Martino –
Nov 1945–Jul 1962+

V.V. Selivanovsky –
Aug 1962–Dec 1962

R.G. Joukoff –
Jan 1962–Dec 1973

Dr. P.A. Urtiev –
Jan 1974–1985

M.A. Danilevsly –
Jan 1985–Present

74 THE APPRENTICESHIP

I left the Scout camp early. Two days before it was over, so I could start my apprenticeship on time – 5 January 1959 – and missed out on good fun with the girls, where more kissing was being practised without the Scoutmasters knowing about it.

I quickly found that there was a pecking order, based on one's skills, to become a master toolmaker. Although I was one of the best in metalwork and technical drawing in my class in high school, after two weeks in the apprentice school at STC[62] I was graded about ninth in the intake of 10 first-year apprentices. My ego sagged, particularly when the assistant apprentice-master told me that I would be lucky if I ever became a toolmaker.

Nevertheless, like everyone else, I was put through one of the most rigorous five-year training programmes in the company, which was probably among the best in the state at that time. It was

62 Standard Telephones & Cables, an Australian/British subsidiary of an American International Telephone & Telegraph Company, decades later became French-owned Alcatel. Between 1959 to 1977, Harold Geneen operated the Multinational Company from New York, an American business executive who built the International Telephone and Telegraph Corp. (ITT) into a worldwide business conglomerate in 11 countries. During his tenure as president and CEO of ITT, the company came to exemplify the modern international corporation, with business interests in bakeries, Hartford Fire Insurance and Sheraton Hotels.

not unknown for the best toolmakers to progress to senior management levels, including one at that time – Tom Lord – who was one of the directors. The company employed about 3,000 people. Every year there was an intake of would-be toolmakers, fitter and machinists, electrical fitters, electricians, telegraph mechanics and engineering cadets – production/industrial, mechanical, electrical, electronics and communication types, at certificate, diploma and degree level.

During the next five years, I would spend time in most of the workshops of the company located at Botany Road, Alexandria, and even four months at the moulding shop tool-room in Liverpool. I would learn the basic art and science of press and sheet metalwork, component assembly, automated capstan and turret lathe production. How to machine tool-parts on every known machine such as: lathes, milling machines, horizontal and vertical shapers, surface and cylindrical, tool and jig grinders and spark erosion machines. How to: test and inspect very fine and accurate tools and piece parts using a scientific process known as engineering metrology. Further skill development included heat treatment of metals, engineering drawing and design and finally how to build and repair press tools.

It was considered one of the top trades one could learn at that time. Very often toolmakers went on and received further qualifications in mechanical or production engineering and sometimes even management. That was the route that I took and somehow muddled through, with some inner voice telling me that I wanted to learn more.

During my first year of apprenticeship, after work I trained in boxing welter-weight-division at the Newtown Police Boys Club, trying to emulate my father. After six months, I was disappointed with my progress. In a few two rounds training fights I would do well in the first round but run out of steam by the middle of the second round. My breathing needed much improvement and probably significantly much more training. I even did better in the on and off Greco/Roman wrestling which came more naturally to me than boxing. But my father was a great boxer and not a wrestler. Boxing had a greater appeal to me. I also wanted to improve my academic knowledge and needed to study a year part-time in higher maths and science in order to be accredited for entry into Mechanical Engineering at a Technical College. While I was considering what to do, my sister's boyfriend, Vlad Anikijenko, who also worked with me at STC as a metallurgist gave me this advice: "What do you want to be – a boxer or an engineer? As an engineer, you will raise your status and be able to support your family better than as boxer and a tradesman. The odds of becoming a great boxer are slim and you could become punch-drunk and get cauliflower ears. On the other hand, the company will probably support you in furthering your education even while you are still apprenticed to a toolmaker, or at least after you complete your apprenticeship successfully."

Along the way, I met some very interesting people whose advice I often took and profited from. From the bottom of the pecking order, somehow I progressed. By the time I finished my trade I was married, a corporal in the CMF and studying part-time second year Mechanical Engineering Certificate (the following year I converted to Production Engineering, which I was better suited for) at Sydney Technical College. Two months after that I was the first out of my intake group of 10 to be promoted to a Production Planning Assistant, located in a clean engineering office environment but still spending half my time in workshops and assembly lines – solving problems. The prophecy of my apprentice master was partly true. I was not going to be a toolmaker. I did, however, in time become a production-planning engineer, not a boxer.

75 CITIZENS MILITARY FORCE (CMF)

(Historical information about our First Reserves in this chapter, is based on the *Reserve Forces Day* Commemorative Booklet 1998 illustrated on p245.)[63]

Australia's military history began with the British marines, who came with the first fleet to operate the penal colonies and to set up outposts on the east coast of Australia. British Garrison troops remained in Australia for nearly one hundred years.

On Norfolk Island, in 1788 and 1794 there were brief levying enlistments of free-settler citizen force members to assist law and order. In neither case were these formally constituted forces.

September 1800 saw the raising of the first formally authorised forces in New South Wales, initially by levy of prescribed free persons, by Governor Hunter. They were known as the Loyal Sydney and Parramatta Associations and the Governor appointed their officers with fifty rank and files in each establishment.

Raised to assist in both defence and local law and order arenas, they evolved into a volunteer force over their intermittently active lives from 1800 to 1810. It is from this Corps that the Australian Army (and particularly the Reserve's) claims descend.

Britain eventually realized the need for greater empowerment

63 Refer Reference for acknowledgement

by the colonies to assume increased defence responsibilities. This realization only came after persistent requests, first by Governor Macquarie in 1814 and then by Captain MacArthur in 1825 and 1851. Britain's growing awareness of Australia's increased vulnerability, combined with the outbreak of the Crimean War in 1854, prompted the formation of volunteer forces in New South Wales, Victoria and South Australia. Since that time, part-time forces continued to be in existence in Australia despite the fluctuations of public interest or budgetary constraints.

The Inaugural Reserve Forces Day held on 1 July 1998 celebrated fifty years service to the nation by Reservists since its reformation after World War II. As the War ended, the combined numbers of the three services – Army, Navy and Air Force, dropped from a peak of 681,220 in 1944 to 50,732 by 1949. A number of dignitaries observed the Parade. The most decorated and respected was the former Governor of NSW – Sir Roden Cutler VC AK KCMG KCVO CBE. He was the National Chairman of this Historic Occasion.

Historically the Reserve or Militia tradition has been the mainstay of Australia's military forces. After World War II, units were disbanded as they returned to Australia. From 1947 an Australian Regular Army (ARA) was established. The old pre-war militia was also reformed to continue the proud service of citizen soldiering by backing up and augmenting the Regular Army. It was renamed as the Citizen Military Forces (CMF). The end of World War II did not herald an era of peace. Australian service members continued to be engaged in occupation duties in Japan. When North Korea invaded South Korea on 25 June 1950, Australia was one of a number of United Nations member countries, that went to the aid of the South Koreans.

The 3rd battalion, Royal Australian Regiment, formed from units of the second AIF on 26 July 1950 and later reinforced by Regular Soldiers, was committed to the Korean conflict.

This conflict marked the beginning of a significant Regular

Army for Australia and the three battalions of the RAR became the nucleus of Australia's postwar army. They provided the standing force required for immediate action in a national emergency.

During 1950 to 1953 when the three battalions of the RAR served in Korea, the Australian Government introduced National Service in 1951. Under this scheme, all 18-year-old men were required to serve 98 days full time training followed by three years part-time service in the CMF. Trainees could elect to serve six months full time in the RAN, ARA or RAAF as an alternative to the CMF service.

The Korean conflict saw an increase in defence expenditure and the permanent force expanded to nearly 57,000 with 91,000 in the Citizen Forces. The latter had further expanded to 95,000 by 1956 because of the National Service policy.

By 1961, with the nation's population at approximately 10 million, the Permanent forces had dropped to 46,000 and the Citizen forces to 35,000.

A new recruitment drive in 1961 encouraged me to join the CMF and a Scout friend of mine, Wally Wayne, to join the regulars.

In the meantime, the Australian Government had committed elements of the three services to the quelling of the terrorist uprising in Malaysia and to the development of the Pacific Islands Regiment in Papua New Guinea.

76 I'M IN THE ARMY NOW

In March 1961, I joined the CMF in the Royal Australian Electrical and Mechanical Engineers (RAEME) Corps.

The Corps of RAEME has had a short but glorious history. It was only officially established in 1942 (the year of my birth) when the repair facilities of the Ordnance Corps (AAOC) and the Service Corps (RASC) were combined to form the Australian Electrical and Mechanical Engineers Corps (AEME).

The first of December 1942 is generally acknowledged as the Corps's birthday because this was the date of the Order declaring the creation of AEME.

In 1948, His Majesty King George VI recognised the dedicated performance of the AEME tradesman during World War II, when he granted the Corps the title 'The Royal Corps of Electrical and Mechanical Engineers'.

I joined the CMF against my mother's wishes. It was the only time that I ever blackmailed my poor mother. In those days, I needed my mother's signature, as I was only 18. She refused on the basis that if there were a war I would have to go. I of course assured her there would not be any war in the short term. Anyway, if there were I would not be on the front line, as RAEME was a supporting and not a fighting unit. However, I told mum if she would not give her approval now, when I turned 21 I would join a fighting arm like the commandoes. She signed immediately. I felt terrible in doing it. Fortunately, Vietnam did not occur until my discharge four years later.

About 18 months after I joined, our RAEME group was broken up into Light Aid Detachments (LAD). We were attached to different fighting arms and supporting services such as: Armour, Artillery, Anti-Aircraft Batteries, Transport and so on. I was attached to the 7th Field Regiment Royal Australian Artillery. We were referred to as 7th Fd. Regt. RAA LAD – (RAEME) – CMF.

The fortnightly camps and weekend bivouacs provided the basic training for young men like me to be at the ready if the need arose. It had sufficient realism and challenge to be of interest to me. It included: reconnaissance, the repair and recovery of vehicles and equipment and exercises in the various operations of war (such as Defence, Ambush, Seek and Destroy) with blank ammunition and Inter Regimental Artillery exercises. In addition, there was target practice twice a year at the rifle range where small arms were fired. Sometimes we had special weekend exercises like attacking the enemy along a river route with the use of zodiac inflatables. Another was our field base workshop under siege by enemy guerrillas, i.e. returned Australian Regular Army advisers from Laos who were aware of the unfolding events in South East Asia prior to the Vietnam conflict. They gave us a taste of the real situation by keeping our unit awake, several nights in a row under pretend enemy fire and other enemy trickery.

During my time in the CMF, I had completed four fortnight annual training camps, about 20 weekend bivouacs, Junior and Senior – Non Commissioned Officer (NCO) exams, two heavy vehicle driver courses, Small Arms and Field Gun Artificer courses. For the last one and a half years as a Corporal Small Arms Fitter my duties included: small arms repair, service on the rifle range, repair of generators, battery chargers, minor repair to vehicles and other equipment in training camps and attending field firing practice of 25 Pdr. Field Guns, while attached to the 7th Fd. Regt. RAA. It was about that time that another NCO and I were offered the opportunity of applying for Regular Officer Candidate School at Portsea, Victoria. I was ready to sign up the following day; however, my wife-to-be at that time clearly spelled out my two choices – a regular army career or marriage. Women can be ruthless! I guess my love for Alexandra won. And although I often reminded her of my sacrifice for her, she sacrificed several times over when she put up with raising two children while I continued my part-time studies for many years to come. She might also have saved my life as Vietnam was around the corner. In the process of my over involvement with the army, my part-time studies suffered and I had to repeat some subjects.

By the end of 1964 whilst on the verge of receiving my third stripe, reluctantly my army career ended. This was due to my new role, as a husband and a father-to-be, as well as the earlier promotion that I received from a tradesman to a junior engineer, which required my commitment to complete my part-time studies in Production Engineering satisfactorily.

Reserve Forces 50 year Commemoration Medal

77 VIETNAM

In 1964, owing to the deteriorating strategic situation in South East Asia, the Australian Government re-introduced National Service to expand its military forces. At the request of the South Vietnam Government and in consultation with the United States Government, Australia sent an infantry battalion to South Vietnam in 1965.

By 1967 a force of 8,000 personnel were deployed in South Vietnam. This force was maintained until wind-down and withdrawal took place between 1970 and 1972. A large number of National Service Conscriptees saw service in Vietnam, as did members of the CMF. Among regular army servicemen were two friends of mine (photo on p246). Staff Sergeant Walter Wayne was one of my closest friends from my Scout days. Wally introduced me to Sergeant John Binham, who is a very colourful and interesting person and who in turn wrote a book on his wartime experiences, *Three Wars a Soldier – Korea, Malaysia and Vietnam.*

78 REVIEW AND CHANGE

A review of the CMF in 1974, aimed at making it a more effective and viable force in Australia's defence, resulted in its renaming as the Australian Army Reserve. The review called for the Army Reserve to operate under the same functional command structure as the Regular Army, with direct representation in each of the three commands.

Part-time volunteer Australian servicemen have served as United Nations Peacekeepers, as crews of naval vessels sailing between Australia and overseas posts and on flood disaster rescue and relief. They have served on full-time duty, attached to units of the Regular components of the Australian Army as well as with the British, United States and other armies overseas.

At the turn of the 21st century, the 25,000-strong Army Reserve is an important element of our national defence and standby as a well-trained volunteer force backing up the Australian Regular Army in its primary role of national defence. It is comprised of people from all walks of life and from every corner of the country, with more than 250 Army reserve units based in cities and towns throughout Australia.

The Australian Army Reserve, together with the Australian Regular Army, forms one of the largest and most diverse organisations in Australia; an organisation involving men and women who are doing something for themselves and for their country. The beginning of the 21st century saw Australian Reserves again alongside their Regular counterparts in new conflicts, namely: East Timor, Iraq, Bougainville and the Solomons.

Perhaps if more young men and women today served in such organisations as the Army Reserves, the Scout Movement, the Peace Corps or other similar organisations there would be less civil disobedience and street crime. Certainly, both the Scouting Movement and the Army Reserves gave me my start in life and set values for me for the rest of my life.

79 MYSTICISM AND THEOSOPHY

By my late teens and early twenties, I was into all sorts of things. The Scouts, the Army Reserves, part-time studies, reading books that I could seldom understand: psychology, astronomy, politics, comparative religions and the teachings of the mystics. I guess I was searching for greater meaning to life, often at the expense of sleep, relying on my abundance of energy.

Mysticism and theosophy for a while provided me with great interest. The mystics that caught my attention were G.I. Gurdjieff, P.D. Ouspensky and to a lesser extent Helena P. Blavatsky.

Mysticism sometimes has been accused of passing off psychological states for metaphysical experiences. However, the psychological base has never been questioned seriously. Perhaps it is more proper to call it autology – the science of self. If the word psychology is to be retained, it must be in the original sense of the word now discarded. Early last century the contrast between the old and the new has been well expressed by the Russian philosopher and mystic P.D. Ouspensky:

> *Never in history has psychology stood at so low a level, lost all touch with its origin and meaning, perhaps the oldest science*

and, unfortunately, in its most essential features, a forgotten science, the science of [man's] possible evolution.

Mysticism is that science in which the psychology of man mingles with the psychology of God. The major change or orientation is from the level of the profane to the sacred, an awareness of the divine in man and outside.

A Methodist leader – John Wesley – revealed the source and goal of such a psychology in the 18th century. His dying words were "The best of all is this: that God is with us."

According to the teachers of Eastern mysticism a mark of mystic life is the great excess or influx of energy and enlarged awareness, so much so that the man who obtains the vision becomes, as it were, another being. Mansions of the mind, maqam-place (Arabic), and bhumi-land (Sanskrit), open up to the gaze of the initiate, a traveller of the worlds. This means a renewal or conversion until one knows that the earth alone is not man's teacher. The mystics begin to draw their sustenance from super sensuous sources. They have drunk the Infinite like a giant's wine, and a hidden bliss, knowledge, and power begin to sweep through the gates of their senses.

Gurdjieff (1872-1949), a Greco-Armenian mystic and philosopher, founded an influential quasi-religious movement. The details of his early life are uncertain, but he is thought to have spent his early adult years travelling in northeast Africa, the Middle East, India, and especially Central Asia, where he was exposed to various spiritual traditions. He moved to Moscow about 1913 and began teaching there and later in Petrograd (St. Petersburg). He returned to the Caucasus at the outbreak of the Russian Revolution in 1917 where some of his followers rejoined him.

Gurdjieff established the Institute for the Harmonious Development of Man in 1919 at Tiflis (Tbilisi), Georgia; which was re-established at Fontainebleau, France, in 1922. Its members, many from prominent backgrounds, lived a virtually monastic life, except for a few banquets, at which Gurdjieff would engage in probing dialogue and at which his writings were read. Ritual exercises and dance were also part of the regimen, regularly accompanied by music composed by Gurdjieff and an associate. Performers from the institute appeared in Paris in 1923 and in four US cities the following year and brought considerable attention to Gurdjieff's work. P.D. Ouspensky introduced Gurdjieff's teachings to Western readers in an understandable intellectual form. Gurdjieff's basic assertion was that human life as ordinarily lived is similar to sleep; transcendence of the sleeping state required work, but when it was achieved, an individual could reach remarkable levels of vitality and awareness. The Fontainebleau centre was closed in 1933, but Gurdjieff continued teaching in Paris until his death.

I never reached that transcendental state but my understanding of life was perhaps a little more enriched. Instead of fragmentising my interests, I increasingly began to focus my energies into work, part-time studies and raising a family. I also decided that preoccupation in the supernatural was not my prime call and that perhaps as in my mother's case over 30 years earlier, the words of Sir Arthur Conan Doyle had a point when he said: "Obsession with the supernatural has been the ruin of many an exceptional intellect."

80 REHABILITATION

Reading an extract of my father's file often drained me of emotion. While we suffered in Harbin, he suffered in a GULAG in Kazahstan. The physical and mental anguish of both my parents is too difficult too describe. But at last he was to get some restitution. Below is an excerpt from the KGB files made by an intermediary. For authenticity apart from translation no attempt is made to change the grammar or the vocabulary used. As a result of my father's protest his case was reviewed in 1963.

1963 Protest

Resulting from a protest by the accused and in order of surveillance arrangement over the case of Vassilieff V.A. as handed down by the troika resolution of the PP OGPU of the Moscow Region dated 13.07.33. The case is now being reviewed.

Vassilieff V.A. was declared guilty under the article 59.3 of the Criminal Code of the RSFSR and convicted to three years internment.

Based on the supplementary resolution by the same troika his belongings were confiscated. Together with Vassilieff V.A.

and as part of the same case there were six convictions in all including Haritonov D.E. and Azarov A.P.

Vassilieff V.A. was accused of; that in April 1933 together with a former representative of the operational sector of the PP OGPU of the Moscow region – Haritonov D.E. (sentenced to receive capital punishment) under a pretext of a search of the premises with the aim of personal gain committed a burglary of Mr. Lobanov's flat. From whose premises manufactured goods were removed and that Lobanov himself was placed under unlawful temporary arrest.

The verdict against Vassilieff V.A. is considered incorrect and is subject to be revoked on the following basis:

The case does establish that Vassilieff V.A. indeed one time accompanied former OGPU agent Haritonov D.E. at his request and participated in the burglary. However, Vassilieff's V.A. testimony and review of the evidence shows that he was acting in the blind and was unaware that Haritonov was organizing burglaries under the guise of searches ...

Dated 19 November 1963

Signed Deputy General Public Prosecutor A. Mishutin

A further extract from the KGB file: In 1947, Vassilieff V.A. was sentenced a second time under article 58-4 of the Criminal Code – RSFSR by a Special Meeting under the auspices of the MVD (another forerunner to the KGB) USSR:

Comrade Vassilieff lives in Kazakhstan, Karagandskaya Region, in the city of Timirtau, Gertsina St, House No 1 flat 34. He was released after nine years in a GULAG. His rights have been restored. For the past eight years, he has worked as an engineer.

At 50 years of age through a friend of his who worked at the Union Newspaper – *Izvestia* – Vassilieff wrote to a newspaper. Copy of the letter is attached to his case file.

A brief outline of his letter:

Dear Alexei Ivanovich,

In January 1931 when I was 17 years old, I came to Moscow. My father remained in Harbin. A year and a half after my arrival he died in a Japanese gaol owing to torture by the Japanese Gendarmes...

Once Haritonov called me out, showed me an official search order of premises, and offered me to accompany him as an official search witness. (Tr. note: you would not want to refuse a KGB request particularly if you are young and naïve.) Haritonov completed the search and found nothing but for some reason took a few meters of calico. Soon it became clear that Haritonov was a rogue and performed illegal removal of valuables from premises that he searched. In the capacity of official search witnesses he recruited his acquaintances, those that he thought he could trust. I turned out to be such a convenient person as I related to him with extreme trust and respect ....

By an unfortunate chance,[64] *my GULAG turned out to be within close proximity of the Manchurian border. Together with two others, I escaped and crossed the border into Manchuria. I was guided by one motive to prove my innocence. As soon as I arrived in Harbin, I approached the Soviet Consulate with the respective request of my innocence. I was simply tossed out and refused a hearing.*

At the start of World War II, I again approached the Soviet Consulate with a request to be sent to the front even as a

64 In order to acquire full acquittal – rehabilitation I believe my father tried to imply his regret in escaping from the GULAG to strengthen his case for a full exoneration.

member of the penal battalion, again the Consulate ignored me and replied that the homeland could do without people like me.

After my escape, during the days of difficulty and low morale I beat up a Japanese Gendarme and was forced to flee from Harbin to Shanghai. There I vegetated until 1945. (Tr. note: the term vegetates was probably used to please the authority that period in Shanghai was perhaps the best in his life.) When our Red Army occupied Manchuria, I together with my family and with great difficulty returned to Harbin in order to return to the motherland. (Tr. note: he trusted another apparatchik – Stalin who promised to forgive everyone their sins if they returned and helped to rebuild the motherland.) I was met simply – arrested and sent to Alma-Ata Kazakhstan where I was incarcerated together with the Japanese in a Prisoner of War (POW) Camp. For a long time they could not find an appropriate article under which to sentence me, then they dressed me into a Japanese uniform and declared me a POW accusing me of fighting against the motherland. From my overall state and the condition I was in, I contracted typhoid after which I was kept in solitary, questioned and requested to confess that I was a spy. From a healthy and a strong former athlete of 180 cm tall, I was reduced to a skeleton of 46 kg. For lack of evidence my case was sent to Moscow where I was convicted by a special meeting and was finally sentenced for 10 years under article 58.4.

I was released after nine years and as they say paid for my guilt. But you can only pay for your guilt if you're guilty, an innocent person has nothing to redeem.

My father was tortured to death by the Japanese Gendarmes, my wife and children are under torment and starvation in Harbin, because of me, as I brought them there in order to take them to the motherland ...

At the present time I am on leave in Moscow, which I

specifically took to personally deliver to you this letter and to wait for a reply. I live in: Kazakhstan SSR, Karagandskaya Region, in the city of Timirtau, Gertsina St, House No., 1 flat 34.

I shall remain in Moscow until 26 August 1963 at Spartak St, House No. 7, flat 34.

Signature
7-9-63

The publication of the above letter in the newspaper is recorded as unknown by the authorities. However, a copy of the letter was on file. The letter apparently gave a stimulus for a speedy resolution of Vassilieff's rehabilitation, as the General Prosecutors' Office of the USSR reviewed it together with the attached documentary evidence regarding his case.

Certificate of Rehabilitation from 6 December 1963 is issued by the Moscow Regional Court on 30.11.63, rescinding the resolution No. 1530 by the Troika representing PP OGPU of the Moscow Region from 13 July 1933 and 4 October 1933 in regard to Vassilieff Vladimir Alexandravich, DOB 1913, former employee chauffeur at the auto depot of the Narkomindela USSR and the case against him for lack of evidence is dismissed.

President Moscow Regional Court A. Korotkov

Vassilieff V.A. is thereby totally rehabilitated and exonerated from the two convictions; he is to be compensated by the Federal Bank of the USSR for the value of his confiscated belongings during his arrest in 1933. His belongings and their value are outlined in his case file for the return after his release, as also are the appropriate bank documents for the transfer of the financial amount due to him.

7 FAMILY, CAREER AND COMMUNITY

1965-1980

81 ENGINEER OR MANAGER

An inner force kept on pushing me to improve and develop myself further. Following the example of two of my senior colleagues at STC – Ken Milton and Barry Elliott – after completing Production Engineering I did another four year TAFE course in Management. It gave me a more rounded view of business enterprise. I studied Industrial Psychology, Theory and Practice of Management, Financial, Personal, Production, Marketing and General Management in a teamwork atmosphere.

Also, following the advice of my Senior Engineering colleagues I decided to move around, widen my expertise and get my bum burnt – for only then you really learn your profession, rather than staying with the one company, no matter how good the company is. Each time I moved, I improved my salary and expertise and got my bum burnt. I spent a year with Centre Industries – Spastic Centre as a Project Engineer, then almost two years with AWA[65] as a Production Planner-Senior and finally with my lifelong Semi-Government Authority – MWS&DB[66] – Sydney Water. I joined the organisation as a Management Services officer – an Internal

65 Amalgamated Wireless of Australasia. A large Australian-owned Communication and Electrical Consumer goods, manufacturing Company – no longer in existence.

66 Metropolitan Water, Sewerage & Drainage Board.

Management Consultant. After ten years and internal deregulation I diversified into other fields. Introducing Ergonomics in the Waterboard. Hence I became known there as a Father of Ergonomics. Then I moved on as a middle manager in various roles, sometimes acting for lengthy periods in senior management positions. My areas included Occupational Health and Safety, Environmental Resourcing, Human Resource Planning and Project Management, Support Manager in an International Clean Waterways Consortium and finally as a Business Administration Manager in a Utilities Planning Unit. In 1981, I was pleasantly rewarded when the Institution of Engineers, Australia invited me to become a full member as Professional Engineer. A membership which I kept until well after my retirement.

It was an interesting career full of excitement, change, new developments, at times disappointment, but overall I felt I made a worthwhile contribution to the organisation. When I retired, the organisation was left with about 4,000 people, less than a quarter of the size when I started in 1971.

82 FAMILY OR COMMUNITY

With my hectic involvement in Scouting, Army Reserves and part-time studies, it is a wonder I had time enough for work let alone to find a soul mate. By the age of 19, I was devastated when my first relationship – puppy-love with a girl-guide from Melbourne lasting 12 months – ended unsuccessfully. I was then even more determined to pursue my educational development with greater zeal and to leave affairs of the heart for another time. It was about five months after in May while on an army course, that I went to a party and met a girl, whose girlfriends – Larissa Shevchenko and Elena Zolotorenko – were in my Scout Group. These two girls had been trying to set me up for a while with a friend of theirs, as I was becoming much too serious and not the same cheerful and high-spirited youth that I used to be. Their efforts proved to be not in vain.

What gave them the initial idea was that our Christian names were the same – Alexander and Alexandra (Shurick and Shura). Larissa further told me that Shura was dux of the year of Marrickville Junior High, which they both attended prior to Shura Matriculating from Fort St. and enrolling in a Pharmacy/Science Degree at Sydney University. As I got to know Shura more, a number of similarities and/or coincidences began to emerge. Apart from our similar names and being a friend of my friends, her mother, Dasha Wownenko, was a former school colleague of my Group Scoutmistress, Marina Alexeiva, back in the 1930s in Paris, France, and they came out to Australia on the same ship, the *SS Kastelbianko.*

Unlike the parents of my previous girlfriend, Dasha and Ivan accepted me as I was – a toolmaker apprentice (and not an Engineer or a Doctor-to-be). I for some time avoided telling them that I was studying part-time to become an Engineer, as I wanted to be accepted for who I was, not for whom I might be one day. Only some time later when her parents noticed that our relationship was becoming quite serious did her father casually ask me, whether I had considered continuing with my studies, after I had finished with toolmaking at the end of the year. He was pleasantly surprised when I said that I was concurrently completing my second year Engineering Certificate at TAFE. Shortly thereafter, my request for his daughter's hand was accepted, although with some initial reservation that we were too young – which we were. However, her parents finally gave in. This increased my resolve to continue my professional development in order to be able to give the best to my future family.

On 26 January 1964, we were married at Croydon Archbishop's Chapel by Rev. Nicholas Golubev. My wife and I were blessed with two children – a pigeon pair – son Vladimir-Vlad, born on 5 November 1964, and daughter Elena-Helen, born 10 January 1968. As a result of early marriage, Shura gave up her University studies in Pharmacy and converted to second year of Biology Certificate at TAFE. But, soon after, she became pregnant with our first child requiring her to give up both her studies and her career. During the first year of marriage we had to make many adjustments. Her parents offered us cheap accommodation until we saved enough for our first home deposit. However, in April that year while I was away in my Army camp in preparation for anticipated hostilities in Laos or Vietnam, I received a telegram that my wife's father died unexpectedly. I terminated my training and was immediately brought home.

Ivan Wownenko, a large kind man, at the age of 61 died from a heart attack on his way to work. Needless to say the family was distraught for a long time. I was left as the only male in the house with three women – my wife, mother-in-law and Babushka Elena. Being young I was not always sensitive to their needs. It was a trying but eventful time. By the end of the year, as mentioned earlier, I had resigned from the Army Reserves, passed four and failed a couple of my engineering subjects and become a father. There was also a new man in the house – young Vova. His birth was received with much joy and helped compensate for the earlier loss in the family.

As hard as it was for Shura and her kin, we needed to make a break and get out on our own. About two kilometres away at 63 Ferry Road, Glebe, we bought our first house a two-storey semi about 65 years old. It was not much, but it was ours. I promised Shura that in about five years time we would upgrade and get ourselves a better house. Prior to our daughter being born, we bought our first car – a three year old 1964 EH Holden, a lemon, but we kept it for five years until I bought a former Waterboard two-year-old automatic station wagon. It was a beaut!

By the end of 1970, at the age of twenty eight, I completed my Management Studies. In all I studied at TAFE for twelve years and achieved one trade and two Certificates – Associate Diplomas. I thought I had enough of studying for the rest of my life. As I promised Shura, by Easter of the next year we moved to a garden suburb at 32 Robin Street, Carlingford. It was to be our family home for almost 30 years until my retirement. My professional development helped me to read economic signs and I could see that manufacturing was gradually being pushed overseas. As I was one of the last to join the AWA Engineering office, I would be one of the first casualties if the crunch came. We would probably lose our newly bought home, as we had no one to turn to if I was unemployed. The feeling of insecurity and the desire to move into the field of Management intensified my research of the job market. Meanwhile the clouds were gathering and factory staff were being laid off. Finally I was offered a Management Consulting position at the Waterboard where I started in September, 1971. By December of that year one third of the Engineering and drafting staff were laid off from AWA and similar retrenchments in other companies followed. I felt that somebody above watched over me.

The previous year after I finished my studies I returned to my Scouting activities. The whole family attended the Scout Summer Camp. Shura, with some reservation, came along too, to keep the family together but could think of other things to do. Soon after I also began taking our children to Saturday Russian Church Shool at Croydon.

As usual I did not engage in half measures. My Scouting involvement over the next five years resulted in Shura and I drifting apart. Also by 1971, after nine years of home duties and now that both children were at school Shura, went back to her laboratory work as a Laboratory technician at Sandoz Pharmaceuticals (now Norvatis) . This was further exasperating our relationship, as until then I was often spared household chores and just did the essential home maintenance jobs and some gardening. Now I had to pull my weight domestically as well. The relationship was heading for a showdown.

Meanwhile my sister separated from her husband. She left him with the eldest son – Nicholas – who was about eight years old at that time, and kept with her their seven-year-old daughter Katya and young John, who was then about two years old. My reluctance to interfere in my sister's affairs caused my senior relatives to ostracize me. Throughout this, my mother somehow kept her head and was at peace with all of us, at the same time helping my sister as much as she could.

Prior to my sister's marriage breakup and after much effort, in 1971 I was able to acquire on mum's behalf a pleasant housing commission unit for her at Malabar Heights at about the time of her retirement. She finally had her own place. Her own refrigerator, TV, telephone, and other home necessities, which until then she could not afford. While still at AWA, I was able to assist her with some items like the TV, radio and fridge with a staff discount. Her fortune teller's prediction was coming to pass. She was living a life like cheese rolling in butter as compared to the postwar years in Harbin. But there was still one more prediction that had not come to pass.

83 THE KNIGHT RETURNS

...The moment's come for sweet awakening:
Once more before me you have stood,
A transient vision of perfection,
A dream of lovely womanhood.

My heart beats fast with exultation
And once again with rapture glows;
The thrill of awe, and inspiration,
And life, and tears, and love it knows...

A. Pushkin[67]

In early August 1975 while at work my wife phoned me. It was one of those times when I was attempting to give up smoking. Shura suggested that I sit down prior to continuing with our conversation. Then she read out a telegram: "Your father is arriving tomorrow morning on a flight from Moscow via Singapore." I sat down and asked for a cigarette from one of my colleagues and began to rapidly consider all that had happened and what now needed to be done to deal with this happy but unexpected situation.

---

67 To A.P. Kern 1826 (trans. by Walter Arndt)

For many years now, my mother, then my sister and now myself had all attempted to bring my mother's beloved – our father – out to Australia. Each time there was a refusal from Moscow. On this occasion, things looked very promising and I wrote to my father asking him to tell me as soon as approval was given, so that we could appropriately prepare for his arrival. To find out by phone the day before his arrival after 30 years of separation was not exactly what I was expecting. After further discussions with Shura, she advised me that although my sister, my relatives and I were not on speaking terms I should advise them of the fact, which I did.

I immediately spoke to Valerie. All was forgotten as though we did not have any prior misunderstanding. She advised me not to tell Mum immediately but to slowly prepare her over a week. Against my own judgement I agreed, as mum's wellbeing was important to both of us. I cannot remember now whether I directly or through Valerie informed the senior relatives of my father's coming.

Early next morning, Shura and I picked up Valerie on the way to the airport and went to meet our father. As we looked at the arrival passengers coming out of the Immigration exit, I saw a reasonably tall man in a brown hat and coat and said to my sister and wife that's our father. We quickly walked up to each other, looking one another over. He was just under six foot, about two inches (five centimetres) taller than me, and said "What happened, shorty?".

We then all embraced, chatted, picked up his baggage and went to our car. Then, in stages, I dropped off my sister and then my wife at their respective workplaces and finally brought my father home. I explained to him that we were being on the cautious side with mum and would gradually explain to her of his homecoming and that they would meet within a week, which he fully accepted. We then had a cup of tea, followed by a shot or two of vodka accompanied by black bread and tinned smoked salmon. He was impressed. I was already prepared by an older friend of mine – Kon Alexandrow – that my father would be very tired after a long and exausting journey, so when he asked me if he could go to sleep for a while I quickly agreed. He awoke just after school hours as the children, followed by my wife, came home. After dinner and much chatter we all went to bed. My father shared the bedroom with his namesake – grandson. I kissed him, saying "Goodnight, papa". He responded by saying: "It has been a long time since I heard that."

That night I could not fall asleep. Apparently neither could my father. About an hour after retiring I heard him get up, go to the living room and light our kerosene heater. August nights were rather cold. My wife said, "Go on, go and join him. I know you want to." We sat together and, over cigarettes in the middle of the night with the red glow of the heater, discussed our deep feelings.

"What a dreadful price our family had to pay for my mistake," he said.

"But we are all together now," I responded. After more deep and meaningfuls, we embraced again, shed tears and finally parted and went to bed.

Over the next few days I bonded with my father and shared him with neighbours and close friends who dropped in. By Soviet law we had to go to the Soviet Consul at Edgecliff, where he had to register his arrival. My father had a sense of humour, and as we arrived and walked in to the Consular chambers, we were asked how could we be helped. He immediately responded in his strong Moscow accent: "Regards from Moscow!" Following that exclamation, the two functionaries behind their desk immediately jumped up and responded:

"Greetings, *tovarish* (comrade)!" My father then, letting them off the hook, replied: "I have come to register," after which the embarrassed officials, realising that it was just a common individual and not a high level official, became more businesslike.

I also took my father to my office and introduced him to my boss and colleagues, mentioning that he, still in his semi retirement, was a fellow industry employee – a Treatment Works Engineer from the Moscow Waterworks. I asked my boss to try and get the Vice President's approval in order that I could take my father on a tour of the Warragamba Dam and the Burragarong Lake. To my pleasant surprise approval was promptly given.

The most emotional moment of the visit was when at the end of the week I was bringing mum home from the station. By that time, mum had already worked out what was going on. Our precautions were probably unnecessary. As mum walked in to our living room, dad stood up from the lounge suite and they embraced and then sat down arm in arm. I went to the kitchen-dining room to make them a drink and broke down. After I collected myself, I again came out thinking that my life's ambition had been rewarded in seeing my parents together again. A line from an old Russian song played out in my mind – "Oh my grey-winged eagle, where have you been flying for so long?"

My cousin Milla was acting as an intermediary in trying to organise a reunion between my father and other relatives, as I was still boycotted by the seniors. We agreed that when I had finished taking dad around the countryside and had gone back to work in two weeks time that he would be delighted to meet the rest of the kinfolk and stay with the Koliagins for a few days. After their reunion and dad's return to our place, Uncle Misha began to ring us to speak to my father but never acknowledged me. I finally mentioned it to my father.

"I know Misha has always been your close friend and by now you know the situation here. I have been shunned by my senior relatives for some time now, but when Misha rings my home acting like I do not exist and just says: 'Put Vova on the phone', that is going too far. I will not tolerate his rudeness any longer, despite our difference in age. I did not do anything to any of them. Whatever misunderstanding there was, was between my sister and myself and it all started when my Aunt Tina began to dictate to me and I responded saying: 'Aunty, when you and the Koliagins have family quarrels, I do not take sides. On the contrary, I have usually attempted to encourage both sides to let bygones be bygones and make up'. This was of course interpreted as a rebuke from a young pup in his early thirties to a senior Aunt in her sixties and was never to be forgotten for the remainder of her life. Whatever she said to the Koliagins I do not know but from then on I was shunned by the rels. I am still hurt and I do not want to ruin your holiday, but if Misha wants to ring here and talk to you, he will pay me the necessary courtesy or not bother to ring again."

My father looked at me in a comprehending way, possibly realising that he missed my boyhood days and that he was talking to a grown man, something that the rels still failed to realise.

"Shurick," he said, "You can rely on me. I will make things right." And he did. From then on not only was Misha courteous on the phone, but he actually initiated conversation with me. Tina of course would never be moved. But I accepted that as her loss. Soon after we held a party for all the relatives that could come. It was a cherished moment which probably healed past wounds. My feelings were always very strong towards the Koliagins and I was glad the rift was over.

As my father's visit was drawing to an end, I asked him to consider remaining in Australia. His response was: "I promised back home I would return." His response made me lose my cool.

"And what about the NKVD promise that you would return in five minutes after they took you away back in Harbin? And mum stood for three days by the window waiting for your return? And the aftermath? What it did to her?"

"I know all that, son, and I am dreadfully sorry about my stupidity. But now I have a new life. I have been cleared of all blame. I am a full Soviet Citizen. Former GULAG interns can retire at 60 with a Government pension equivalent to two thirds of their former salary and I can supplement it with casual work. I am tired of being a second class citizen as we were in China or how I was in the USSR until my full pardon. If you succeeded getting me permanent residency, who would give me a job at my age of 63 and my poor knowledge of the English language? Where would I live? You know my weakness for vodka and complain that I drink a third of a bottle a day. Well I drink twice as much as that at home".

"I cannot guarantee everything, but I could probably get you a job such as a storeman at the Waterboard and you could live with mum in her Housing Commission unit. As far as vodka is concerned, well, you would have to work on that and at least you would be with your family," I said.

"No, son. I do not want to depend on anybody or live off anybody. I do have some pride left." Our conversation ended. I could see that I would be unable to convince him to stay, and I was not insensitive to his pride and his desire to live in the USSR as that was where he always wanted to be.

In his last few weeks, he wanted to take home with him as many material goods of high quality as he could. It was a trait common to many other visitors from the USSR who had an opportunity to see how the West lived. They wanted to return home taking back capitalist goods of value for the status that it brought them – some of which they could sell for up to five times its original price. Apart from a suitcase of clothing that we were able to give my father to take with him plus some personal effects, he, like a child, was hoping I could give him things like a Mumiya journalist camera, Parker pen and sun glasses of the best quality among other things. Most of these we could not afford ouselves for many years to come. Mum Bought him an attractive English hat. At this point I could not stop myself commenting to my father. "How can you take all these things? And what have you given to mum, who waited for you most of her life?" After his excuses I made a point of telling him: "I left you the spending money that you brought and tried to supply you with most things including a return ticket home. You could have given mum something as a going away present[68]."

When finally dad left I was left with very mixed feelings. My

68 In his defence he did bring all his kin presents when he arrived from Moscow.

sister was even more upset and did not want to discuss him at all. My mother as usual was very meek and told me not to wory about anything. About a week after she rang me and said she was worried that she might be pregnant. This time I told her not to worry and said that it was most unlikely at her age.

84 HOW TO BEND WITH THE WIND

Shortly after my father's departure and the renowned sacking of the Whitlam Government by the Governor General, my wife and I had our own falling out. All the previous pressures that we both went through nearly resulted in our marriage break-up. In retrospect one can see things more clearly. It was the compounding effect of many years of self denial and hard work, with Shura bearing the brunt of bringing up the children and me working by day and studying by night and the immediate return to community work upon the completion of my studies – with Scouting and Saturday School for the children. Adding to the strain was the cost of bringing my father out to Australia, which was largely carried by us. The pressure upon our marriage at this time was intense and in no way relieved by my feud with my relatives. Thus, with Shura's return to the workforce it ultimately resulted in a serious breakdown of communication, with both of us seeking our separate ways.

But even when we thought that we stopped loving one another, the thought of our children living in a broken home prevented us from taking the final step of separation and we, together with our children, decided instead to go on our first overseas cruise – on a Russian/Ukrainian Ship the *Taras Shevchenko,* for 16 days in the Pacific. That cruise resulted in giving us the lift that we needed, something that we repeated four years later. Other factors that influenced our decision to stay together was Shura's close family upbringing and me growing up without a father and always wanting one.

As the years went by, we learnt how to communicate better and above all to put the wellbeing of our children above our own, learning in the process that: it is easier to give than to take. I also gave up my active involvement in Scouting and contented myself with the Saturday School, where I was elected President and the most Reverend Father John Stukacz became the School Director. These were two pleasant but hard working years and a time in which I had my first success in community management and diplomacy when, as the leader of the management team, I brought about the amalgamation of two small schools. This also afforded me a chance of maintaining a remote interest in Scouting, by encouraging students to join the Scouts and on occasion attending their functions.

85 THE NEVER-ENDING CURSE

Soon after our return, I noticed mum was beginning to show the signs of mental deterioration. She had been well for seven years since her last breakdown and I began to believe that the worst was over. But now with increasing inattentiveness, glassy stares, depression and paranoia, it was clear that she had declined. She confessed that she had stopped taking her medication. So after yet another series of lengthy discussions with the hospital authorities and much emotional exhaustion, mum was re-committed to the Gladesville Mental Hospital. This was the seventh time that this had happened to her in 23 years.

It is always hard to commit someone that you love to a mental institution and particularly difficult to deal with the situation leading up to actual admission. In each case, mum did not think that she required any treatment and the verbal abuse that one had to endure while attempting to do the best for her is best left unsaid. Her mental state was in a way comparable to a play acted by Russell Crowe in the movie *A Beautiful Mind,* where the patient lives in an imaginary world of paranoid behaviour – fearing and suspecting harm from sources that are not present. It did not occur to my mother that she had a dreadful affliction derived from her experience of the NKVD, that could only be relieved by proper care and medication. As a result, I went back to smoking after seven months of abstinence.

At that time, institutionalised mental health was in the early stages of being dismantled. New policies were being advocated with greater reliance on self care. It was a stupid policy, as mental patients are usually admitted because of their failure to reason logically. How were they expected to cater for their own wellbeing if all that it took was to forget to take their prescribed medication and they were once again on the slippery slide to their abnormal behaviour. And so it was with mum: after stabilising her condition during the next two months, her doctor was ready to discharge her. I pleaded with him to keep her in longer, as it was unlikely that she would continue taking her medication once released. So he humoured me by keeping her for about a week longer.

About three months later, in the second week[69] of January 1977 when my family and I returned from a Scout camp, my sister rang, informing me that mum had collapsed and died in her flat a few days earlier. I was devastated, but over the next two days I organised mum's funeral. She was one month short of her 64th birthday.

I believe that mum reached a stage in her life where life no longer mattered. Her children and grandchildren were safe and established. She had gained, despite a lingering apprehension, what she set herself out to achieve and had also been momentarily reunited once more with the love of her life – everything that the fortune teller had promised her during the dificult days in Harbin had come to pass. What else was there to live for? Did the feelings of loss and despair of December 1945 resurface in her mind? One can only speculate. Which of course I did. To console myself I chose to believe that God was merciful and spared my mother any more pain – she had had her share. We Christians believe that God only

---

69 Mum died about 14 Jan. 1977 from thrombosis of pancreatic vein, causing internal hemorrhage.

sends us those trials and ordeals that we are capable of withstanding, and if they are too great or superfluous, then He spares us from any further pain.

Klava throughout her life was a good, decent and meek person, always putting the wellbeing of her children above her own. Accordingly her inscription reads, "Blessed be the Pure in heart for they shall see God."

8 FAMILY, CAREER AND COMMUNITY II

1980-1995

86 THE GRADUATION

In August 1974 a paper of mine was published on *Variable Working Hours* in the *Australian Machinery and Production Engineering.* It was adapted from a comprehensive report which I prepared for the Sydney MWS&DB. The paper recommended a change from the conventional working hours of nine to five or akin to, and adopt a more flexible approach of starting and finishing times with rostered days off. Examples were cited from a few pioneering organisations, mainly in Europe and a few in Australia, with a number of productivity improvements outlined with resulting benefits to both – employees and employers. Following the MWS&DB and other pioneering leaders, other public and private organisations gradually introduced the scheme in one form or another. Our scheme evolved into a nine day fortnight[70] with variable starting and finishing times. The scheme benefitted me in a way I could not foresee a few years later.

The one benefit I took up in post Whitlam Government years was free education. In 1979 at the age of 36 I went back to part-time studies. I enrolled in Business Studies at the NSW Institute of Technology (NSWIT), housed mainly in the old Anthony Hordens

70 Working longer hours each day and building up a credit of hours – providing a rostered day off each fortnight.

building (now gone) and the tower building on Broadway, both within walking distance of my workplace. With the employer's agreement I was able to break up my fortnightly rostered day into a half a day off for study purposes each week. In my first year of two semesters I passed Macro and Micro Economics, Management, Remedial and Advanced Mathematics, as I found calculus and matrices challenging initially. Accounting, which I did not particularly like, I gave away after eight weeks – so as not to affect my yearly average score. I realised that in not taking on the full three subjects per semester it may take me more than six years to finish my degree.

Fortunately I found another way. Two of my younger colleagues, Jeff Morris and Geoff Burne (future senior managers), were enrolling in post graduate business studies at the Kurringai College of Advanced Education[71]. Jeff Morris was already a graduate in Commerce but Geoff Burne, like me, was an undergraduate Production Engineer. Hence I made the necessary applications at NSWIT.

As a post graduate management aspirant I had to fulfil the following criteria: have formal qualifications in an acceptable field from a university or technical college, work in a management-related field, sit for a Princeton Test at the University of NSW and provide a letter of support from my employer.

After fulfilling all of the above, I was admitted the following year at the NSWIT in the post graduate School of Business on probation – failing any subject in the first semester meant losing my candidature. Following two years of intense studying with an additional three hours paid study leave by MWS&DB each week, I graduated second in my class, receiving a Graduate Diploma in Business Administration majoring in Public Administration and was conferred the next year – 1982.

I was invited to complete another two years and receive a Master

---

71 Later Kurringai College of Advanced Education and NSW Institute of Technology; amalgamated and became known as Sydney University of Technology – UTS.

of Business Administration – MBA. Although I was right in the swing of things and had the academic *bug,* my inner self told me that I could not continue to ask my family to sacrifice and put their life on hold for me. My wife who stood by me all this time deserved some life too. Our son was to sit for his Higher School Certificate that year and our daughter the following year would sit for her School Certificate. It would be a madhouse and too much strain to put on my wife, although she was not complaining.

So for the next eight months I was a real husband and father, worked hard at work and home and did all the preparatory work to have an inground swimming pool installed that winter.

87 THE CLUB

My best intentions of providing a peaceful family life did not last long. The Russian Club Limited (RCL), of which I was soon to become an active member, was experiencing management problems.

A brief account of the Club history shows how important the Club had been to the Russian community as new migrants integrated into the new land. In fact, probably all clubs of ethnic origin serve a similar purpose – a means of assimilation for new arrivals.

The Russian Club is probably the second oldest Russian institution in Australia, following the Russian Orthodox Church. It has always played an important role in the life of the Russian community within the state of New South Wales. Originally known as the *Russian House,* it was founded in 1924 and for many years was located in the centre of Sydney – George Street – when I first went there in 1956 and in Pitt Street before then.

In the 1920s, there would not have been more than about 200 Russian migrants living in Sydney. Many of their kin were scattered all over the globe – Harbin, Tienjin and Shanghai, Paris, Berlin and Belgrade, San Francisco, Chicago and New York. Then, as now, the Club provided a meeting place for people of a similar background enjoying: homeland cooking and drinking, a variety of concerts and performances and various subjects of interest to the people in the process of assimilating in their new homeland. It also became the home of the first Russian library, the first string orchestra of folk instruments and a venue for lessons in Russian to children. For a while even, a place of worship for Russian Orthodox services on Sundays.

Some of the names are still remembered today. Mrs. I.A. Davidenkova, now a centenarian, was at that time the first teacher. Her husband Y.A. Davidenkov, an architect, was the Club's first President and continued for a period of about twenty years until 1944. The couple actively supported the Russian Club for many years. Mrs. Davidenkov still celebrates her birthdays at the Club with many well-wishers attending.

In 1926, the Russian Club organised a reception for the Jaroff Don Cossack Choir and for Anna Pavlova's ballet ensemble, which toured Australia with great success. The Club also entertained famous Russian artists from Europe and the USA, and in 1960 had the honour of receiving King Peter II of Serbia.

After World War II, following the influx of thousands of Russian migrants from Europe and China, the Club expanded and moved to No. 3 Albert Road, Strathfield, in 1957.

The Strathfield area was fast becoming a Russian Community centre, sprawling in all four directions. The Cathedral of Saints Peter and Paul was also built in Strathfield in 1953. The Club President during 1944 to 1963 was then N.P. Hokhloff.

Through the efforts of a large number of people, the Club developed into a premier organization in the Russian Community of NSW. Until the formation of the Russian Ethnic Community Council of NSW in 1994, the elected President of the Club was usually regarded as the first representative of the Community.

The Club, as most Russian organizations that found refuge in Australia, having experienced Communist persecution – avoided contact, sometimes almost to an extreme – with any pro-Soviet organizations or even those that had a blurred position between right and left leanings.

As Russians, like other foreign immigrants, assimilated in the new country, only some chose to follow the left-leaning Australian Labour Party. Back in the 1950s and 60s and even later, the ALP still maintained a strong Socialist position. Memories of its former leader, Dr. H.E. Evatt, with other less distinguished members supporting the Australian Communist Party's right to exist, caused much tension in the Club and resulted in left-leaning Russians being denied membership from it. Hence left-leaning Russians were not welcome in the Club.

In 1982, there was gossip in the Russian community that some of the Board members and its President were making friendly overtures to the Secretary of the Russian Social Club which fraternised with Soviet Consular officials. It was claimed that the Club Board was entertaining the idea of renting Soviet films from the Russian Social Club which were alleged to have been received from the Soviet Consular officials. This all took place shortly before the Canberra Coombs/Ivanov affair, during the *Cold War*, when Gorbachev and *Perestroika* were still years away. The Russian community was up in arms. The Board had to be ousted, new members elected and a strong signal given that the Club had no desire to play palsy walsy with the reds.

Consequently a new alternative Board was swiftly organised under the leadership of a former Club President, Igor M. Nesteroff, a civil engineer and a son of a former Russian Imperial Naval captain with a strong community-committed wife and a few former respected Board members. The remainder were respected novices chosen from the community. Amongst these I was selected to be the new Vice President of the Board. Young – barely 40 – idealistic, energetic and a fresh recent business graduate. I was keen to put some of my ideas into practice. Little did I realise the long and hard sacrifices that had to be made. Neither did my wife, who gave me her blessing and her support throughout the long road ahead.

The alternative Board won by an overwhelming majority and immediately got to work. Among the objectives of reuniting the community, improving the Club facilities and facilitating a new social structure, we had to reduce a debt of almost $100,000, which for that time was a lot of money, requiring much hard work. Igor was a good President and a mentor. From the beginning, he empowered me with significant authority. I did not consciously realise his reason for doing so, until someone mentioned to me during the second term that I was being groomed for President. By now I was more seasoned and did not know if I wanted the job. But ultimately I agreed.

Now there were eleven Board members, plus a President and a Vice President (VP), all elected separately. Every Director had his responsibility and most of us were in the Club several days a week. By taking over paid jobs as volunteers we saved a lot of money during the next few years. However, the exacting and unremitting demands made on office bearers resulted in a high turnover of directors. After two years as Vice President I was elected as one of the youngest Presidents.

While still a VP, one of my responsibilities was to run fortnightly Friday night Discos. Two principal Directors that used to help me were Nick Gileff and Victor Tischenko. On these days I would arrive directly from work at about 6.00 p.m. and remain until about 2.00 a.m. The other Directors and helpers would arrive shortly after I did. My wife Shura, Nick's wife Kalya, Victor's wife Natasha and many other ladies of the Ladies Committee helped on a rostered basis to run the new coffee shop – *Teremok* – that we set up. The Ladies Committee, comprising of wives and friends, significantly contributed to the running of the Club. They were in fact like a secondary Board. This gave me the idea of modernising the management of the Club by inviting women to join the tradionally all male Board. Two of the outstanding directors that I had during my Presidency were women – Antonina Johansen and Tanya Chernisheva.

As Scoutmasters, Nick Gileff and I were not happy seeing some young people drinking themselves stupid during the discos, so we introduced bar closure by 11.30 p.m. on those nights. This resulted in only a small decline in alcohol sales, but significantly reduced broken glassware and youth brawls by the end of the night.

Another innovation was hot meals – *piroshki* and pizzas provided by the Ladies Committee during discos. An active Committee member, Tamara, used to arrange surprise guests like TV personalities from *Sons and Daughters* which always increased youth attendance. At that time children were allowed under the supervision of attending parents. Our own children loved coming.

By the time I became President, I wanted desperately to bring an end to the remaining rift which existed in the community, continue with the introducion of economic and social reforms for greater efficiency and effectiveness and make the Club better known to our local, State and Federal politicians. To this end, we organised local businessmen's dinners for advice and participation, youth programmes, a variety of balls and concerts and where possible we refrained from holding rowdy nights during the Holy of the Holiest weeks – the Great Lent prior to Easter. We were rewarded by our Archbishop frequently visiting us to give lectures on subjects of interest and seldom declining invitations to any special occasions. We were also privileged to have entertained a large number of politicians, some of whom became honorary members.

After four long years on the Board, two of them as President, I was worn out and reluctantly resigned at the end of my second term. The legacy that I left was an almost debt-free Club, a united community – despite the political inclinations (apart from card carrying communists) of its membership – with a strong senior citizen and youth participation. In addition, both Scout organizations and the Vitiazi were brought closer together by participating more regularly in a new youth hall that was built by Club members and enthusiast friends. With these developments came a renewed interest in the Club's various activities, with its regular participating interest groups and a highly informative quarterly Club journal. But it was the Senior Citizens that gave me the greatest active support. My senior relatives – the Koliagins – were over the moon that their little nephew was so prominent and active in the Russian Community. During my presidency they became regulars at the Club. Uncle Misha took out membership and I made certain it was renewed each year. Serving my community gave me the greatest reward one can receive.

Nadia at my father's grave in Moscow USSR – 1983 (Plot 83 No 6054)

88 A LETTER FROM MOSCOW

Between my days at work and evenings at the Club, there was little time for anything else. One day late in May, when I arrived home tired after work my wife handed me the day's mail. There was a letter from Moscow, but not in my father's handwriting. The letter appeared to be from a close friend informing me that my father passed away on 3 May 1983, four months short of his seventieth birthday. At that moment, I do not remember what else the letter said. I do, however; remember a comment made shortly after by our son to my wife: "Now papa has no mama or papa left!" Sometimes out of the mouths of children come meanings in a nutshell. My wife responded to him by saying: "He has us dear, and we won't let him get too unhappy."

Some time later, I re-read the letter. In essence it filled in the missing link of my father's other life … .

Shortly after Vladimir's release from the GULAG in 1954, he met Nadezhda Timofyevna Pogozhena (Nadia) whom he remembered from High School in Harbin. She had moved to the USSR some time in the 1930s. Nadia's husband Valentine was killed during the war, possibly during the Stalingrad offensive. She survived with their son, Oleg. Nadia later remarried, but left her second husband as he was an alcoholic. After meeting Vladimir, she cared for him and helped to nurse him back to health. She also encouraged him to find his family from whom he was torn away, and correspond with them. They stayed together as close companions for the rest of his life. In my father's last letter (26 January 1983) to me on the last page she introduced herself as his temporary carer, preparing me for the worst, telling me that he was very frail and his time was near and that she would notify me if anything happened. She also said that his speech was impaired and that he did not comprehend everything. At that time I was still unaware of their relationship. In that same letter my father congratulated me on my graduation, wished the family all the best and expressed pride in his grandchildren. As I look back, it was obviously his final farewell to us. He also told me of his ailing health, his difficulty in walking and that he would not survive without a carer, as he would not go to a nursing home. From recollection I think his heart finally gave out. Nadia corresponded with us briefly over the next year and later sent me slides of his grave with her standing beside it and a place prepared for her when her time came.

There was at least one more item left in the unfinished saga of my father's life which I would only find out after Perestroika.

89 IT'S FSB - NOT KGB OR MGB OR NKVD OR OGPU OR THE CHEKA

After Perestroika and the collapse of the USSR, the KGB was dismantled following the unsuccessful coup against President Gorbachev in August 1991, which was assisted by the head of the then KGB. The KGB was systematically stripped of its extensive military units as well as many of its domestic-security functions by President Yeltsin and replaced by a more moderate domestic successor – the FSB – a similar pancake transferred to a different plate with less horseradish (less severe).

In 1998 through an intermediary I was able to have access to the former KGB files. My go-between was allowed to read and copy only by hand, however, about six pages from the historic case file, numbering 320 pages, of my father dating back to his original arrest in 1933. This is the new Russia where limited Freedom of Information is now allowed.

It is from these files with great emotional pain that I was able to reconstruct my father's history in the USSR. Perhaps apart from his love of his homeland, however misguided, while being stateless in a foreign land that in turn was occupied by a ravenous aggressor, it was the psychological urge to clear his name that pushed him the second time to place his family in harm's way and blindly follow the call of Joseph Stalin – "Come home all is forgiven". It is hard to judge as about half of the Russians then living in China one way or another ended up in the USSR, many of whom did not live to tell the tale.

90 THE RETURN

My return to China as a participant of the International Conference on Ergonomics Occupational Safety and Health and the Environment (ICEOSHE) October/November 1988 is a story to be remembered. (Since then of course much has changed, particularly in the preparation for the 2008 Olympics in Beijing. However, a trip down memory lane will illustrate what travel to China 20 years earlier was like.)

The Conference and Post Conference tours arranged by the Darling/Downs Institute of Advanced Education jointly with the Chinese Society of Metals were great successes. The tours could even be described as a miracle.

To arrange a Chinese trip was no easy matter, believe me. Their tourist service infrastructure left much to be desired. The official China International Travel Agency (CITS) was then in a pre-dawn stage, e.g. you quickly found out that they did not know basic things like train schedules between cities, or the names of many of the hotels. They had greater difficulties in booking you into a hotel than you would have had yourself. Much of the time, they could not get you any airline tickets to go anywhere, usually because it was either too early or too late. In fact, if you were lulled into a false sense of security because some other carrier like Qantas booked the schedules for you through CITS, the chances were that you would be in for a rude awakening. When in the early hours of the morning you found yourself in a foreign country with nobody to meet you at the airport, and you were not booked into a hotel and the tickets that were supposed to be waiting for you for a joining flight were not there, you were certain that CITS was involved.

My initial intention was to arrive a week earlier in Beijing and as arranged skip over to Wuhan where I would do some consulting and return on 22 October, well in time for the Conference.

As you learn very quickly in China, what you buy is not necessarily, what you get.

On Saturday 15 October 1988, we left for China. The trip was uneventful apart from such minor things as late departures, no safety instructions, unintelligible messages, and clogged toilets.

The first real crisis came when nobody met us at Beijing Airport at 1.00 a.m., so after some negotiations we got a taxi to our hotel, Beijing International. This is where a continuum of crises began. "Very sorry, no reservation for you at this hotel. Are you in the right hotel? What conference? What is ICEOSHE? Are you attending the Chef's Conference? No? If you pay we find room."

"But I already paid for everything."

"*Sorry, you pay again.*"

"Oh God! 2.00 a.m. Here is my credit card, give me a room."

The next day or rather an interrupted extension of the previous night was a repetition of the nightmare when we tried to pick up our airline tickets to Wuhan. No air tickets! A morning dogfight followed! An afternoon stroll to Tian An Men Square lowered my blood pressure.

Sunday morning I began ringing China CITS who immediately blamed Qantas/Jetabout for our misfortunes. They, Qantas, were at fault because they did not adhere to CITS's bureaucratic process of ticket reservations. That is, it was simply not good enough to order and then confirm your travelling intention, you had to re-confirm. And there you had it; the blame was apportioned. Qantas was the culprit. CITS was clean as a whistle and the customer was 'stuffed'. So this was China!

On the other hand, Qantas went out of their way with phone calls, telexes to and from Sydney. By the end of the day, Qantas sent me a driver, a car and an interpreter to take us to Beijing Railway Station in the hope that we might have had some luck getting on the train as we could whistle Dixie for at least the next two to three days before we could hope to get any airline tickets (and that was one-way only).

If you had never been to Beijing railway station you had not missed anything. The station had to be seen to be believed. A mass of humanity: mostly sitting or lying on the bare dirty floor – everywhere. Waiting: you had to literally step over people. Reminiscent of wartime – with refugees waiting for a train – any train. It was all so sad.

After one hour and lengthy haggling, I decided I would not be going anywhere. The Wuhan visit would have to wait for another day. The best that was offered was to leave my wife behind and receive a single one-way ticket, standing all the way for 18 hours with the possibility of lying down in the lavatory for short periods of time. Now, if this was Sydney, I might have considered it, but toilets in China, well that is quite another story, which I will touch on later in this expose.

By next day, we had overstayed our welcome at the Beijing International. We were promptly evicted. After two days in Beijing, I wanted to go home. But there were no tickets available.

Qantas came to the rescue. A Qantas rep was so affected by our misfortune that she offered to share her apartment in the diplomatic compound with us for the next four days until the rest of the Australian contingent started to arrive. From then on we began to live, travel, see, feel, eat, shop etc. in and around the city prior to the Conference.

Beijing was an enigma. It was a large, flat, grey dusty city, which was rich in historical and cultural relics inherited from its fascinating past. It had wide streets, with special lanes for bicycles, of which there were millions. Traffic was chaotic, driving etiquette non-existent. The pedestrian had absolutely no right of way. Pedestrian crossings were convenient areas to be picked off in.

The Forbidden City (Imperial Palace) was and still is huge. Roaming through it rekindled scenes from *The Last Emperor.* The trip to the Great Wall, 70 kilometres away, was interesting. The Ming Tombs were not. The Temple of Heaven was heavenly. It has the famous echo circular wall, 65 metres in diameter, which is supposed to have amazing acoustic properties.

You are supposed to be able to whisper while standing close to it and it will be heard at the other end. It was amusing to see thousands of Chinese trying the same trick simultaneously, all with faces pressed against the wall. One of the highlights of the cultural part of our trip was the magnificent Summer Palace, some 10 kilometres away. It had a beautiful setting on a lake, a variety of architectural styles and lovely, evocative names to its various features such as Palace of Kindliness and Tranquillity, Garden of Harmonious Interest, Hall of Benevolence and Longevity. It was very well-maintained and definitely worth visiting.

But yet there was another problem, like the currency system in China. The Chinese Yuan was and at the time of writing still is not negotiable outside the country, just like the Rouble in Russia used to be and the Government was after foreign currency to buy things from the West. So you had to change your money into special Foreign Exchange Certificates (FECs), which must be used to pay hotels, Friendship Stores (the equivalent of *Berioska* in Russia) etc. The rules were not clear. Some said that foreigners were prohibited to use anything but FECs but you had to carry local money, as some places do not accept FECs (restaurants, road stalls etc.). The exchange rate was about 3 FECs to the $A. However, since the foreign dollar was prized, there was a black market on FECs, which would give you nearly two Yuans to one FEC. So all those in the know wanted to get paid in FECs and the foreigners wanted, wherever possible, to pay in Yuans. This gave rise to constant haggling with taxis, restaurants, shops etc.

How do we get Yuans on the black-market? Do not worry, we are told, you'll be approached. And approached we were, in Beihai Park. "You want to change money?" asked a passer-by. "Yes," I said. We haggled and then agreed on the exchange rate and he started looking around furtively. It was not clear whether this activity was legal or not, but he certainly acted guiltily.

"Follow me," he said and led me to a public lavatory. Now let me tell you this. Public conveniences in China are very far removed from your neighbourhood bank. In fact, they surpass even the worst examples of conveniences you may have been exposed to. We walked in. Three men were there in various working postures, studying us with interest as he counted out the money. Suddenly, a fellow traveller with a video camera in hand walked in to check on the status of the big financial transaction. This frightened off my man, and he rushed out. Later, he pulled me aside into some bushes, counted out the money as I watched carefully. We exchanged wads and he rushed away. A bit later, another guy accosted my fellow traveller, rushed him off into the bushes and another deal was completed.

It was only a bit later that my companion thought that the wad in his pocket felt small. So we stopped to check, and, sure enough, the guy had done some sleight-of-hand and half the money was missing. I marvelled at his gullibility while Alexandra insisted that I check my money. Sure enough, the same had happened to me ... and both of us had watched them count out the money! Sadly I recalled the saying: there is no fool like an old fool, you just can't beat experience and China had always been notorious for its tricks and tricksters.

Some impressions: The standard of living was very low. Although there were few beggars visible compared to the old days, the people work for a pittance. A monthly wage of the equivalent of Aus$50-60 was the norm. Although, standard goods were very cheap – Aus$

for a pair of jeans, 40 cents for a bag of chestnuts, Aus$3-4 for an average dish in a Chinese Restaurant – the earnings to cost ratio was not good. As the costs were so relatively low for foreigners, the Chinese charged us higher rates wherever they could. For example, train and plane fares were charged at more than triple the price. There were special sections for foreigners in most good restaurants, where they were given English menus at inflated prices. On the one hand, although the visitors could afford it, it was annoying to think that one was being exploited.

During the four days, we covered a lot of territory thanks largely to an arrangement we made with a taxi driver. He ended up being our guide and travelling companion as well.

We visited Tienjin (Tientsin) where I lived for two months as a boy prior to coming to Australia 37 years ago. I did not recognise anything, other than possibly the 'Large Park on Water'. Tienjin is one of the three largest cities in China and together with Shanghai and Beijing is under the central administration. Also like Shanghai and Guangzhou (Canton) it's a large port city.

Technical details of the Conference are omitted here so as not to bore the reader with scientific methodologies. Suffice to say, that it was excellent and a sequel further down the track requested. The conference attracted 360 delegates from five continents – 33 countries, 124 oral presentations, 33 workshops, technical seminars and posters were on display. The subject matter was very diverse. My subject was Manual Handling in the Sydney Waterboard. (The papers are available in a two-volume conference proceeding, and a separate workshop proceedings booklet.)

The conference venue not only provided the opportunity to exchange information in the usual way, but also gave the opportunity to forge and renew many new and old acquaintances. It linked people from associated disciplines, enabling them to widen their horizons and provide an insight into understanding how vital our work in ergonomics and occupational health is on the international plane. In my case, it was also a catalyst in providing a clearer vision of the morrow and giving me the opportunity of building a bridge between my own and a related organisation.

After the conference, some of us stayed on for a tour, which extended from 29 October to 10 November. It included Xian Shanghai, Hangzhou, Guilin and Hong Kong. Of course some people had to be different, causing all sorts of inconveniences to their spouses and CITS. Michael Patkin went lecturing to some God-forsaken outpost of Changsha and joined the group on the tail end of the trip in Guilin. I almost choked the living daylights out of the CITS representative because the Beijing nightmare nearly reoccurred as I left for Shanghai for some consulting on 28 October, rejoining the group three days later after they all (less Michael) arrived from Xian.

My wife documents the Xian impressions:

After Alex's departure, I was anxious about our rendezvous in Shanghai two days later as some arrangements had already fallen through, but Alex assured me that nothing else could possibly go wrong. A whole day was spent in Beijing visiting the biggest Lamasery, Hong He Gong, with lunch at the jade factory. Then a visit to yet another Friendship Store but there were no signs of departure for Xian (which should have been about midday).

At last, we arrived at the airport, but the plane was delayed. Our National Guide demanded two Yuan each for locks on our luggage, (she already held the keys) and 20 Yuan for excess luggage (no receipts could be given). We paid up as we were all very tired after a long day and cramped flight, many suffering from the 'Beijing Bug' (a most unpleasant virus) and so Xian at last. It was about 10.00 p.m. as we stood in the street waiting for the local guide to arrive before our luggage could be released. The Xian Hotel proved to be one of the best on tour, but by 11.00 p.m. after a boxed dinner, we were exhausted and went to bed. The next day, we discovered that only two suitcases were lost (sent to another hotel) and one bag had been torn and an electric razor stolen — so much for our locks.

The day's events made up for the mishaps. We travelled through the flat, dusty countryside to the misty mountain with its numerous palaces and pavilions near steaming hot Huaqing springs. The ancient matriarchal village was next and after lunch the awesome sight of the Terracotta Army. The nearby markets offered a dazzling array of local handicrafts.

We met in the hotel foyer prior to dining at the luxurious Tang Dynasty Restaurant. However, our enjoyment of the evening's activities, including a first class traditional cultural performance, was dampened by the news from our 'friend', the National Guide, that we would have to leave Xian at 5.30 the next morning. Our protests were of no use.

We staggered out of the hotel with a breakfast box, deprived of a whole day's sightseeing. On the plane another box with more goodies: a dried fish snack, tea and biscuits baked in pork fat, as well as a little red CAAC bag, which still serves to remind us of the airline's 'flexibility' in scheduling.

We were back to civilisation. The Shanghai Sheraton was a luxurious oasis, but by 12 noon we were on the move again until after dinner. Alex was already in the room when I returned and he was bubbling over with tales of the wonderful time he had in Shanghai. "Oh, did you have a nice time, dear?" he asks. We were together again in Shanghai.

Shanghai you cannot confuse with any other Chinese city. Even in 1988, as in the colonial times, it was more prosperous, and more dynamic than any other; its skyline boasted European style towers; its shop windows and food stalls seized your attention and it is the largest city in China with, then, nearly 12 million inhabitants. Subsequent to our visit, it has expanded even further, with a modern skyscraper city emerging across the Huangpu in the former Pudong ship building District. Shanghai has no exceptional historical attractions to offer but nonetheless still draws millions of tourists. Foreigners associate the present city with its past reputation. A banking and commercial centre and largest seaport in China, it was also known as an El Dorado for adventurers and opportunists and for its bars, drugs and prostitution. During our visit, about 10,000 factories poured forth a pall of choking gas and smoke, which the Government is still striving to clear up. But Shanghai continues to have a special appeal to visitors as a sophisticated, businesslike metropolis – all the more colourful for its nostalgic associations.

The first place tourists usually make for is Nanking Road (Nanjing Lu) – the largest business street in Shanghai, perhaps even in China (where, for example, there are cafes that serve gateaux) – and then they go on to the Bund, the bustling promenade, once the Wall Street of China. Along this esplanade by the Huangpu River, the multi-storey buildings of the former colonial powers are located. Here one can see hundreds of shadow boxers at 6 in the morning with old masters instructing the young people in the art of Kung Fu boxing.

The Shanghai Club, the Cathay Hotel, Customs House, the Hong Kong Shanghai Bank all still stand proudly. All renamed, of course. The Cathay Hotel is now the Peace Hotel, where the ghostly auras of such dignitaries as Noel Coward and Somerset Maughan still linger on. I stayed there three nights and had dinner there on the last night. On the ground floor is a bar/coffee shop which features a Glen Miller-type orchestra, playing old favourites. They sounded and looked like they had been playing there for the last 50 years. Dull, mechanical, uninspiring!

I also went up to the top of Shanghai/Broadway Mansions. This afforded a panoramic view of Shanghai, the Bund, and the river. So, *muchos* photos and *muchos* feet of video.

The Shanghai Hilton is on Avenue Haig (Huashan Lu) where it meets Route de Say – Zoong, about a block from where we used to live. Sassoon's Marble House still stands in all its glory, surrounded by spacious gardens. The French (Jesfield) Park is intact except for the zoo. My cousin Marina who baby-sat me at the time, used to hear the lions roaring from her house, but they have compensated for that by erecting a giant statue of Marx and Engels. Route Vallon looks prettier, all tree-lined. Many of the streets are in fact tree-lined, giving the old French concession a cosy, European look.

The Cathay Theatre on Avenue Joffre (Huihai Road) has now been converted to a clothes shop in the old foyer and into the Cathay Restaurant upstairs. The Doumer Theatre remains, although it has a new front and at the time of our visit was showing *Waterloo Bridge* with Robert Taylor and Vivien Leigh ... in Chinese.

The Russian Church in Rue L. Lorton (Xiangyang Lu) was a sorry sight with broken windows and dirty; it was a storehouse for metal pipes and fittings. Rue L. Lorton was also a shocking shambles, with food stalls, piles of coal and garbage. However, it was to be renovated shortly. Unfortunately, the Chinese Communist Government shows insufficient respect for history.

The tourist attractions we were taken to, as a group, were jade carving, carpet weaving, silk factories and a commune.

On Melbourne Cup day, Michael Middleton from Geelong and I organised a sweep, hoping to at least cover some of our expenses, even if at the expense of our travelling companions from the US, New Zealand and Europe. As fate would have it, and as industrious as we were, we could not get any results until we were back home. Yes, by now, you guessed it; the bloody foreigners won all the prizes.

From there on it was easy sailing. We went by train, first to Hangzhou, one of China's most scenic cities and famous for its silk. Then a cruise along the scenic West Lake, a city tour, the Pagoda of Six Harmonies, a stroll through a colourful Huangong Park, a visit to the tea plantation, and finally ivory carvings and fan-making factories.

Then on to Guilin considered by many to be the most scenic

area in China, boasting mountains, caves and limestone formations, structured many millions of years ago. The peaks of this 'stone forest' are often shrouded in mist creating an eerie atmosphere. Guilin is situated on the Li River where a canal built 2000 years ago connects the Li Pearl and Yangtze Rivers.

We cruised a whole day on the Li River and took in the natural beauty of mist-shrouded crags, bamboo groves and rapids, which have inspired Chinese painters and poets for centuries.

The flight to Hong Kong was quick and tension releasing. We loved our trip but were ready for Western civilisation. Our remaining three days were at leisure for relaxation and bargain hunting in the duty free shops. Kowloon was the true metropolis of the colony with wonderful antique shops, world-renowned tailors, jewellers, and exotic restaurants, nightclubs topped by thousands of coloured neon lights, and signs, which, at night, turned the streets of Kowloon into a fairyland. Local attractions in Hong Kong included Victoria Peak, Repulse Bay, Stanley Markets, Aberdeen Fishing Village, Ocean Park, the New Territories and much, much more. Standing on the Peak viewing Victoria Harbour and Kowloon in the distance, I recalled my last visit there in 1951 on the way to Australia from China.

The conference and tour had their ups and downs, but in general were very good. Like the USSR and now Russia, China is undergoing significant political and physical restructuring. This is witnessed by massive construction projects, buildings, roads and associated infrastructures. Almost 20 years later, owing to the coming of Beijing Olympics, the intensity of construction has intensified even more. The trip was a revelation. People's emotions were touched more than once. We were often humbled by, and at times cried at, what we saw. Practically everyone in our group of 30 suffered from a respiratory *bug*. Towards the end, the very cohesive group was becoming tired, irritable and cynical. If asked what were the three worst and best things about China, in order, I would say: hygiene, bureaucracy and petty corruption; cultural relics, its simplicity and scenery.

Would I go back? Definitely (particularly if I could share my usefulness) but I would avoid at all costs CITS and of course CAAC.

91 POLITICS

Although my interest in politics began in my youth, my academic development in political affairs and government was initiated by working for a semi-government authority and, in particular, graduating and majoring in Public Administration during that time. Having lived under a communist government and experiencing its horrors, I did not want to be associated with any political party that had leftist leanings. So when I was invited to join the Liberal Party Strathfield Branch by its President, George Popowski, while on the Board of the Russian Club, I understandingly accepted.

Subsequent to leaving the Board of the Russian Club, I also transferred to a local branch of the Liberal Party in Carlingford, and by then had more time to give to the grass roots of Australian politics. After about a year in the branch and on retirement of its President at the Annual General Meeting I was *bushwacked* by the committee ring leaders and elected Branch President. Whilst the idea did not occur to me, I was honoured to be chosen for something that I believed in and my appetite for politics was further encouraged. Over the next three years I applied my recently acquired skills from the Club and Graduate School and began to network our Branch with the Federal and State Politicians – Philip Ruddock, Bronwyn Bishop, Michael Photios, Andrew Tink, Wayne

Murton and others. I also had the privilege of being on the selection committee of some of our politicians; namely Dr. Brendan Nelson and Bronwyn Bishop, when she moved from the Senate in 1993 to the safe seat of Mackellar in the House of Representatives.

Our Branch continued to be one of the two top performing branches of a total of eight in the Parramatta Conference, where I also took an active part as one of the two vice presidents. Attending the State Liberal Party Convention two to three times a year allowed the grass roots representatives to interact with the Federal and State politicians, thereby acquiring first hand information of proposed policies and initiatives.

Some of the ideals that appealed to me about the Liberal Party were characterized by its attitudes rather than by precise ideology. Central to Liberal attitudes is its trust in rationality, faith in the idea of progress, regard to individualism, its emphasis on human rights, and an eagerness to emancipate underprivileged groups. The Liberal Party also champions individualism, free trade, and private enterprise and opposes the centralizing and over-indulgence of the power of the state. It pursues policies of active social reorganization, by promoting social justice in order to prevent abuses of private power. As well it extends the role of the state in fields such as education, social welfare, and industrial relations.

After spending over 10 years in the Liberal Party I would be foolish to give the impression that only the Liberal Coalition has all the answers. In our system of government we have the opportunity to try out the opposition when the encumbent party gets on the nose. From my experience and study of former Australian Governments since World War II, I believe that we had four great Prime Ministers; two Labor – John Curtin and Joseph Benedict (Ben) Chifley – and two Liberals – Sir Robert Gordon Menzies and John Winston Howard. As interesting as grassroots politics was, my involvement in it was soon to be overtaken by another equally important undertaking.

92 THE MULTICULTURALS - HOW TO CATCH A FISH

Grass roots politics was interesting and absorbing and not as demanding as my former Club activities. I was able to carry on with my professional involvement in the Ergonomic Society outside of business hours and still have time left over for family and home care. Alexandra and I even had time to fit in a couple of overseas trips to South East Asia since our China trip. Life was good! But good things come in small doses.

One day the phone rang (come to think of it, it always rang). The caller introduced himself as Bill (Vadim) Jegorow, a former Lord Mayor of Ashfield with strong ALP connections. After brief introductions, he asked me, "Have you had a good rest since your club activities?" I was immediately on my guard. A person I have not officially met, who has strong political ties and is sort of a power-broker, does not ring me up to enquire about the state of my health.

"Yes!" I answered. "But other things keep me busy."

"Good!" he said, and then went straight into his pitch. "The Russian Community is not well represented in NSW." Being himself of Russian origin he pointed out to me, that about 80 per cent of the ethnic population in our state was represented in the Ethnic

Community Council of NSW, of which he was a proud founding Chairman and still a current member. "The Russians however," he went on to say, "have abstained in forming an umbrella body to represent themselves to our three-tier Government structure. Have you any idea why?"

"Not really," I answered. "Suffice to say that the Russian community has not had good experience with governments in China, Europe or the USSR and consequently prefers to keep a low profile, be self-sustaining and avoid asking favours from anybody."

"But that's just it," kept on Bill, "the whole purpose of umbrella bodies is to provide a better two-way communication between the Government and the electorate. If the Russians do not participate in this process their needs cannot be accommodated. The whole process becomes skewed to meeting only the needs of the interest groups that are represented. Do you realise that 25 per cent of our society is ethnic-based and about 40 per cent of the families have one or more parents born overseas. Even the Liberals now back the principle of multiculturalism which Gough Whitlam was instrumental in introducing. As a person of Russian origin I am devastated that as a father of the Ethnic Community Council in our State I have been unable to persuade our community to follow likewise. That is why I am turning to you as a community leader to help in setting up such an umbrella body."

Although Bill was beginning to get through to me, the memories of the workload in the Russian Club were still fresh and I did not want to get involved again where community demands exceed my available time. Right now my life was once again balanced and I had no intention of getting lassooed for another cause. "Bill!" I responded with my pitch, "I agree with the things you say. I do work for a semi-government organisation and am aware of current policies. But my spare time is limited – I am a President of the Carlingford Branch Liberal Party. In my professional career I am involved with the Ergonomic Society as a National Councillor, and I just finished being an interim committee member, helping to set up a technology-related organisation at the University of NSW. So apart from my home and worklife I am busy enough."

"That's good!" he said, "as people who are not busy would not know how to organise such a venture. Look I will try to appeal to your idealism. As a person who spent so many years in the Russian community and at a time when USSR has finally collapsed and a new Russia is emerging, for which I am sure you have been waiting most of your life, wouldn't you like to represent your community in NSW and get an opportunity to interact with some of the Russian dignitaries who will regularly visit Australia?"

Bill was a good persuader and a fisherman. He knew that he almost had me but he also knew he had to give me a little slack. "Look," he said, "if you will lead and set up an interim committee with a group of volunteers who already agreed to participate ... " and he rattled off some of the more known names that I could relate to, "then when you finish your preparation and present a plan of action I am sure that at a meeting of the Russian Community a new board can be elected on your advice."

"How long do you think that will take?" I asked.

"No more than three months, Alex."

93 RUSSIAN ETHNIC COMMUNITY COUNCIL

After three months of preparation, on 31 May 1994 our Interim Committee presented its findings and recommendations to an audience of over 400 people at Ashfield Town Hall. Apart from the Russian Community there were representatives from the three tiers of Government. Edna McGuill represented the Ethnic Community Council of NSW.

I found it one of the most inspiring meetings that I had attended in my community career. Not only were all our recommendations accepted, our Foundation Committee with a couple of changes in members was endorsed by the general meeting to continue and develop a constitution within the next 12 months. By then not only myself, but most of the Committee was hooked line and sinker to continue and develop this new umbrella body. By now the Committee comprised the following members:

> President – A. Vassilieff JP, Vice Presidents – T. Hartung and N. Nicobadze.
> Secretaries – S. Krestovsky and T. Shliapnikoff. Treasurer – N. Lobastoff, Public Officer – O. Litkens. Committee Members – A. Davidoff, T. Gluvchinsky, A. Ho, L. Lapardin, D. Lloyd JP and K. Savchenko. Consultants – W. Jegorow MBE and A. Konovets JP.

It was a hard-working Committee and it made significant achievements in its first three years. During that time about half of the membership was renewed. Some of the major achievements included: a new Constitution, a number of fund-raising events such as the one for the Sakhalin earthquake appeal, Russian/Australian student exchange, fostering immigration and welfare needs, establishing links with Australian and Russian Governments.

Of course, after about a year in the Russian Ethnic Community Council (RECC), I gave up my activity in the Carlingford Branch Liberal Party. By now I knew my limitations and could not preside over two organisations at the same time and still remain a normal person at work and at home. As a gesture of gratefulness to me, Michael Photios, the NSW Minister of Multiculturalism, invited our RECC to organise a reception night at the NSW Parliament House for about a hundred representatives of the Russian Community. The Russian Community felt very honoured to be welcomed in such style for the first time and so did the Russian Consul General, to whom the RECC extended the ministerial invitation. This event provided all the guests the opportunity to interact with several members of Government and their Parliamentary colleagues and was repeated once more the following year.

I must also say that in my opinion Multiculturalism has an important place in the Australian community. We all migrated to this land from somewhere. Multicultural communities help to fill a transition gap while each new community assimilates to their new home. But even after assimilation it is still pleasant to revisit one's roots – retaste one's former culture, cuisine, folklore and just hear one's mother tongue. For the religious the beliefs are usually intergenerational and will continue whatever language it is in. Belief in a Higher Being is complementary to our existence in the performance of good in this life and hopefully the life thereafter. If it becomes harmful to others then maybe we have not understood the basic teachings of our own religion and instead are substituting our own undesirable vices for the religion that we profess to believe in.

For most migrants the adopted land becomes their land, as does the language and the common values. My advice to those who cannot assimilate even after two or three generations is: do not stay here, this land is obviously not for you. Find another place where you will be more content.

94 BALLS

A colourful aspect of the Russian community is perhaps their ability to ceaselessly organise spectacular Balls. Since the time of the Russian diaspora, the Russian community, whether in Harbin, Shanghai, Berlin, Paris and now here, carried with them this amazing gift – the organisation of Balls. This gift had its roots in the gala events of St. Petersburg and Moscow. The community organisers carried that trait with them wherever they went.

I can still see and hear (frequently to the background waltz of *In the Hills of Manchuria)* the splendour of these events that I have attended and often organised over the past 50 years. The Jubilee Grand Ball, the Traditional Graduation Ball, New Year's Eve Ball, Easter Ball, Unification Ball, the Association of Engineers Ball, Ball – Masque, the Spring Ball, the various youth balls – Scouts, Vitiazi and Saturday School Balls and the unforgettable Tatianas Ball, its origin dating back to the Russian University students in pre-revolutionary Russia, and many, many others.

What these events lacked in the splendour, pomp and ceremony, compared to their predecessors in St. Petersburg and Moscow, they made up for in their spirit, diligence and an unending frequency of new causes to celebrate.

These splendid events provided the opportunity for raising

funds for the various community groups, while providing them with the opportunity for a get-together in a nostalgic atmosphere. Nostalgia is something we are very good at and have plenty of experience in! It also provides a medium for the better understanding of the Community by the Government dignitaries frequently invited to these functions.

More recently, since Perestroika Russian dignitaries have also been invited to attend. The Russian dignitaries had expressed amazement that in the Land Down Under there are Australians of Russian descent, who speak and sing Russian and know their history, religion, and their culinary delights, customs and traditions often better than their counterparts in Russia. This is a living testimony of the Soviet era heritage – Destruction of the Past. Fortunately now the Russian people are once again earning and learning their past.

The fact is that most of these Russians did not become dinky-di Aussies overnight. They gradually integrated their cultural heritage into the Australian way of life in a lengthy assimilation process tempered by a natural inclination to refresh ancestral links in a characteristically human way. The Military Tatoo, the Orange and the Green, Octoberfest, Chinese New Year, Christmas and Hannukah, the Orthodox and Catholic-based Easter illustrate our difference and yet our unity. The introduction of Multiculturalism into the Australian way of life took a long time to arrive. However, the Labor Government deserves the credit for its initiative. It has delivered much good. But like all good things there is a tendency by some to swing the pendulum too far in the opposite direction. Integrating Multiculturalism into the Australian way of life does not mean polarising or dividing up Australia into separate or introverted Shires or States. One official language, one flag and one Government at each level is what most new arrivals learned to expect, respect and support.

After three years as the foundation President of the RECC and another two years in an advisory role as its Immediate Past

President, I ended my active community involvement. My drive was fading and it was a signal for me to devote my remaining energy to my wife and by now my extended family.

In 1998, a number of Russian long serving community leaders were awarded a 50-year diocesan jubilee medal by His Grace Archbishop Hilarion, the Archbishop of Australia and New Zealand of the Russian Orthodox Church Abroad.

The bestowing of honours in Sydney was at the end of a church service at the Russian Orthodox Cathedral of Saints Peter and Paul at Strathfield. I stood in the church with my wife among a number of friends and colleagues and was honoured to hear my name called out, followed shortly after by another name – that of a lifelong friend who was soon to become a Chief Russian Scout in NORS. As the ceremony continued, I reflected on the previous decades of my community participation. I saw myself as a fourteen-year-old Scout, dressed in the appropriate Scout uniform of khaki shorts and short-sleeved shirt with an orange scarf, the colour of the (campfire) flame around the neck. Beside me, stood my friend – Nick Gileff – from our Kookaburra patrol. He remained an active lifelong Scout while I diversified into other community activities, but still remain a Scout in spirit. As they say, once a Scout always a Scout. I also think that my community life has been one good Ball.

95 WHEN A GIRL MARRIES

On 1 September 1990, our daughter Helen (Lena) married her first true love – Gregory Cook (Grisha as we lovingly referred to him in Russian). I was just eight days short of my forty-eighth birthday. The whole event began to dawn on me when my daughter and I were being driven in the bridal car to the Ukrainian Orthodox Church in Flemington. I finally realised that our little girl – now twenty-two – was going to leave us and start her own new life. Just as it should be! And yet my emotions were getting the better of me.

Her whole life was flashing in front of me. Her loud piercing screams as a baby were even louder than her older brother Vladimir. When she was one year old I had to take a week off from work while Alexandra had her appendix removed. I followed Alexandra's instructions to the letter in keeping Helen well fed and free of nappy rash. Vlad was easy going as he was already attending pre-school. I remembered the time when she was three and we had just moved to Carlingford. She unexpectedly darted out across the road, as we were saying goodbye to Babushka Dasha, to show to the neighbours' children a present she had received, and a shaken young driver barely pulled up in time in his VW. We were eternally grateful to God for not taking her from us.

Her beautiful, curly red hair made her easy to identify when she played up during lessons in class or assembly. In high school, where Alexandra was Science Assistant, she would sometimes hear, while walking past a classroom, her bubbly sociable daughter giggling and chatting as a frazzled teacher called the class to order. While during a break at Saturday Russian School, Helen's teacher would address me: "Mr Vassilieff, your daughter and her friend Joanne had to be separated once more."

"I will speak to her again?"

"Yes! And also speak to your son, as he and his friend Misha urinated out of the window not to get wet; they claimed it was raining this morning."

Helen grew up strong willed and has proved to be tenacious and brave when confronted with life's problems. She made a great career for herself working in Human Resources, after completion of her Higher School Certificate and her Business Secretarial Diploma. During her time at Williams Secretarial College, she met her Greg, a panel beater by trade. Four years later, there we were in the car.

As Helen was named after her Cossack grandmother Elena, who, together with her daughter, son-in-law Ivan, and her granddaughter Alexandra, all attended the Ukrainian Orthodox Church in Flemington, Helen wanted to hold the wedding ceremony there in their honour. Father Alexander – the Parish Priest – knew the whole family for many years, since Alexandra was a small girl and he the new assistant Priest.

Besides, as we told some of our relatives, the Ukrainians were more progressive than we Russians. They had pews inside the church, something that the mixed guest list would appreciate as Orthodox weddings can exceed an hour and non-Orthodox guests begin to crumple to the floor.

Father Alexander and I became very friendly from the start. Although I stole one of his parishioners, I would always accompany her to the Ukrainian church on special occasions. Initially, the remembrance service for her father and later her grandmother and lastly her mother. He even teased me once, knowing that I was an active Russian community participant, and would say, "You know you are not a bad Moscovit (a Russian in Ukrainian). In fact you are only partly Russian, as your maternal kin used to live in the Ukraine." I knew he was complimenting me. Russian/Ukrainian rivalry is akin to the English/Scottish joshing.

The service with the accompanying Ukrainian choir was delightful, very moving and progressive. It was performed in three languages for everyone's benefit – Ukrainian, Russian and English. The reception at the Elim Function Centre in Burwood brought back many fond memories of our own reception over twenty-seven years before. This was another time when the Vajinsky clan and some of their relations were formally together. Musya and Misha Koliagin, Sasha Dobrovidoff and Jim Yanchevsky. They were the last of the Mohicans. Jim took the photo.

It was the last time that the elder kin would be present together for a formal gathering. Within a few months Sasha, who was the eldest, passed away. The others followed over the next few years. Musya remained as the matriarch of the clan until she passed away in 2001. Musya was spared the agony – the death of her youngest daughter – Mischelle Saint Claire (born Vera Koliagin) who died the following year in July 2002. Vera is the first cousin to join our ancestors, bringing home the fact that life is unpredictable and brief.

9 THE NEW GENERATION

1995-2005

96 THE OLD WORLD

In September 1996 I took seven weeks' leave, my longest break in 37 years since I commenced work. Shura and I toured Britain and Europe by a Trafalgar Coach. It was a marvellous trip. We fell in love with Britain and both of us were very impressed with France and Germany, while other countries, particularly Italy and Austria, left memorable impressions.

It was in Innsbrook that Alexandra experienced a feeling of deja-vu. Whilst shopping and sight-seeing we approached a street corner. Suddenly she exclaimed, "There should be a Salamander Shoe store across the road!" She looked up and sure enough there it was. Alexandra then recounted her memory of forty-eight years ago when her mother took her there to buy her some shoes after visiting Alexandra's grandfather in Oberammergau. Prior to this incident we stopped briefly in Oberammergau and attempted to find her kin and almost succeeded, but time was against us. We left a message in a delicatessen with the owner, who turned out to be a distant relative of Alexandra's Aunt Olga and her daughter. Perhaps this episode, combined with our overnight stopover in Munich, and then a walk through Innsbrook, jolted Alexandra's childhood memory which surfaced at the moment of approaching a long forgotten site. Years later Alexandra bought herself a pair of Salamander shoes on Norfolk Island, perhaps as a reminder of this flash of time gone by.

Unfortunately that branch of Alexandra's family did not respond to the message or to the letter and old photographs that she wrote in German, with the help of our friend Harry, on our return to Sydney. Harry, who is originally from Germany, told us that Bavarians can be very suspicious of the unknown. Perhaps Alexandra was after some financial inheritance. Or something else. Who knows. But perhaps they were just content in their present world and were not wishing to open it up to any distant relations, who by now are nothing more than strangers.

97 THE END OF A CAREER

All good things come to an end and by the end of the 1990s Sydney Water, like many other large private and public corporations, was accelerating its downsizing. All levels of management were enticed to consider their future – a strategy of musical chairs was often the order of the day – eventually when the music stopped one or more chairs were gone. By 1998, my chair as a Business Administration Manager in the Utilities Planning Services of Sydney Water was gone. I was disheartened and left to ponder my future. By now, I was a seasoned executive with diversified experience with a lot to offer – varying from Production Engineering and Management Consulting to Strategic Planning, Human Resource Management and Occupational Health and Safety. My last few years were highly dynamic. I was part of an executive group developing and operating a new branch that became part of the Sydney Water Retail Business known as Utilities Planning Services. We originally set this unit up as a consortium of international water treatment consultants, which was part of a seven billion 20 year Clean Waterways Programme to clean up Sydney/Illawarra and the Blue Mountains. The change in Government led to changes in our organization and eventual downsizing of our unit. Solutions to water recycling were already in progress. So had the Unit remained in tact there may not have been a need for a desalination plant down the track.

I was not ready to go, but what could I do? Necessity is a mother of invention! I suddenly remembered recently attending an executive breakfast at Darling Harbour where the audience were informed of the coming 2000 Olympics. The person I was seated next to was a Human Resources General Manager for SOCOG – the Sydney Organising Committee for the Olympic Games. He told me how SOCOG was planning to attract executives in the months ahead by secondment and/or contractual arrangement Australia-wide, in order to meet the challenge of the coming Games. So I picked up the phone and my quest for a secondment to SOCOG started.

98 THE OLYMPICS

The goal of Olympism is to place everywhere
Sport at the Service of the harmonious
Development of man, with a view to
Encouraging the establishment of a peaceful
Society concerned with the preservation of human dignity.
Extract from the Olympic Charter, "Fundamental Principles"

On 15 February 1999, I commenced my secondment at SOCOG Headquarters in Jones Street, Ultimo, the former Herald building. The arrangement was simple. As a surplus employee, I was placed under the Olympic Management and Development Program for Senior Management, for a period up to the completion of the Olympic and Paralympic Games, as a Project Manager-Venue Staffing, while still remunerated by Sydney Water.

A large proportion of the management staff at SOCOG were former sporting personnel, including Olympians, and many of the others were young future hopefuls. In general the atmosphere was in a state of constant hype and driven by anticipation, in a fast-paced go-go zone. Naturally not everyone could take the pace and farewells were not uncommon. In the next six months I experienced several test events including Mini-Olympics – events ran concurrently and sequentially to get the feel of the pressure and the unexpected side effects. There was a continual feeling of euphoria.

By late July I began to feel the pressure. The go-go style of modern management was rapidly becoming unattractive to me. Prioritising was the order of the day – deciding which stack of emails not to answer, which meetings not to attend, how late to finish work and what files to read in the train on the way home. I began to wonder whether I wanted this lifestyle for the next fifteen months, with the expectation of even longer hours during the Games. So when a new and improved offer of redundancy came from Sydney Water I almost felt a sense of relief.

In August I stepped down from the role of Venue Staffing Manager and took on the more simplified one of Project Management until my negotiated departure date (26 November 1999). A more contented way of finishing off the 20th century. Thus bringing to a peaceful conclusion the ferment of perplexity that overtook my working life at the end of the 20th century.

Prior to leaving SOCOG I was accredited as a Russian/English Language Specialist as part of the 100,000 Volunteer Workforce for the coming Games. However, I ended up in a different role yet again. The following year I was offered a paid position, on a contract basis as a Team Leader Spectator Services for both the Olympics and Paralympic Games.

Sydney Games attracted over 10,000 athletes from 198 countries competing in 28 sports. From aquatics, archery, shooting and athletics to a variety of ball games, water sports, cycling, equestrian, and gymnastics as well as a selection of weightlifting and arts of defence. More importantly, the Games left a legacy which all Olympic Games strive for, namely the promotion of the values of the Olympic spirit so as to develop a peaceful and better world through sport.

Two weeks after the Olympic Games, this Legacy was further

enhanced and possibly exceeded by the Paralympic Games. The passion, grit and determination, only overshadowed by the humility of these athletes, demonstrated to the rest of us that even with imperfect bodies and/or mind we can still reach for the stars.

Unfortunately the Legacy of 2000 was short-lived. Almost twelve months to the week, 11 September 2001 saw the commencement of terrorist hostilities on a global scale and to which the Alliance of the Willing – US, UK and Australia and a number of others responded with a war on terror. In particular against the nations of Afghanistan and Iraq.

The war against terrorism still goes on today, making us all aware of the unbalanced world in which we live these days. However, the world at large again took time out and enjoyed the Olympic spirit at Athens in August 2004.

In retrospect I am proud to have been associated with the Olympic movement late in my life. The Olympic Games had a beneficial effect, particularly for Sydney. They helped to elevate Sydney to the status of a modern international city in the Southern Hemisphere.

99 THE GOLDEN YEARS

After the Olympics I was, for a time, involved in voluntary work at the Sydney Airport as a Golden Ambassador – Meet and Greet Guide – providing interpreter assistance to visitors from overseas as and when required. It was an experience that I enjoyed, but I had to give it up as there were other demands on my life at that stage.

Now in retirement, after a total of 41 years in the workforce and almost as long in community work, I still do some casual work while nurturing the hope to travel. As we await the opportunity, Alexandra and I developed an interest in the Arts. She paints and attends the opera and the ballet when she can, while I commit "Roots and Heritage" to paper for posterity. All this of course is subject to our devotion to the needs of children and grandchildren as the family grows.

Finally in the late northern spring and early summer of 2007 Shura and I visited our roots – a 15 day cruise from Saint Petersburg to Moscow. We experienced many great feelings and places. Above all it was great to see Russians resurrecting pride in their heritage, speaking freely and many once again turning to God away from the cult of Marxism and Leninism. This is demonstrated by countless churches, monasteries and palaces being restored to their former magnificence, in the cities as well as villages. Also a week before our departure the Russian Orthodox church abroad reamalgamated with the Moscow Patriarchate, as the faithful are no longer in persecution and the olive branch was extended both by President Putin and the Moscow Patriarch Alexi II to the Russian Orthodox church abroad. The act of agreement was signed in the recently rebuilt cathedral of Christ the Savior in Moscow. The former cathedral was blown up by the bolsheviks and in its place Stalin had built a swimming pool. In the 1990's the cathedral was once again rebuilt to its former splendour. Many Russian Orthodox faithful abroad contributed to its reconstruction.

Russia still has a long way to go. All it needs is political stability during its dynamic socioeconomic change. Unfortunately ordinary working people and those retired find this very hard to comprehend. Our heart goes out to them wishing them the earliest possible success and happiness.

100 AND SO WE ARE BLESSED

Eventually we became grandparents, but not before our son Vlad also decided to tie the knot. Our little boy had grown up as all boys do and became a man.

Vlad very much enjoys the outdoors – a passion which he acquired since his childhood from his early scouting days. He is an industrious and practical person and began with building billycarts as a boy and grew up rebuilding many old cars. In his youth, he cycled, surfed, skied and bush-walked and he still cycles with his family and takes them skiing a few times a year. As a hobby, he finds pleasure in home projects.

Although, Vlad does not enjoy reading or has the time to, and finished his Higher School Certificate with a mediocre pass, he still made us proud, as he did not give up. Over the next several years, he completed his Mechanical Engineering Associate Diploma, an Electrical Trade Certificate and by his early thirties graduated with Distinction as a Bachelor of Manufacturing Technology.

At the age of twenty-five, together with a few of his close mates – former students of Carlingford High School – he toured Europe for five months and skied in the snowfields. During his early days, he combined his greatest passion skiing and working in the Thredbo snowfields, but eventually the snowfields had to give way to the city life and his engineering career.

Although Vlad left home for the first time at about twenty-two years of age, he kept on returning. We were relieved when finally at the age of thirty-three he left us for good and married a lovely girl by the name of Nicole Fetingis. Nicole, like Vlad, is of Ethnic descent. Her father Alfred is Lithuanian and mother Johanna a Kiwi – New Zealander.

Vlad was married at the Russian Orthodox Cathedral of St. Peter and Paul at Strathfield on 8 February 1998. As mentioned earlier, there are no pews inside the Russian Orthodox church and we were anticipating that some guests might not last the full service. The Priest, Father George, accompanied by the Archdeacon, Father Boris, now performs the service in two languages to enlighten couples that are increasingly less fluent in the language of their ancestors and are of mixed national background.

Alexandra and I are now proud grandparents of four lovely grandsons – two Cooks and two Vassilieffs. The Cook boys were born – Benjamin 15 January 1999 and Jordan 30 June 2000. The Vassilieff boys were born – Matthew 2 November 2001 and Luka 18 December 2003. The feeling of a strong bond between the cousins is encouraged and greatly appreciated by the parents and grandparents alike. The boys are a delight. The pleasures grandparents experience are: firstly, to enjoy their grandchildren and, secondly, to hand them back to their parents.

As grandparents, we frequently help when things become difficult. The Cook grandparents live on the mid north coast and are unavailable for support. Nicole and Vlad can rely on both the grandparents Fetingis's and us. Hence, at times we feel overstretched, but love for one's family requires a will and commitment, something that has been demonstrated to us by our kin more than once throughout our family's Odyssey. It also reminds me of a Chinese proverb – that a measure of one's will is the difference between the possible and the impossible.

101 THE LEGACY

We look forward to the future
Which so soon becomes the past
R. L. Frost

This story is the legacy my wife and I leave to our children, their children – Ben, Jordan, Matty and Luka – and their children's children. We have been married for over 40 years and, God willing, Woody Herman's jazz-soundtrack *The Golden Wedding* will be played at our 50th.

Over the years, I recall many people asking, "What has it been all about?" when approaching the end of their journey. In this respect I don't have those qualms or questions, I have answered them to myself and my descendants as I wrote my family's Odyssey – *Odysseya*. Some memories were deeply buried in my conscious and sub-conscious mind – images, sounds and feelings, which in my intervening years I suppressed as much as I could from my conscious thoughts. In a way it was cathartic and sometimes painful to confront them and see them from a new perspective.

In retrospect it has been an interesting and satisfying journey. Fortunately my wife and I were spared many of the unpleasantries confronted by our kin. As war babies, we were at the tail end of World War II and the postwar years and were only slightly scarred by it. I sincerely hope that future generations will not have to endure the horrors of war.

Unfortunately, it seems that the succeeding generations seldom take much notice of their predecessors, often believing that they know better and ignore the lessons of the past. The 19th century Russian novelist Ivan Turgenev, in his novel *Fathers and Sons,* offers both an even-handed visual rendering of the radical nihilists[72] and a figurative discourse on the conflict of generations. The generational conflict is again frequently illustrated by younger people believing that older people are fools, but when they themselves age they are often astounded to discover how wise their parents were. Thoughts to this effect were once expressed by the 19th century American novelist Mark Twain.

For whatever it is worth, I would like to reiterate what some great people have said in the past: Love is the most powerful weapon. Conversely, be afraid to hate. To husbands and wives, do not be afraid to argue. By overcoming the arguments you will get closer together. Do not have any expectations of others, but give to them whatever you can. Humility is greater than pride and age usually leads to the door of Wisdom.

Today, most of the Vajinsky descendants are known by different names and most of them have settled in Australia: Boiko, Cook, Moss, Nash, Smith and Vassilieff. We still have a strong bond and most of us get together regularly. Whereupon, over a glass of wine, we exchange old stories passed down to us by our ancestors. The previously heard stories end up boring our spouses and other rels out of their minds.

In writing this book, when I did not have all the facts, I relied upon tradition and tried to get into the heads of my ancestors through deductive reasoning. So any errors in misinterpretations

72 A philosophy that represents a crude form of positivism and materialism, a revolt against the established social order; it negates all authority exercised by the State, by the Church, or by the family. It based its belief on nothing but scientific truth.

of the real events are entirely mine and are due to incomplete information and/or analysis of past events.

I am indebted to my ancestral heritage which has influenced the decisions I have made in life. I am also grateful for the convergence of events – which some may call fate – that have brought my wife and me together, for it has culminated in the fulfilment of all my aspirations.

As colonists and/or adventurers I wonder whether Ivan Vajinsky, or the earlier Alexander Vassilieff, and their spouses ever considered that their journeys or that of their descendants would take them outside of Russia and later China to a new, not well known Land – *Down Under.* They were men and women with wills of steel – hardened and tempered by their long journey. This strength helped them to adapt to their new land. Even when they were down and out, they still summoned the courage to keep going. Indeed it was people like them, who made Australia what it is today. Above all my wife and I are grateful to our adopted land Down Under – Australia, which gave us the opportunity to grow and flourish and make this country our home for over 55 years and an optimistic future for our descendents.

Maybe that's why my kin, after a lengthy assimilation process, were able to blend and not feel out of place in this new land of pioneers as described by the 19th century Australian bushman, originally from Narambla near Orange:

They came of bold and roving stock that would not fixed abide;
They were the sons of field and flock since e'er they learned to ride;
We may not hope to see such men in these degenerate years
As those explorers of the bush – the brave old pioneers.
An excerpt from the Pioneers
Banjo Paterson

And closer to more recent times, to end my story, I cannot think of a song that better describes the hardened and tempered Australian spirit in this Land – Down Under, *'I am Australian'* (written by Bruce Woodley and Dobe Newton and sung so beautifully by Judith Durham and The Seekers).

The song rises like a flame and brings forth images of the Dreamtime of the original owners, surrounded by the red soil of the outback. One can visualize the rock of Uluru, the gum trees, the outback dust, and the dry and wet seasons. To this land people came from all the lands on Earth. After years of toil and hardship, the Depression and going off to wars to defend their shores of freedom, still more people came and from all of them a new nation arose, sharing a dream and singing with the one voice that we are all Australian.

APPENDICES

1. Detailed Ancestry of the Vassilieffs and Vajinskys, Bogachevs, Kolesnikoffs and Wownenkos

1.1 Descendants of Alexander Vassilieff (I)

1. Alexander Vassilieff (I) (b.1870-Russia; d.1920-Harbin China)
 sp: UNKNOWN
 - 2. Alexander Vassilieff (II) (b.1894-Russia; d.1932-Harbin China)
   sp: Alexandra Shuvalov (b.1894-Russia; m.1912;d.1970-USSR)
   - 3. Vladimir Vassilieff (b.1913-Harbin China; d.1983-Moscow USSR)
     sp: Klaudia Vajinsky (b.1913-Blagoveshensk Russia;m.1938;d.1977-Sydney Australia)
     - 4. Valerie Vassilieff (b.1939-Shanghai China)
       sp: George Moss (b.1931-USSR;m.1961(Div);d.2003-Sydney)
       - 5. Nickolai Moss (b.1963-Sydney)
       - 5. Katy Moss (b.1965-Sydney)
       - 5. John Moss (b.1970-Sydney)

       sp: Joseph Mahnovetsky (b.1926-Harbin China;m.1980)
       - 5. Raphael Mahnovetsky (b.1979-Sydney)
     - 4. Alexander Vassilieff (III) (b.1942-Shanghai China)
       sp: Alexandra Wownenko (b.1944-Berlin Germany;m.1964)
       - 5. Vladimir Vassilieff (b.1964-Sydney)
         sp: Nicole Fetingis (b.1972-Sydney;m.1997)
         - 6. Matthew Vassilieff (b.2001-Sydney)
         - 6. Luka Vassilieff (b.2003-Sydney)
       - 5. Helen Vassilieff (b.1968-Sydney)
         sp: Gregory Cook (b.1965-;m.Sydney;m.1992)
         - 6. Benjamin Cook (b.1999-Sydney)
         - 6. Jordan Cook (b.2000-Sydney)
 - 2. Lidiya Vassilieff (b.1891-Russia; d.1960-USSR)
   sp: Nikolai Vishnevsky (b.1895-Russia;m.1915)
   - 3. Lev Vishnevsky
   - 3. Lidiya Vishnevsky
   - 3. Galina Vishnevsky
 - 2. Sergiey Vassilieff (b.1897-Russia; d.1970-probably San Francisco USA)
   sp: UNKNOWN
   - 3. Nikolai Vassilieff
   - 3. Nina Vassilieff
 - 2. Nikolai Vassilieff (b.1901-Russia; d.1942-likely Stalingrad USSR)
   sp: UNKNOWN
   - 3. Nikolai Vassilieff

1.2 Descendants of Hereditary Noble Ivan Vajinsky ne Yaninov

1. Hereditary-Noble Ivan Vajinsky ne Yaninov (b.1825-St Petersburg Russia? d.1885-Kiev Ukraine?)
 sp: Unknown
 └ 2. HN Nikita Vajinsky (b.1850-Kiev Ukraine; d.1916-Kiev Ukraine)
  sp: Evdokia (b.1850-Ukraine/Russia ?;m.1874;d.1904-Herson - Ukraine)
  ├ 3. Naval Capt/Navigator Hereditary Noble Vasily Vajinsky (b.1875-Ananieve (Herson Pro; d.1944-Harbin China)
   sp: Pauline Ivanov (m.1902(Div))
   ├ 4. Eugenia Vajinsky (b.1906-River Shilka (Sretensk) Russia; d.1993-Sydney Australia)
    sp: Vladimir Boiko (m.1923(Div))
    ├ 5. George Boiko (b.1923-Harbin China; d.1987-Brisbane Australia)
     sp: Daphne Wray (b.1933-Jamaica W.I.;m.1950)
     ├ 6. David G. Boiko (b.1951-Costa Rica)
     ├ 6. Michael G. Boiko (b.1953-Costa Rica)
     ├ 6. Stephen F. Boiko (b.1954-Costa Rica)
     ├ 6. John R. Boiko (b.1955-Costa Rica)
     ├ 6. Anthony B. Boiko (b.1957-Jamaica W.I.)
     └ 6. Angela J. Boiko (b.1959-Jamaica W.I.)
    sp: Jack Woolard (b.1900;m.1930;d.1980-Sydney Australia)
   ├ 4. Natalia Vajinsky (b.1908-Russia; d.1980-Krasnoyarsk USSR)
    sp: Ivan Kulinich (b.1905;m.1928)
    ├ 5. George (b.1929-Harbin China)
    └ 5. Nicholas (b.1931-Harbin China)
   sp: Natalya Ivanovna unknown (m.1919)
   └ 4. HN Valentin Vajinsky (b.1919-Harbin China; d.1963-Nahodka USSR)
    sp: Unknown
    ├ 5. Vajinsky (b.1960-Nahodka USSR)
    └ 5. Vajinsky (b.1962-Nahodka USSR)
  ├ 3. Hereditary Noble Boris Vajinsky (b.1883-Ananieve (Herson Province) Ukraine; d.1935-Harbin China)
   sp: Efrasinia Burdel-Budze (b.1887-Odessa Ukraine;d.1973-Sydney Australia)
   ├ 4. Valentina Vajinsky (b.1909-Khabarovsk Russia; d.1990-Sydney Australia)
    sp: Alexander N. Dobrovidoff (m.1933(Div))
    ├ 5. Marina Dobrovidoff (b.1934-Harbin China)
    sp: Dimitry Yanchevsky (b.1917-Chelyabinsk Russia;m.1946;d.1995-Sydney Australia)
   ├ 4. Maria Vajinsky (b.1911-Blagoveshensk; d.2001-Sydney Australia)
    sp: Michael N Koliagin (b.1912-Vladivostock Russia;m.1935;d.1994-Sydney Australia)
    ├ 5. Milla Koliagin (b.1936-Harbin China)
    └ 5. Vera Koliagin (b.1941-Shanghai China; d.2002-Newcastle Australia)
   └ 4. Klaudia Vajinsky (b.1913-Blagoveshensk Russia; d.1977-Sydney Australia)
    sp: Vladimir Vassilieff (b.1913-Harbin China;m.1938;d.1983-Moscow USSR)
    ├ 5. Valerie Vassilieff (b.1939-Shanghai China)
     sp: George Moss (b.1931-USSR;m.1961(Div);d.2003-Sydney)
     ├ 6. Nickolai Moss (b.1963-Sydney)
     ├ 6. Katy Moss (b.1965-Sydney)
     ├ 6. John Moss (b.1970-Sydney)
     sp: Joseph Mahnovetsky (b.1926-Harbin China;m.1980)
     └ 6. Raphael Mahnovetsky (b.1979-Sydney)
    └ 5. Alexander Vassilieff (III) (b.1942-Shanghai China)
     sp: Alexandra Wownenko (b.1944-Berlin Germany;m.1964)
     ├ 6. Vladimir Vassilieff (b.1964-Sydney)
      sp: Nicole Fetingis (b.1972-Sydney;m.1997)
      ├ 7. Matthew Vassilieff (b.2001-Sydney)
      └ 7. Luka Vassilieff (b.2003-Sydney)
     └ 6. Helen Vassilieff (b.1968-Sydney)
      sp: Gregory Cook (b.1965-;m.Sydney;m.1992)
      ├ 7. Benjamin Cook (b.1999-Sydney)
      └ 7. Jordan Cook (b.2000-Sydney)
  └ 3. HN Eugene Vajinsky (b.1880-Ananieve (Herson Province) Ukraine; d.1900)

1.3 Descendants of Don Cossacks - Taras Bogachov

1. Don Cossack Taras Bogachov (b.1815-Rostov-Don? d. (?)
   sp: Unknown
   - 2. DC Feodor Bogachov (b.1840-Rostov-Don; d. (?)
     sp: Unknown
     - 3. DC Ignatiy Bogachov (b.1865-Rostov-Don; d. (?)
       sp: Theodora (b.1870-Rostov-Don;d.(?))
       - 4. DC Elena Bogachev (b.1891-Rostov-Don; d.1972-Sydney)
         sp: DC Gregory Kolesnikoff (b.1889-Dmitryevka; m.1911; d.1948- (Oberammergau)
         sp: Ivan Wownenko (b.1902-Ivanovka Dniepropetrovsk Ukraine;m.1932;d.1964-Sydney)
         - 5. DC Daria Kolessnikoff (b.1912-Rostov-Don; d.1989-Sydney)
           - 6. Alexandra Wownenko (b.1944-Berlin Germany)
             sp: Alexander Vassilieff (III) (b.1942-Shanghai China; m.1964)
             - 7. Vladimir Vassilieff (b.1964-Sydney)
               sp: Nicole Fetingus (b.1972-Sydney; m.1997)
               - 8. Matthew Vassilieff (b.2001-Sydney)
               - 8. Luka Vassilieff (b.2003-Sydney)
             - 7. Helen Vassilieff (b.1968-Sydney)
               sp: Gregory Cook (b.1965-; m.Sydney;m.1992)
               - 8. Benjamin Cook (b.1999-Sydney)
               - 8. Jordan Cook (b.2000-Sydney)
       - 4. DC Andrey Bogachev
       - 4. DC Ivan Bogachev
       - 4. DC Efimiy Bogachov
       - 4. DC Matrona Bogachov

1.4 Descendants of Don Cossacks – Jacob Kolesnikoff

1. Don Cossack Jacob Kolesnikoff (b.1860-Rostov-Don;d.(?))
  sp: Olga (b.1855-Rostov-Don;d.(?))
  - 2, DC Gregory Kolesnikoff (b.1889-Dmitryevka (near Rostov-Don); d.1948-Oberammergau Germany)
    sp: DC Elena Bogachev (b.1891-Rostov-Don;m.1911;d.1972-Sydney)
    - 3, DC Daria Kolesnikoff (b.1912-Rostov-Don; d.1989-Sydney)
      sp: Ivan Wownenko (b.1902-Ivanovka Dniepropetrovsk Ukraine;m.1932;d.1964-Sydney)
      - 4, Alexandra Wownenko (b.1944-Berlin Germany)
        sp: Alexander Vassilieff (III) (b.1942-Shanghai China;m.1964)
        - 5, Vladimir Vassilieff (b.1964-Sydney)
          sp: Nicole Fetingis (b.1972-Sydney;m.1997)
          - 6. Matthew Vassilieff (b.2001-Sydney)
          - 6. Luka Vassilieff (b.2003-Sydney)
        - 5, Helen Vassilieff (b.1968-Sydney)
          sp: Gregory Cook (b.1965-;m.Sydney;m.1992)
          - 6. Benjamin Cook (b.1999-Sydney)
          - 6. Jordan Cook (b.2000-Sydney)

    sp: Pavit Krach
    - 3. Olga Krach
      sp: Joseph
      - 4, Petra
        sp: Muller
        - 5. Unknown
        - 5. Unknown
  - 2. Pilageya Kolesnikoff (d.1908)

1.5 Descendants of Ukrainian Arhip Wownenko

- 1. Arhip Wownenko (b.1875-Ukraine; d. (?))
  sp: Ecapitolina Hartschenko (b.1875-Ukraine;d.(?))
  - 2. Ivan Wownenko (b.1902-Ivanovka Dnepropetrovsk Ukraine; d.1964-Sydney)
    sp: DC Daria Kolesnikoff (b.1912-Rostov-Don;m.1932;d.1989-Sydney)
    - 3. Alexandra Wownenko (b.1944-Berlin Germany)
      sp: Alexander Vassilieff (III) (b.1942-Shanghai China;m.1964)
      - 4. Vladimir Vassilieff (b.1964-Sydney)
        sp: Nicole Fetingis (b.1972-Sydney;m.1997)
        - 5. Matthew Vassilieff (b.2001-Sydney)
        - 5. Luka Vassilieff (b.2003-Sydney)
      - 4. Helen Vassilieff (b.1968-Sydney)
        sp: Gregory Cook (b.1965-;m.Sydney;m.1992)
        - 5. Benjamin Cook (b.1999-Sydney)
        - 5. Jordan Cook (b.2000-Sydney)
  - 2. Maria Wownenko
  - 2. Micola Wownenko
  - 2. Olga Wownenko
  - 2. Marfa Wownenko
    sp: Unknown
    - 3. Victor (b.1925-USSR; d.1944-USSR)

2. From Chapter 4

2.1 The Cossack Clans

1. Amur Cossacks
2. Astrakhan Cossacks
3. Don Cossacks – The Great Don Cossack Clan
4. Enisey Cossacks
5. Orenburg Cossacks
6. Semirechen Cossacks
7. Siberian Cossacks
8. Terek – Kuban Cossacks (originally separate clans)
9. Transbaikal Cossacks (Zabaikal'skie kazaki)
10. Ural Cossacks (originally known as the Yaik Cossacks)
11. Ussuri Cossacks
12. Cossacks in the Caucasus

N.B. Zaporozhian Cossacks were disbanded under Catherine II. Later, together with some of the Don Cossacks, they became the basis of the Kuban Cossack Clan,

2.2 Some Descriptions of the Cossacks

- Russified leftovers of Genghis Khan's undefeatable horsemen
- A *peasant-warrior*
- Military service people, something like a warrior cast
- Runaway serfs who established their free communities on the borders back in 15th century
- Pioneers of new lands
- Descendants of all the waves of invaders who passed the route from Asia to Europe (through the area known as The Great Steppe), who settled down in the steppes of Southern Russia and Ukraine where they mixed with the Slavic people
- *Robin Hoods* of Russia and Ukraine

- ❖ The knights of Orthodoxy
- ❖ Trappers with special duties to guard the borders
- ❖ Legendary fighters in the service of the Tsars
- ❖ Farmers with special duties to guard the borders
- ❖ *Cossacks are the best light troops among all that exist. If I had them in my army, I would conquer the world* – Napoleon

2.3 The Wide Steppe – An Old Cossack Song (A rough translation by the author)

In the wide steppe of Central Asia
We were surrounded by a foe
For three whole days with the *busurmanin* (the infidel)
We broiled in battle with the gallant foe
    We marched and marched along to battle
    As we brought death to the enemy with our own blood
We marched as our ranks declined
Our Cossacks dying one by one
Surrender was not on our mind
And we were mowed down like the grass
    We marched and marched along to battle
    As we brought death to the enemy with our own blood
But then a bayonet flashed on the horizon
The reinforcements were coming near
And all remaining sighed with gladness
As grateful Cossacks crossed their hearts

3.0 From Chapter 24 – The Viking Incident

3.1 The Russian Squadron

Battleships: Tsesarevich (flag of the Squadron Commander), Retvizan, Pobieda (flag of Rear Admiral Prince Ukhtomsky), Peresvet, Sevastopol, Poltava and Petropavlovsk.

Armoured cruisers: Bayan, Gromoboi, Rossiya (broad pennant of Captain Rentsenshtein) and RYURIK.

Cruisers: Bogatyr, Askold, Varyag, Pallada, Diana, Boyarin, and Novik.

Gunboats: Otvazhnyi, Gremyashi, Gilyak, Mandzhur, Koreyets, Bobr and Sivuch.

Old cruisers, of no fighting value: Zabiyaka, Razboinik, and Dzhigit. Torpedo cruisers: Vsadnik and Gaidamak.

1st and 2nd Destroyer Divisions, in all 25 destroyers.

One Torpedo Boat Division, consisting of 10 torpedo boats.

Auxiliary cruisers: Lena and Angara.

Minelayers: Yenisei, Amur, and Bogatyr.

Hospital ships: Angara, Mongolia and Kazan.

Of these, the armoured cruisers Rossiya (broad pennant of Captain Rentsenshtein), Gromoboi, Rurik, the cruiser Bogatyr and 10 torpedo boats were stationed at Vladivostok. The cruiser Varyag and the gunboat Koreyets were at the disposal of the Russian Ambassador at Seoul in Korea. All remaining ships were concentrated in the fortress of Port Arthur.

The Gunboat Koreyets

Launched in 1886, 1437 Tons, 13.3 knots

2 – 8" guns (Short barrelled), 1 – 6" gun (short barrelled) 4 – 9-pounders

2 – 47 mm guns. 1 – Landing party gun

Crew: 176

3.2 The Japanese Fleet

The whole of the the combat-worthy Japanese Fleet was united under one command and was designated the "Combined Fleet". It was composed of three squadrons:

1st Squadron: Commanding, also the Commander–in Chief of the Fleet: Vice Admiral Togo Heihashiro.

1st Battle Squadron – battleships: Mikasa (flag of the Commander-in-Chief), Asahi, Fuji, Yashima, Shikishima, Hatsuse, and the despatch vessel Tatsuta.

3rd Combat Squadron: Commanding: Rear Admiral Dewa Sigenori;

Cruisers: Chitose, Takasago, Kassagi and Yoshino.

1st, 2nd and 3rd Destroyer Divisions, a total of 11 destroyers; 1st, 2nd 3rd and 14th Torpedo boat Divisions, a total of 15 torpedo boats.

2nd Squadron: Commanding: Vice Admiral Kamimura Kikonojo.

2nd battle Squadron: armoured cruisers: Idzumo (flag of Vice Admiral Kamimura), Azuma, Asama, Yakumo, Tokiwa and Iwate. Despatch vessel Chihaya.

4th Combat Squadron: Commanding: Rear Admiral Uryu Sotokichi.

Cruisers: Naniwa, Akashi, Takachiho, Niitaka.

4th and 5th Destroyer Divisions, a total of 8 destroyers.

9th, 17th, 18th, 19th, 20th and 21st Torpedo Boat Divisions, a total of 22 torpedo boats.

Attached to these two Squadrons were 17 steamer transports.

3rd Squadron: Commanding: Vice Admiral Kataoka Sichiro.

5th Combat Squadron: cruisers Itsukushima (flag of Vice Admiral Kataoka Sichiro), Hashidate, Matsushima, the old battleship Chin Yen and the despatch vessel Yayeyama.

6th Combat Squadron: cruisers Idzumi, Suma, Akitsushima and Chioda. Commanding Rear Admiral; Togo Masamichi.

7th Combat Squadron: coast defence ships: Fuso, Hei Yen, Sai Yen, gun boats Kaimon, Tsukushi, Chokai, Atago, Oshima, Akagi, Maiya, Uji, Banjo, and the despatch vessel Miyako. Squadron Commander: Rear Admiral Hosoya Sukendzi.

6th, 7th, 10th, 11th, 12th, 15th and 16th Torpedo Boat Divisions, in all 27 torpedo boats. In addition, the 3rd Fleet had 4 Steamer transports attached.

4 How the Czar is crowned.

Some time ago, a workmate of mine handed me a copy of newsprint that he found under the linoleum of his mother's house when he was helping her to clean up. The newsprint is a form of a time capsule that I thought was appropriate to include in the Appendix, as it was written and interpreted through the eyes of an Australian or British Journalist about 120 years ago:

> Thursday 24 May 1883. From unknown Australian/British newsprint:
>
> 'Alexander III. Will be crowned in Moscow on Sunday, the 27th of May. As the coronation is one of the most brilliant ceremonies in the world, a description of it (from a Russian source) may be read with interest.
>
> 'The great ceremony has always been performed in the Church of the Holy Assumption, within the walls of the Kremlin, at the ancient town of Moscow. Arriving at the Church, the Czar and his wife are shown to ordinary thrones near those of the bishops, and the special service immediately begins.
>
> 'After the first lesson is read, the Metropolitans conduct the Emperor and Empress to a canopy of scarlet velvet, richly embroidered in gold, the principal figure being the double-headed Russian eagle. Under his canopy is an elevated platform, upon which are the historical throne of the Czar Vladimir Monomah and an ordinary armchair for the Empress, also a table upon which are the sceptre and crown of Constantinus Monomachus, a sword and a mantle of ermine.
>
> 'The nobles now advance from the south of the Cathedral, and surrounding the platform draw their swords and place them at the feet of the Czar. The Bishop of Kazan then asks

the Emperor in a loud voice if he is a true believer, to which he replies by reading the Lord's Prayer and the Apostles' Creed of the Greek Church. The Bishop next says: If there be any of you here present knowing any impediment for which Alexander son of Alexander (or other name) should not be crowned; by the grace of God Emperor and autocrat of –

'All the Russias, of Moscow, of Krell, of Vladimir, of Novgorod; Czar of Kazan, of Astrakhan, of Poland, of Kherson-Taurida, of Grusii (Georgia); Gosoudar of Pskoff: Grand Duke of Smolensk, of Lithuania, of Volhynia, of Podolia, and of Finland; Prince of Estonia, of Livonia, of Courland, of Semigalia, of the Samoyedes, of Bielostok of Corelia, of Foer, of Ingor, of Perm, of Viatka, of Bulgaria, and of other countries; Master and Grand Duke of the Lower Countries in Novgorod, of Tchernigoff, of Riazan, of Polotsk, of Rostoff, of Yaroslav, of Bielosersk, of Odourk, of Obdorsk, of Kondisk, of Vitelsk, of Msttilaff, and of all the countries of the North; Master Absolute of Kastalnisk, of Kabardinsk, and of the territory of Armenia: Sovereign of Mountain Princes of Tcherkask; Master of Turkestan, Heir presumptive of Norway, and Duke Presumptive of Sleswick-Holstein, of Sternmarne, of Dithmiase, and of Oldenburg,

'Let him come forward now, in the name of the Holy Trinity, and, show what the impediment is or let him remain dumb forever!

'This is repeated three times, and upon no objection being raised he lays his hand upon the head of the Czar, who immediately kneels. At this point the Metropolitan of Moscow takes the mantle of ermine from the table, and throws it over the kneeling Czar, saying: "Cover and protect thy people as this robe covers arid Protects thee". The Emperor replying, "I will, I will, I will, God helping;" and kissing the prelate's hand.

'The Bishop of Novgorod now places the sceptre in the

Czar's hand, saying, "May thine hand which holds this wither the day thou art unjust" The answer being, "Be it so;" after which the Bishop of Kieff places the crown upon the Emperor's head. At this point the Empress kneels beside her husband, who partly covers her with the cloak of ermine, and also holds his crown above her head for a few seconds, without, however, placing it upon her head. The Czar and Czarina remain in prayer for several minutes amid a deadly silence, and the instant they rise to their feet bishops, nobles, deputations, clergy, and all present kneel to them, shouting: "Long live the Czar!"

'The hundreds of thousands who are outside take up the cry, the heralds sound their trumpets, guns are fired, and bells are rung. The Czar commands the people to rise, and is again surrounded by the nobles, who receive their swords back from the Imperial hands, the Emperor saying: "It is thy country's", to which the noble replies: "And my Czar's".

'Mass is again resumed, and the Emperor proceeds alone to the altar, passing through the Golden Gates of the Iconostas, which are closed behind him, thus hiding him from view. Here, after partaking of the Holy Communion, the Metropolitan of Moscow anoints his head, temples, eyelids, lips, nostrils, ears, breast, and hands, saying: "Behold the seal of the Holy Ghost; may it keep thee ever holy."

'The Gates of the Iconostas are reopened. The Czar appears before them, and is hailed with shouts of "Thou art verily by the Lord anointed."

'The Empress advances to the sanctuary and kneels to her lord, who bids her rise and they walk out of the cathedral arm in arm. At the door is a gilded chariot, drawn by 12 white horses, into which they enter, the princes, other members of the imperial family, foreign monarchs, guests, etc., entering other State chariots. The procession again forms as it did on approaching the Kremlin, and with its new additions moves slowly through the gaily-decorated town. According to an old custom, the Czar's carriage instead of being guarded by troops is surrounded by 100 maidens belonging to the best Russian families all dressed in white and holiday garlands of flowers. Court balls and receptions begin in the evening and last for a fortnight, after which the Court returns to St. Petersburg.'

REFERENCES

IN RUSSIAN

Anniversary Collection Polytechnic No 10 – *Youbileyniy Sbornik Polytechnic No 10* 1969-1979 Sydney

Association of Engineering Graduands of Harbin Polytechnic Institute

Association of Realists A Memoir Collection Of The 1st Harbin Russian (Realist) High School

F.S.B. (former **KGB)Files** *The Case Of Vladimir A Vassilieff – GULAG Rehabilitee* (sentenced 1933 –escaped, re-sentenced 1945-1954) Moscow 1999

Jiganov V.D. Capt Russian Imperial Forces (Ret) *Review Of The Past No 14* Sydney Jan 1975

Jiganov V.D. Capt Russian Imperial Forces (Ret) *Russians in Shanghai* Shanghai Apr 1936

Joukoff R.G. St. George Pathfinders (ORUR) *Commemorative Anniversary Album* Melbourne 1987

Melihov G.V. Manchuria the Far and Near Moscow 1991

Ostrovsky M. *Russian History* Peking 1919

Petrov V.P. *Shanghai On The Huangpu* Washington DC 1985

Sergeevsky B.N. The Past Of Russian Land – *Proshloye Ruskoy Zemli* San Francisco 1954

Sermons of St. John of Shanghai and San Francisco *WORD – Slova* San Francisco 1994

Syrov S. Pages From History – Stranitsi Istorii Moscow 1975

Vasys/Krypton/Iswolsky/Taskin Russian Area Reader (contents and preface in English) New York 1977

IN ENGLISH

Berlin The Nicolai Guide Berlin Germany June 1993

Chambers Encyclopedia 1895 Vol IX Philadelphia

Cossackweb.com

Encyclopedia Britannica 2001 Standard Edition CD-ROM

Klyuchevsky V.O. *The Raise of the Romanovs* (translated from Russian) USA 1970

Mandich D.R. et al Russian Heraldry and Nobility USA 1992
Nash G. *The Tarasov Saga* Sydney 2002
National Executive of the Reserve Forces Day Committee *Reserve Forces Day – 50 Years Of Service To The Nation 1948-1998* Sydney 1998
Obolensky D. et al *The Russian Chronicles* London 1990
Plotto A.V. Serving The St, Andrew Flag Paris 1998
Solzhenitsyn A. *The GULAG Archipelago 1918-1956* Harper and Row Publishers Australia 1974
Stephan J.J. The Russian Fascists Tragedy and Farce in Exile, 1924-1945 Harper and Row Publishers New York 1978
The Russian Scout News No 3 Yale Sta. Conn USA July, 1958
Vassilieff A. *Ergoes Tour China* Ergonomics Australia Vol 3 No 2 Apr.1989
Vassilieff A. *From The Far North Via The Central Kingdom To The Downunder* Lindfield Rotary Club taped presentation Sydney 1991
Vassiltchikov G. et al The Berlin Diaries 1940-1945 of Marie Vassiltchikov
Ware T. *The Orthodox Church* Penguin Books 1963